THE
FITZGERALD
LEGACY

Reforming Public Life
in Australia and Beyond

Edited by
Colleen Lewis, Janet Ransley and Ross Homel

First published in 2010 from a completed manuscript presented to
Australian Academic Press
32 Jeays Street
Bowen Hills Qld 4006
Australia
www.australianacademicpress.com.au

National Library of Australia cataloguing-in-publication entry:

Title:	The Fitzgerald legacy : reforming public life in Australia and beyond / editors Colleen Lewis, Janet Ransley, Ross Homel.
ISBN:	9781921513350 (pbk.)
Notes	Includes index. Bibliography.
Subjects:	Queensland. Commission of Inquiry into Possible Illegal Activities and Associated Police Misconduct. Police corruption--Australia. Political corruption--Australia. Law reform--Australia. Crime and the press--Australia. Organized crime--Australia.
Other Authors/Contributors:	Lewis, Colleen. Ransley, Janet. Homel, Ross.
Dewey Number:	364.132309943

Cover image © istockphoto.com/DenisTangneyJr

For Alana, Isabel and Marko
CL

❧·❦

For Doris and Rod
JR

❧·❦

For Lewis — the new generation
RH

ACKNOWLEDGMENTS

As editors, we are indebted to the authors of these chapters for their contributions and for the cheerful and professional way in which they responded to our many requests. We also appreciate the time several colleagues spent peer reviewing these chapters and for their insightful comments. The Key Centre for Ethics, Law, Justice and Governance, Griffith University has supported the project on several levels and we thank the Director, Professor Paul Mazerolle and Carmel Connors in particular for that support. Our sincere thanks also to Stephen May and his colleagues at Australian Academic Press, it has been a pleasure to work with them.

Colleen Lewis, Janet Ransley and Ross Homel

CONTENTS

Continued over

CONTENTS
continued

LIST OF
TABLES AND FIGURES

Public administration presents many challenges, a number of which are analysed in this excellent book. This brief introduction notes some structural and systemic flaws in the most critically important element in public administration, the political process.

Whether or not all humans have the same basic 'nature', we possess a number of common, if sometimes contradictory, characteristics. Self-interest and fear of the different and unknown, especially other races, religions and cultures, are almost universal, but many also share noble aspirations including peace, security, justice, equality and personal, political and economic freedom.

It often serves our individual long-term interests to pursue mutually beneficial altruistic objectives collectively. Many nations now accept that majority rule, through representatives elected to take decisions and actions on behalf of and for the benefit of the entire community, is the best system of government. Elected leaders are intended to subordinate their own interests and even to act contrary to the wish of the majority when that is necessary in the public interest. However, most democracies recognise the compelling force of self-interest and that, because of the pressures of populism and personal or political advantage, effective constraints on the exercise of power, including the power of the majority and the power of its elected representatives, are needed to protect individuals and minorities. Almost all countries with values similar to Australia enshrine essential constraints on the misuse of power in a constitution or sometimes, less effectively, in a statutory bill or charter of rights.

Parliamentary sovereignty, the foundation of Australia's rudimentary and anachronistic 'Westminster system' of representative democracy, is based on history rather than reason. Voters are entitled, indeed compelled, to choose a government every few years. Beyond that, the electorate is little more than an audience to a substantially rule-free political contest. The rights of citizens are largely unprotected by legal constraints on official power which elsewhere are considered a hallmark of democracy. For example, the Commonwealth Constitution provides for a universal franchise but does not dictate fair elections; assures judicial independence but does not require due process and trial by jury for even the most serious offences; and guarantees freedom of political communication and a qualified freedom of religion but does not protect freedom of speech and freedom of association. Laws are not invalid because they are contrary to the public interest or unjust.

Those who seek to justify the current position rely on two complementary arguments; namely, that potential political consequences deter official excesses and abuses and that a law establishing fundamental rights would transfer power from elected politicians to 'unelected judges'. Neither premise withstands scrutiny.

In mature democracies, independent, impartial courts are responsible for enforcing valid laws and determining whether laws are valid. The proposition that it is undemocratic for judges to decide whether laws are valid because judges are appointed, not elected, mischievously obscures the real issue, namely, whether human rights are legally protected or exist only at the whim of a government chosen by the majority.

Relentless social change and perceived security threats make conformity and order attractive, and many are indifferent, or even attracted, to gradual erosions of the freedom of those who are different and easily misunderstood. Even if an opposition has different policies, voters who are not directly affected by a law or official action are generally more concerned with day-to-day financial and other personal considerations than with the impact of injustice on individuals or minorities. When erosions of liberty occur incrementally, as has occurred in Australia, the risk of a political backlash is low. Changes in government because of unjust laws or other abuses of power occur only in exceptional circumstances, usually when a pattern of official misconduct is sufficiently egregious to overcome community inertia.

Political pluralism and political parties are common features of democratic societies but very few Australians are members of a political party. In Australia, parties come and go, but two dominant parties have become entrenched. It is now extremely difficult, if not impossible, for another competitive political force to emerge because of the financial advantages held by the two major parties and the critical role that money plays in political activity. Under the legislative scheme which provides public funding for political parties most money goes to the two major parties, which also receive most private funding because one or other of them is practically certain to win government and therefore better able to provide value for money donated. The probably irreversible dominance of the two major parties makes it imperative that neither subordinates the public interest to its quest for power.

The exploitation of gaps in the law, with each party lowering its standards in order to compete, is producing an amoral political culture: 'whatever it takes' — 'winner takes all'. Small groups control each of the two major parties and indirectly the national destiny. Parliament is effectively subordinate to the Executive, which is not directly elected by voters. Rigid party discipline ensures that, apart from infrequent 'conscious' votes, parliamentarians vote as directed. Careerists with little or no experience outside politics learn their craft in party administration, politicians' offices and supporters' organisations prior to party preselection and entry to parliament. Dynasties are emerging as politics become, for some, the family business. When conduct is legal and the political price is not too high, ethics become irrelevant or worse, a sign of weakness and ignorance of 'realpolitik'.

Misleading or deceptive conduct is barred in commerce but secrecy and misinformation (euphemistically called 'spin') are routinely employed by politicians. Political debate is often marked by spiteful, juvenile point-scoring and attempts to discredit each other, inevitably discrediting all participants. 'Media management' insults and confuses the electorate, which is denied the comprehensive accurate information which is essential to the proper functioning of democracy. Access and influence can be purchased. Patronage is dispensed to supporters and used to silence potential critics. Most, if not all, conventions concerning standards of political conduct which the Westminster system once incorporated are now obsolescent, bi-partisan support for fundamental institutions is periodically abandoned for political advantage and social division and prejudice are occasionally used as political tools.

Social capital is easily dissipated. Principled leadership is essential to preserve our confidence in and support for each other and social cohesion. Public figures are role models and their standards percolate into the community. As the population increases, communities become larger and more diverse and economic disparities widen, people who consider themselves powerless outsiders readily become disillusioned, cynical and apathetic and lose trust in government, the integrity of its process and (often very difficult and potentially controversial) decisions and fundamental institutions.

Reform is always difficult. Vested interests whose activities might be adversely affected inevitably oppose reform strenuously. Political reform is especially difficult because it must be endorsed by politicians who control and benefit from the current system and have little or no incentive to concede part of their power. Nonetheless, even if for solely pragmatic reasons, some political leaders are taking steps to improve political standards. However, public demand for a bipartisan commitment to political reform is essential. The American author Norman Mailer suggested that democracy is 'a state of grace that is attained only by those countries which have a host of individuals not only ready to enjoy freedom but to undergo the heavy labor of maintaining it'. This book is a significant contribution to the task.

G.E. (Tony) Fitzgerald
Griffith University
November 2009

1

The State We Were In

Colleen Lewis, Janet Ransley and Ross Homel

In 1992, Sir Harry Gibbs wrote of the *Commission of Inquiry into Possible Illegal Activities and Associated Police Misconduct* (hereafter referred to as the Fitzgerald Inquiry):

> No commission of inquiry in Australia has been more remarkable in its outcome than that conducted by Mr Fitzgerald QC, as he then was. The transformation of the inquiry, from an investigation of alleged crime and corruption involving five suspected criminals into an examination of almost every aspect of the system of government in Queensland, and the general acceptance of the inquiry and its recommendations, were made possible only by the ability and determination of Mr Fitzgerald himself, and by the constant attention which the media gave to the issues which he raised. Because Mr Fitzgerald believed that the corruption which he investigated was the symptom of a more general illness of the body politic, he sought, by his recommendations, not merely to reform the system of criminal justice and to combat corruption, but also to improve the standards of public administration, and to render the workings of Parliament more democratic. (Gibbs, 1992, p. xiii)

Gibbs was not only a former Chief Justice of the High Court of Australia and Justice of the Supreme Court of Queensland, but he had also conducted the ill-fated 1963–64 National Hotel Royal Commission. That inquiry found no evidence of misconduct against several of the same police officers who later admitted to Fitzgerald that they were in fact corrupt at the time (Fitzgerald, 1989).

The allegations dismissed by Gibbs' inquiry did not disappear, but were contained by a supportive government, captive bureaucracy and supplicant media. Further inquiries into related matters in 1975 by two Scotland Yard officers, the 1976 Lucas Inquiry and the 1985 Sturgess Inquiry had no more success than Gibbs in exposing the true state of Queensland public life (for discussion of these inquiries see Fitzgerald, 1989, pp. 32–48, 68).

This chapter summarises the situation in Queensland prior to the Fitzgerald Inquiry, and in so doing establishes an historical context for other contributions to this edited collection. It describes the nature and extent of corruption and abuse of power in the Queensland Police Force (QPF), the absence of effective police accountability structures and processes and the inappropriate relationship that developed between police and government, which in turn fuelled the feeling of immunity that had pervaded the Force. The chapter also examines 'politics' Queensland style, characterised by a gerry-mandered electoral system, an irrelevant and ineffective Parliament, unchecked conflicts of interest, poor administration, a politicised public sector, and an authoritarian and autocratic style of government.[2]

Queenslanders were told the Fitzgerald Inquiry would take approximately six weeks. It lasted for two years. It sat publicly for 238 days, examined 339 witnesses and received 2,304 exhibits (Fitzgerald, 1989, p. 40). Its records still occupy some 250 linear metres of storage space (CMC, n.d). It went far beyond any previous inquiry into policing or corruption in Australia and established a benchmark for future inquiries. As other chapters in this book will demonstrate, its legacy is still being felt 20 years later.

The Lead-Up to Fitzgerald

Over a number of years Queensland's leading daily newspaper the *Courier-Mail* had reported allegations about the link between organised crime and police corruption. In particular, during the early months of 1987, the journalist Phil Dickie was engaged in a sequence of investigations that highlighted the suspicions then the subject of growing rumour in Brisbane (Dickie, 1989). However, it was the graphic depictions of such matters on the Australian Broadcasting Commission's (ABC) national television program *The Moonlight State* that was the catalyst for the Fitzgerald Inquiry. At the time, the Premier Sir Joh Bjelke-Petersen was out of town and it was the Deputy Premier and Police Minister Bill Gunn, who announced that a commission of inquiry would be established to address the issues raised on the Four Corners program. When announcing the inquiry, Gunn explained that 'A series of police ministers have had these type of allegations hanging over their heads. They are not going to hang over mine' (quoted in Dickie, 1989, p. 174).

The first name put forward to head the inquiry was rejected by members of Queensland's legal fraternity (Dickie, 1989, p. 178). They did not want this inquiry to go the way of the four previous inquiries into police corruption and related issues that had been established in Queensland since 1963, referred to above (Whitton, 1989, p. 122). All had proven to be nothing more than an exercise in symbolic politics (Lewis, 1999, p. 122). Instead (in the absence of Premier Bjelke-Petersen) the Deputy Premier Bill Gunn announced the appointment of a little-known former judge of the Federal Court, Gerald Edward (Tony) Fitzgerald. Fitzgerald agreed to head the Inquiry on the proviso that he be given adequate resources, broad terms of reference, independence from the bureaucracy and the power to seek grants of indemnity for informants (Whitton, 1989, p. 125).

The Fitzgerald Inquiry was established on May 26, 1987, to inquire into 'possible activities involving: (i) prostitution, (ii) unlawful gambling, (iii) the sale of illegal drugs, (iv) associated misconduct by members of the Queensland Police Force, and (v) payments by named persons to one or more political parties in Queensland and the purposes of any such payments' (Fitzgerald, 1989, Appendix 6, A37). Its terms of reference, initially limited to the period June 1, 1982, to May 26, 1987, were to ascertain:

- If Geraldo, Antonio and Vincenzo Bellino, Vittorio Conte and Hector Brandon Hapeta were linked with premises used for unlawful gambling, drug sales and prostitution;
- Whether police received financial or other favours in return for the non-enforcement of laws in relation to the premises;
- Whether the Bellinos, Conte or Hapeta made a $50,000 payment to a Queensland political party; and
- If new legislation was needed to better monitor police enforcement and to detect corruption?

The information gathered in the first few weeks caused Fitzgerald to request a widening of the terms of reference to allow for the investigation of people other than the Bellinos, Hapeta, Conte and their associates. The Commission was also given the power to subpoena people in relation to allegations of illegal gambling, prostitution and the sale of illegal drugs. The time frame was extended back to 1 January 1977. In August 1988 Commissioner Fitzgerald again sought and was granted additional powers. The *Commission of Inquiry Act 1950* was changed to allow public servants to give information to the Commission, something they previously had been unable to do. The legislation also tightened laws concerning contempt, perjury and conspiracy and gave the Inquiry the power to raise previous charges and trials. The legislation was amended three further times at the Inquiry's request (Ransley, 2001).

Criminal Activities by Serving and Former Police

Throughout the 1960s it was an open secret that senior police were protecting those who ran illegal activities in Queensland, in particular prostitution, starting price (SP) bookmaking and illegal liquor sales. During this period Frank Bischof was Commissioner of Police (1957–1969). He resigned under a cloud of suspicion involving SP betting operations that had operated with police protection for many years. Suspicions about Bischof's corrupt activities were confirmed in 1982 when former Deputy Premier, Sir Thomas Hiley, publicly described him as '… a grafter of immense proportions' (Procter, 1985, p. 165). Bischof was said to favour a small group of officers who were allegedly his 'bagmen': Terence Lewis, Tony Murphy and Glen Hallahan. One of these officers, Terence Lewis, went on to become Commissioner of the Queensland Police from 1976 to 1989. Corruption and abuse of power by police flourished under Lewis's leadership. After the Fitzgerald Inquiry unravelled that record, Lewis was prosecuted and in August 1991 convicted of official corruption and sentenced to 14 years imprisonment.

The following few examples illustrate the degree to which misconduct and malfeasance had become accepted behaviour for many police.

Under indemnity from prosecution at the Fitzgerald Inquiry, former Queensland police officer and self-confessed bagman, Jack Herbert testified that lying or 'verballing' was normal practice for many police. He explained that:

> When we first arrested anybody we would sit down at the typewriter and it would be a matter of … 'once upon a time there were three bears and now there's thousands'. This was the attitude. You would make up the story as you went along. (*Courier-Mail*, 1988a, p. 1)

There was more fabricating of evidence than putting it down as it happened (Herbert and Gilling, 2004, p. 68).

Ten years earlier, the *Report of a Committee of Inquiry into the Enforcement of Criminal Law in Queensland* (Lucas, 1977) identified police 'verballing' as a serious matter within Queensland Police. Consequently it recommended new safeguards be implemented to counter the problem. When the Fitzgerald Inquiry was established in 1987 none of the Lucas Inquiry recommendations had been implemented.

Herbert told how police would perjure themselves in order to secure convictions and admitted that it was his usual practice to tailor his evidence (*Courier-Mail*, 1988a, p. 1). In his memoirs he recalls that whenever a police officer had to 'describe a fictitious individual we would always describe the barrister who was doing the questioning'. The next officer being questioned would also describe the prosecuting barrister and in doing so would corroborate the first police officer's evidence. Herbert explained that when a person was giving evidence police would arrange for 'a runner' to be in court. The runner, always a police officer, would listen to the proceedings and if a matter came up that he thought another witness should be aware of, the runner would leave the court and warn them. 'That way the witness would know what he had to corroborate' (Herbert and Gilling, 2004, p. 67).

Sacked corrupt officer Noel Kelly gave evidence to the Inquiry that perjury was a common practice among detectives. He recalled how two detectives had asked him to lie to the court and the manner in which he had obliged (*Courier-Mail,* 1988b, p. 4). Police disregard for due process and the truth created the situation where, as Whitton (1989, p. 18) argues, 'Justice and the rule of law were virtually a dead letter: fabrication was endemic in the force'. He went on to explain that: 'The danger this poses for liberty of the subject is incalculable: we do not know how many enemies of the regime, or persons who simply annoyed police, were routinely verballed into prison'.

Systemic police corruption had become a major problem. SP bookmakers told of careers spanning 20 years during which time they were rarely questioned, let alone prosecuted by police (*Australian,* 1988a, p. 8). One SP bookmaker testified that he operated illegally for 10 years (1977–1987) but closed down his criminal activities when the Fitzgerald Inquiry commenced as he could no longer expect to be protected. (*Courier-Mail,* 1988c, p. 4). Herbert gave evidence that approximately forty SP bookmakers received protection from 1980 to 1987, at a cost of between $400 and $1000 per month (*Australian,* 1988b, p. 3).

Corrupt police in the infamous Licensing Branch protected SP bookmakers by ensuring that at least one officer who was part of the 'joke' (a term used by police to refer to their illegal activities) was on duty for every shift. Herbert explained how the carbon paper used by the 'enemy' — the honest police — 'was held up to a mirror so that addresses where raids were to occur could be identified' (*Courier-Mail,* 1988d, p. 4).

A major identification card racket involving police personnel was uncovered in Queensland's Beaudesert area, where the going rate for a false driver's license was approximately $200. Such illegal activity was not confined to Beaudesert (*Courier-Mail,* 1988e, p. 1). A police officer who confiscated illegal X-rated films from a cinema arrived at work the next day to find that the films had been returned to the theatre operator (*Courier-Mail,* 1987a, p. 4). Police would arrive at illegal gambling casinos, casually ask questions and enjoy free drinks at the bar, as casino patrons continued gambling as if the police were not there (*Courier-Mail,* 1987b, p. 4).

Police conduct was particularly brazen in relation to prostitution. Members of the Licensing Branch regularly drank alcohol in massage parlours whilst on duty or visited them after work for drinking sessions. A constable, whose first posting as a plain clothes officer was with the Licensing Branch, told the Inquiry that police spent their shifts travelling from one brothel to the other accepting free alcohol and sex. Prostitutes were booked when their name came 'due' on a police record book. Business would continue as normal when police visited parlours, with potential customers contemplating the 'menu board' whilst police made out the breaches (*Courier-Mail,* 1987b, p. 4).

Police not only expected free sex for themselves but also for their southern counterparts. A prostitute told of an incident when four or five local police arrived at a Maroochydore brothel with six visiting Melbourne police. 'When they arrived there was too many of them and not enough of us. The girls gave free sex to four or five police, the rest left disappointed' (*Courier Mail*, 1987c, p. 4).

Self-confessed corrupt former policeman Harry Burgess, who served in the Licensing Branch from 1979 to 1985, told the Inquiry that one of the two groups who ran Brisbane's brothels was paying police more than $10,000 a month for protection, from which he was receiving $500 a month (*Courier-Mail*, 1987d, p. 1). Burgess also gave lectures at the police officers' course on how to police prostitution and illegal gambling while accepting bribes not to enforce the law (*Courier-Mail*, 1987e, p. 4).

Anne Marie Tilley, who with her partner Hector Hapeta controlled a string of massage parlours, escort agencies and sex shops in Brisbane and the Gold Coast, testified that corrupt police assisted the growth of her brothel empire so they would receive larger protection payments (*Australian*, 1988c, p. 3).

These few examples offer only a brief account of the corroding conduct that was taking place within the QPF prior to the Fitzgerald Inquiry. Other factors contributing to the decay included the deliberate establishment of ineffectual internal and external police accountability processes, the abrogation of responsibility for police accountability by successive police ministers and the inappropriate relations between police and government that meant that Queensland was, in effect, operating as a police state (Whitton, 1989).

Police Accountability: Theory and Practice

In the lead-up to the Fitzgerald Inquiry, Queensland had internal and external forms of police accountability. Reforming Police Commissioner, Ray Whitrod (1970–1976) had earlier created a Criminal Investigations Unit to investigate organised crime, but it soon found itself investigating police suspected of being involved in criminal and organised crime matters (Proctor, 1985, p. 168). Soon after Lewis was appointed police commissioner he created an Internal Investigations Unit to deal with complaints against police. In 1982 the government established an independent civilian oversight body, the Police Complaints Tribunal (PCT), purporting to oversight the police complaints process. It was closed down on the recommendation of the Fitzgerald Inquiry in 1989 and replaced with the Criminal Justice Commission. Both the Internal Investigations Unit and the Police Complaints Tribunal were grossly ineffective forms of police accountability and are best described as shameful failures.

Internal Investigation Unit

The Internal Investigation Unit was no more than an 'artifice' (Fitzgerald, 1989, p. 288). It was not allowed to use surveillance equipment when investigating allegations of police misconduct and had no proactive capacity, which meant it could only react to accusations of police corruption and abuse of power after the event. It was also under-resourced and sometimes staffed by corrupt police. No police officer assigned to the Internal Investigation Unit (honest or corrupt) received any training in internal investigation methods, and the interrogation techniques employed were generally 'pleasant, ineffectual and feeble' (Fitzgerald, 1989, p. 289).

The Fitzgerald Report's (1989, p. 81) assessment of the Unit was scathing. It found it was 'a disastrous failure, inept, inefficient and grossly biased in favour of the police'. Its investigative procedures were described as 'amazing', with Internal Investigation Unit officers disclosing 'the material available to suspected police officers prior to interrogations'. The Report went on to observe that: 'Regularly no more has been required as a basis of findings in favour of a police officer than his denial of the case against him'. The Fitzgerald Report concluded that the Internal Investigation Unit was a 'friendly, sympathetic, protective and inept overseer ... [which] provided warm comfort to corrupt police' (1989, p. 289).

The Police Complaints Tribunal (PCT)

The PCT also proved to be an artifice set up as 'a façade for Government power' (Fitzgerald, 1989, p. 290). Queenslanders were told that it would enhance accountability, but in practice the power of the police and government intent combined to create an oversight body, which for most of its life deflected criticisms and shielded police from accountability for their actions (Lewis, 1999, pp. 118–120).

The PCT was established in response to allegations about police corruption made by two former police officers on the Australian Broadcasting Corporation's *Nationwide* program. The Police Minister, Russell Hinze's reaction to the program was to describe it as a 'soap opera on par with "General Hospital"' (Dickie, 1989, p. 102). However, he simultaneously announced that he would seek Cabinet's approval for the establishment of a permanent police oversight body. This apparent contradiction in Hinze's response can be understood through an examination of the rationale underpinning the establishment of the Tribunal.

The legislation to establish the Tribunal was rushed through the planning and drafting stage and was introduced into the Parliament some two weeks later (Queensland Parliament, 1982, p. 5519). In the Second Reading of the Police Complaints Tribunal Bill, Hinze makes it clear that enhanced accountability was not the motivating factor for the rushed introduction of the Bill. As he said:

> For as long as I have been a member of this house, police have been made fair game for anyone who wanted to make non-specific and sensational allegations with malicious political intent. The government will no longer tolerate open-slather criticism of our Police Force by people who lack the necessary evidence to back up their claims. The proposed tribunal will provide a permanent and independent forum for the hearing of allegations against our police force ... Throughout Australia there seems to be a general trend towards attacking police by making unsubstantiated allegations that capture the headlines and then refusing to supply specific information. The proposed tribunal will put an end to that. Individuals who make allegations against the police will be encouraged to bring those allegations forward for investigation by the Internal Investigations Section, whose record of efficiency is undisputed. If individuals feel that their allegations are not properly looked into, they will be able to take them to the Police Complaints Tribunal. (Queensland Parliament, 1982, p. 5548)

The Act also provided for imprisonment for people who made vexatious complaints and a custodial penalty for registering a complaint which a complainant was subsequently unable to substantiate to the very high criminal standard of proof, beyond reasonable doubt (Queensland Parliament, 1990, p. 1347).

The structure of the Tribunal immediately called into question its ability to be effective. It originally comprised a district court judge (the chairperson), a solicitor and stipendiary magistrate and the President of the Queensland Police Union. In 1985 a new position of deputy chair was created. All members were part time and the term of appointment was for one year, renewable.

The appointment of the President of the Queensland Police Union as a member of the independent police oversight body immediately undermined the legitimacy of the Tribunal. It also created a serious conflict of interest situation for the Union's President as the vast majority of matters brought before the Tribunal involved members of the Union he headed. Despite this, the Police Union President was the longest serving member of the Tribunal. He was appointed for seven terms (Lewis, 1999, pp. 111–112).

The first chairperson served for one year. The second Chair, District Court Judge Eric Pratt was a former Victorian police officer. The Lewis diaries, which were exhibits at the Fitzgerald Inquiry, show that in 1979 Pratt had phoned then Commissioner Lewis about possible elevation to Queen's Counsel and Lewis in turn had phoned a government minister about the matter. Pratt was appointed QC in January 1980. Lewis's diaries also show that prior to Pratt's appointment as chairperson of the Tribunal, the police commissioner was being phoned or was phoning others in relation to the appointment. Other entries in Lewis's diaries indicate a strong friendship between him and Pratt (see Dickie, 1989, p. 104).

Lewis's statement to the Inquiry makes it clear that Pratt was one of his 'special friends', a person with whom he 'could discuss any matter in confidence'. The head of a police force and the head of an independent police oversight body need to have an arms length relationship and government should not be taking advice from the police commissioner on who should head an independent police complaints tribunal (Lewis, 1999, p. 113).

Lack of resources was also a problem for the Tribunal, for while it had the power to investigate in its own right it did not have the resources needed to do so. This meant that the PCT had to rely on the Internal Investigation Unit to conduct its investigations. Former New South Wales Ombudsman, David Landa, when pointing out the negative impact lack of resources has on effective accountability, made the point that 'powers without necessary resources are not true powers' (NSW Ombudsman, 1993, p. 22). Starving police oversight bodies of funds is a strategy sometimes used by governments when they are paying lip-service to accountability (Lewis, 2000). An examination of the Annual Reports for the period of Pratt's appointment as chairperson also indicates that the Tribunal was becoming an apologist for the police.

The Fitzgerald Report described the Police Complaints Tribunal as 'an illustration of an administrative body with the superficial trappings of quasi-judicial impartiality and independence set up as a façade for government powers'. Corrupt police regarded it as 'impotent' and it had 'lost all public confidence' (Fitzgerald, 1989, p. 292). One of the recommendations of the Fitzgerald Report was the closure of the Tribunal.

Politicisation of Police

The dismal failure of police accountability in Queensland in the lead up to the Fitzgerald Inquiry can be attributed in large part to the politicisation of the QPF by then Premier Sir Joh Bjelke-Petersen.

Attempts to politicise the Force began during Whitrod's term as commissioner and eventually led to his resignation in 1976. They began in earnest in July 1971 when the South African Springbok Rugby Union team was to play in Brisbane. Games in other Australian States had been disrupted by demonstrators and Bjelke-Petersen decided to adopt an excessive 'law and order' policy in relation to any possible demonstrations in Brisbane. He did so by announcing a State of Emergency during the Springbok's visit. This gave his government 'unspecified and unlimited powers' for a month (Whitton, 1989, p. 22).

In the most controversial episode during the Springbok visit to Brisbane, approximately 300 people peacefully protested on 22 July outside the hotel where the South African players were staying. Fifteen minutes into the protest police ordered the demonstrators to leave the footpath, but rather than allow them sufficient time to do so, police 'waded into them with fists and boots' and pursued the fleeing protestors down a hill. Two days later the government won by-elections in the seats of Merthyr and Maryborough. Research found that the very large swing to the government in Maryborough was related to the tough law and order stance adopted by Bjelke-Petersen (Whitton, 1989, p. 22). The Premier rewarded police for their tough approach to his law and order policy by granting them an extra week's annual leave (Dickie, 1989, p. 20).

The Premier now had proof that a strong law and order policy was a vote winner, but to continue this approach on an ongoing basis he needed a compliant police force headed by a willing police commissioner. Ray Whitrod did not fit that mould as he believed in the independence of police from arbitrary political control. He understood that a politicised police force would end up being accountable, not to the law, the Parliament or the community but to the Government.

Bjelke-Petersen and Whitrod increasingly clashed over the issue of police accountability. In July 1976, during a street march demonstration, a police officer struck a student on the head with a police baton. The unprovoked attack was captured by a television crew and shown on the nightly news. After some initial investigations Whitrod ordered an internal investigation into police conduct during the march. The Premier intervened and quashed the inquiry. The Premier's actions confirmed what many in the community were coming to believe: that the QPF was being politicised (Hawker, 1981, p. 74).

A month later, the Premier and Commissioner Whitrod were again at odds; this time the matter was over a police raid on a 'hippie commune' at Cedar Bay in North Queensland. Despite widespread criticism of police actions, the Premier refused to hold an open inquiry into alleged police misconduct. His response to calls for an inquiry was to say that they were 'all part of an orchestrated campaign to legalise marijuana and denigrate the police' (CPA, 1977, p. 16).

At this time all promotions in the Queensland Police Force, for the positions of inspector and above, had to be approved by Cabinet. In November 1976, the Premier announced that Terence Lewis, a junior inspector at Charleville would be promoted to assistant commissioner (*Courier-Mail*, 1988f, p. 4). Lewis's name had not been put forward by either Commissioner Whitrod or the Commissioned Officers' Association. Whitrod told the Fitzgerald Inquiry that he was 'flabbergasted' by Cabinet's choice as members of Cabinet were aware of allegations that Lewis was one of former Commissioner Frank Bischof's bagmen. When Whitrod questioned Police

Minister Newbery about the appointment, Newbery is reported to have said: 'Oh, but that was when he was a detective sergeant. He is now an inspector and he wouldn't do that sort of thing now' (*Courier-Mail*, 1981, p. 1).

Whitrod felt that he had little option but to resign from the force over the appointment as he believed that Lewis had been promoted to assistant commissioner so that Bjelke-Petersen could seize control of the Force. With Lewis as assistant commissioner, Whitrod believed he would only be a front man, a shield for what might and indeed did develop (*Courier-Mail*, 1988g, p. 1). Rather then advertise the position of Commissioner, Cabinet promoted newly appointed Assistant Commissioner Lewis to the top job.

Improper Police–Government Relations

Now that the government had a police commissioner willing to do the government's bidding, the Premier escalated his confrontationist law and order policies. Police power was used to break up demonstrations against uranium shipments and political street marches in Queensland. A few months before the 1977 State election, the Premier banned street marches, announcing that:

> The day of the political street march is over. Anyone who holds a street march spontaneously or otherwise will know they're acting illegally ... don't bother applying for a permit. You won't get one. That's government policy now. (quoted in Dickie, 1989, p. 54)

The right to appeal the refusal to grant a permit to march was moved from a magistrate to a superintendent of police (Hawker, 1981, pp. 78–79).

Police were also used during the electricity industry pickets in 1985 to implement draconian legislation. They arrested members of Federal Parliament and clergy who protested against the government's controversial legislation. With Lewis in charge of the police force, the situation developed where the government did 'not even pretend that the police [were] independent from its control' (Milte & Weber, 1977, p. 218). An unofficial 'quid pro quo' for police compliance was the premier and police ministers defending police against allegations of misconduct.

Ministerial Responsibility

The Fitzgerald Inquiry terms of reference covered the periods of tenure of five police ministers: Thomas Newbery, Ronald Camm, William Glasson, Russell Hinze and William Gunn. Throughout their time as ministers corruption and abuse of power within the QPF flourished.

Newbery became police minister in 1976. When he was confronted with allegations of police misconduct he repeatedly defended the police (*Courier-Mail*, 1977, p. 3). Camm took over the portfolio in late 1977 and served as police minister for the next three years. He too defended questionable police conduct. Russell Hinze followed Camm and continued what was becoming the norm for Queensland police ministers: defending police against allegations of wrongdoing and denying that illegal prostitution and gambling were taking place in Queensland. In October 1981 the *Courier-Mail* reported that illegal casinos were operating with impunity in Fortitude Valley. Hinze's response was to say that he did not believe any existed, and anyone who said they had seen one was a 'liar' (*Courier-Mail*, 1987f, p. 4). Bellino told the Fitzgerald Inquiry that he had been operating highly organised, illegal casinos in Fortitude Valley for over five years and that they were returning him $20,000 a week. One of those casinos was nicknamed 'the casino that didn't exist' (*Courier-Mail*, 1987f, p. 4).

Glasson replaced Hinze and initially appeared willing to do something about alleged police corruption. In April 1983 he made a public statement saying he wanted to stamp out prostitution and illegal gambling because they caused the public to be suspicious about police receiving bribes. The President of the Police Union (who was also a member of the Police Complaints Tribunal) said that unless police received an apology from the Police Minister the union would by-pass him and deal directly with the premier. The premier's response was to say that Police Minister Glasson '... must be more careful in the way he expresses himself' and that he would 'be calling him' as Glasson needed 'to be discreet'. A few days later the premier, the police minister and police commissioner met and after the meeting Glasson issued a statement saying: 'If there is corruption in the force it's very minimal' (*Sydney Morning Herald*, 1987, p. 3). It seems that Glasson too had become a defender of the police. This was confirmed when, in response to serious allegations of police corruption made in Parliament by a member of the opposition, Glasson accused the opposition member of seeking publicity 'to flatter his own ego with scant regard for the irreparable damage he does to the reputation of honest, hardworking police officers'. He went so far as to suggest that the accusations might be designed 'to serve the purpose of some of the criminal element who are unhappy about the inroads these officers are making into their activities' (Queensland Parliament, 1994, p. 1503).

In 1984 there were allegations of police corruption in relation to police involvement in child pornography and male prostitution. This time Glasson responded appropriately by establishing an inquiry headed by Des Sturgess QC. Sturgess delivered his report 12 months later, part of it confidential. The confidential section was given to Premier Sir Joh Bjelke-Petersen, the Attorney-General Neville Harper, and Police Minister Glasson. It identified people who were subsequently named in the Fitzgerald Inquiry as being involved in illegal casinos and female brothels (*Sydney Morning Herald*, 1987, p. 3). The recommendations of the Sturgess Report, like the Lucas Inquiry were ignored and it proved to be yet another symbolic gesture by government designed to create an illusion of action while, in effect, maintaining the status quo.

The Lewis diaries show the degree to which the government was involved in operational policing matters and the way in which Commissioner Lewis had become involved with the parliamentary and administrative wings of the National Party government. They demonstrate that for years Lewis was directly linked into mainstream National Party politics. For example, on one occasion the Police Commissioner had phoned another minister, a former policeman, to talk about the actions of his own minister; on another, the commissioner discussed with a National Party trustee and power broker senior government appointments, an electoral redistribution and the Honours lists. Lewis and Bjelke-Petersen discussed internal promotions within the government; government members phoned the commissioner seeking what could be perceived as inappropriate favours and the commissioner sought investment advice from a National Party trustee.

Lewis said that while he was commissioner of police he saw the premier 134 times and that the premier had phoned him 197 times (*Courier-Mail*, 1988h, p. 4). Whitrod told the inquiry that in the six years he was commissioner he had personally dealt with the premier on three occasions (*Courier-Mail*, 1988h, p. 4). Lewis's submission to the Fitzgerald Inquiry also named Premier Sir Joh Bjelke-Petersen, as 'a special friend with whom I could discuss any matter in confidence' (*Courier-Mail*, 1988h, p. 4). Other special friends were National Party trustee and power broker Sir Edward Lyons and former National Party Minister for Transport Don Lane. Lane was later prosecuted, convicted and sentenced to 12 months for falsifying expenses.

Electoral and Administrative Maladministration

The Fitzgerald Inquiry went beyond investigating wrongdoing by police and government ministers. It examined the 'entire system of government and its shortcomings' and became a 'pathologist' of that system (Finn, 1994, p. 32). Chapter 3 of the Report, headed 'The Political Context', described an ineffective Parliament, a distorted and unfair electoral system and a politicised and moribund public service not subject to review or accountability mechanisms.

Of these shortcomings, the electoral system was most fundamental in that it enabled the retention of power by the Bjelke Petersen regime, providing a 'buffer against the possibility of political defeat' (Coaldrake, 1990, p. 157). The zonal electoral system had been introduced by a Labor government in 1949, but was refined and extended by the National Party government. The effect was to weight rural votes at between one and a half and three times the value of urban votes (Reynolds, 1990, p. 246). The system was achieved by the government controlling the appointment of the electoral commissioners, who deliberated in private and reported directly to the premier, rather than Parliament (Fitzgerald, 1989, p. 127). The end result was that the National Party formed government in 1986 by winning 49 seats out of an 89-seat Parliament with 39.6% of the vote (Coaldrake, 1989). Coaldrake (1989) describes how in addition to the zonal system, the government actively engaged in gerrymandering electoral borders, excising particular areas from seats to improve the government's prospect of success in those seats.

Its electoral dominance enabled the government to maintain tight control over Parliament. By the late 1980s, Queensland's Parliament was dominated by the executive. It sat infrequently, for 46 days in 1988 and 36 days in 1989 (Ransley, 1992, p. 154). Contrary to Westminster convention, the Governor had been convinced to prorogue Parliament altogether in 1983 when the coalition broke down and the National Party, temporarily without a majority, faced losing a motion of no confidence (Preston, Sampford & Connors, 2002, p. 100). The Parliament lacked basic mechanisms to scrutinise executive action that were by then well-accepted in other Westminster systems, such as public accounts and public works committees, estimates committees, and an independent auditor-general. The speaker, far from exercising independent authority, had been shown to be amenable to government direction (Coaldrake, 1990). Ministers were allowed to occupy most or even all of question time, and gag and guillotine devices were routinely used to stifle debate. The Opposition was under-resourced and demoralised (Ransley, 1992).

As Parliament became progressively weaker and less relevant, power and authority were increasingly centralised in cabinet. After organisational changes introduced in 1957, cabinet assumed an 'all-encompassing and centralised administrative and procedural control' over the business of government, which 'over time had a debilitating impact' on its effectiveness. It became bogged down in minor administration and procedure rather than policy making (Tait, 1992, p. 125). Ministers received a huge volume of material every week, with little time to read it, and did not regularly receive briefings from their own departmental advisors (Tait, 1992, p. 126). Cabinet and its ministers were involved in detailed decisions about government contracts, tenders, land grants and rezonings and the appointment of a broad range of government positions. This provided the opportunity for the blurring of the making and implementing of policy, and the mixing of public and private interests (Fitzgerald, 1989, p. 125). This situation was exacerbated by the lack of any systemised requirement for the declaration of conflicts of interest by either ministers or senior public servants.

The opportunities for corruption and maladministration were intensified by an environment that emphasised secrecy and lacked mechanisms for administrative review. Queensland was not alone in lacking freedom of information laws at that time, but stood apart in its active hostility to the idea (Chadwick, 1990, p. 182). It also lacked general mechanisms for determinative review of administrative decisions, such as administrative appeals tribunals, and possessed only cumbersome judicial review procedures (Fitzgerald, 1989, p. 128).

Finally, any prospect of an independent public service able to provide alternative advice to government was minimal. The public sector had become increasingly politicised, given that there seemed little chance of the government losing power, and little hope of advancement for anyone who questioned its way of doing business. There was no incentive for reform, or new practices, and instead, a sharing of values between the elected executive and those who advised it (Coaldrake, 1990). This atmosphere was found by Fitzgerald to have supported misconduct and led to a decline in the quality of public administration in the state (Fitzgerald, 1989, p. 130). This occurred significantly in the Justice Department and led to a lack of real critical assessment of government legislation, and a failure to advise on the legal ramifications of government and ministerial misconduct. It also led to a lack of interest in law reform generally and in particular in the area of criminal justice (Fitzgerald, 1989, pp. 139–141).

In summary, the pre-Fitzgerald government can be described as having:

> Close connections between business and politics and a political culture that was autocratic, authoritarian, racist, and oppressive. The government was vulnerable to the pressure of international mining companies and conservative groups opposed to liberal social trends. It was sensitive to State rights and deeply suspicious of Canberra. Supported by an electoral gerrymander and a weak Coalition partner, the Bjelke-Petersen government rode roughshod over conventions of open government. Parliament met rarely and briefly. The police force was seen as a natural ally and extension of government. While it was well known that dishonesty and corruption were endemic, a docile and tame media permitted the status quo to remain predominantly unchallenged. (Preston et al., 2002, pp. 99–100)

It was against this background that the Fitzgerald Inquiry was established and completed and it is these matters which the authors of this edited collection have addressed.

This Book

A striking feature of Queensland pre-Fitzgerald is how intertwined the problems were — how widely and deeply the institutional cancer had spread. Ransley in her chapter on inquiries addresses these matters and explains that

Fitzgerald, like Costigan before him, understood that unravelling intricately linked institutional problems requires the core of the system to be exposed and a reform program that concentrates on fixing systemic issues rather than apportioning blame to individuals. In Fitzgerald's case the problems were about the conduct of public life including the malapportioned electoral system which greatly diminished the operations of the Parliament.

Noel Preston graphically illustrates how despite Fitzgerald's best efforts to raise parliamentary standards and greatly improve scrutiny of the executive, virtually non-existent pre-Fitzgerald, there is still much to be done in Queensland, as well as nationally and internationally, to enhance transparency in public life and the accountability of elected public officials in particular. This theme is also addressed by Ransley in her chapter on the Electoral and Administrative Reform Commission, and by David Solomon who examines progress in relation to Freedom of Information legislation. Ransley evaluates EARC's achievements in its short four-year life and asks whether the Commission should have been retained. Solomon evaluates the extent of the progress made toward Fitzgerald's goal of preventing future governments and the bureaucracy burying decisions by public servants in places the community can not access. For Fitzgerald, FOI was one of the tools needed to achieve open and accountable government and good governance. Solomon explains that while progress has been made it seems there is still much that needs to be done to lift the veil of secrecy.

Fitzgerald found that police corruption in Queensland was multidimensional, manifesting itself in endemic verballing practices, protection rackets, involvement in illegal gambling and prostitution, and a variety of other forms of direct criminal activity that was engaged in, for personal profit, by junior and senior officers including the commissioner of police. Such practices could only flourish because police systems of accountability were woefully inadequate. As several authors have shown, internal police systems and processes were deliberately designed to fail, as was the external independent accountability institution established by the Bjelke-Petersen government to make police accountable for their actions. Police corruption in all its forms was nurtured and amplified by the political, parliamentary and social malaise described so graphically in the following 12 chapters.

Given the central importance of police corruption and abuse of police power to the Fitzgerald inquiry, and the all encompassing nature of the police reform program that forms a large part of the Fitzgerald Report, several chapters are devoted to the many dimensions of policing and the struggle to achieve institutional and cultural change. In Chapter 6, Colleen Lewis addresses the key issue of the politicisation of the policing function and the corrosive effect politicisation had on democratic policing. In so doing, she assesses the effectiveness of three reforms recommended by Fitzgerald to help address the 'thorny' overlap between constabulary independence and ministerial responsibility.

Jenny Fleming's chapter on structural police reform concentrates primarily on reform of the QPF, in particular regionalisation, civilianisation and community policing. But her analysis goes beyond policing. She also addresses the impact Fitzgerald had on broader public sector reform and credits the Fitzgerald program with providing the framework for others with their own ideas for positive public sector reform. Drew and Prenzler also address the matter of civilianisation but their analysis takes place within the broad context of Human Resource Management, including police to population ratios, the promotional system, recruitment and training and education. Their report card on progress in these areas is mixed. Staying with police reform matters, Kerry Wimshurst gives a detailed account of how Fitzgerald's vision for the future of police education lasted a mere three years. Wimshurst, like many other contributors, takes his analysis beyond Queensland and looks at the situation in other Australian states and overseas and questions whether Fitzgerald's vision is achievable and always desirable.

In addressing the role and influence of the police union Richard Evans sees reason for optimism, especially at the national level. However, he points out that in Queensland and Victoria, in particular, there is still ongoing resistance to reform, especially when it is designed to turn the spotlight of accountability toward the conduct of union members. Evans points to the need for unions to move away from supporting negative and myopic aspects of the police culture which, to varying degrees, have been barriers to reform in many jurisdictions in Australia and beyond, and to embrace integrity reforms.

The media's role as the 'fourth estate' is sometimes that of lapdog as well as watchdog. Julianne Schultz demonstrates how media complacency can contribute to declining standards in public life. However, when the media decide to act fearlessly as the community's watchdog, and are given the resources needed to do so effectively, they can be the catalyst for much needed reform. In Queensland, the media played both a lapdog and watchdog role, in that they were part of the problem as well contributing part of the solution.

Along with EARC, the Criminal Justice Commission was an attempt by Fitzgerald to put institutions in place that would implement his reform program and prevent a return to the 'bad old days'. The CJC, now the Crime and Misconduct Commission (CMC), is a unique integrity commission which has influenced the design of public sector integrity models in Australia and beyond. As Colleen Lewis argues in her chapter on the CJC–CMC, the direction the CMC is taking in relation to complaints handling may well have negative consequences for the institution itself.

The genius of the Fitzgerald Inquiry is that the nature of corrupt practices in Queensland was understood almost immediately (at least instinctively) as a pervasive and stable 'sub-system' of 'well-established networks where trust is present on both sides of the exchange relationship,' to borrow from Charles Sampford's words in his chapter on integrity systems. Sampford takes us beyond Queensland and Australia and places state and national integrity systems into a global context.

As the public hearings at the Fitzgerald Inquiry were drawing to a close, it became evident that any reform program would require the establishment of an equally stable and pervasive 'integrity system.' This book is dedicated to documenting and analysing the many attempts to establish such a system in Queensland in the 20 years since Fitzgerald, identifying successes and failures and making some recommendations for further reform. The authors have also, where possible, looked beyond the borders of Queensland to consider the influence of the Fitzgerald model of systemic reform nationally and internationally.

Conclusion

All authors in this book emphasise, in diverse ways, that the establishment and maintenance of effective integrity systems is a task that has no clear end point, and that attempts at reform can themselves stir up powerful forces opposed to change. In the cases where reform failures are documented the challenges for the integrity system are obvious. However, there are perhaps even greater challenges when some major problems seem to be (more or less) under control and success is celebrated — such as with the elimination of the most egregious instances of police and political corruption. It is at these times that we once again need to 'hear the prophetic voice' and look with more discerning eyes at hitherto uncontroversial practices in politics, policing, or public administration.

Such a prophetic voice was once again provided by Tony Fitzgerald on 28 July 2009, after 20 years of public silence, when he introduced the Honourable Arthur Chaskalson as the inaugural Griffith University Tony Fitzgerald lecturer. In commenting on 20 years of reform in Queensland, and in particular on recent trends in government-business relations, Fitzgerald observed:

> Access can now be purchased, patronage is dispensed, mates and supporters are appointed and retired politicians exploit their connections to obtain 'success fees' for deals between business and government. Neither side of politics is interested in these issues except for short-term political advantage as each enjoys or plots impatiently for its turn at the privileges and opportunities which accompany power. (Fitzgerald, 2009)[3]

These and Fitzgerald's other remarks were widely reported in the media, provoking extensive debate. Before long the controversy had triggered a government discussion paper *Integrity and Accountability in Queensland*, as well as a public review. Importantly, the issue was quickly recognised in the press as having national significance and the debate took on a life of its own, detached from its Queensland origins. This illustrates that the media are still an important force in the reform process. It also vividly illustrates the point made by Premier Bligh in her foreword to the discussion paper, "The job of delivering accountability and transparency in government is never done." (Queensland Government, 2009, p. 2)

This book is offered as a record of 20 years of struggle for accountability and transparency in Queensland, and also as a contribution to the ongoing struggle to build effective integrity systems across Australia, and internationally.

Endnotes

1   Sections of this chapter draw on Lewis (1988) *Police Accountability Queensland Style,* unpublished honours thesis, Griffith University, Australia.

2   For further discussion of the pre-Fitzgerald era see generally Coaldrake, 1989; Coaldrake and Wanna, 1988; Finnane, 1987, 1994; Lewis, 1999; Prasser, 1992; Preston, Sampford, & Connors, 2002; Ransley, 1992, 2008; Whitton, 1989.

3   The full text of this lecture can be accessed via the Griffith University website.

References

Chadwick, P. (1990). Freedom of information: How Queensland could do better than the Commonwealth, Victoria and New South Wales schemes In S. Prasser, R. Wear & J. Nethercote (Eds.), *Corruption and reform: The Fitzgerald vision* (pp. 178–202). Brisbane, Australia: University of Queensland Press.

CMC. (n.d.). The Fitzgerald Inquiry. Retrieved 14 September 2009, from http://www.cmc. qld.gov.au/asp/index.asp?pgid=10877

Coaldrake, P. (1989). Changing the System. *Legal Services Bulletin, 14*(4), 159.

Coaldrake, P. (1990). Overview In S. Prasser, R. Wear & J. Nethercote (Eds.), *Corruption and reform: The Fitzgerald vision* (pp. 157–159). St. Lucia: University of Queensland Press.

Coaldrake, P., & Wanna, J. (1988). 'Not like the good old days': The political impact of the Fitzgerald Inquiry into police corruption in Queensland. *Australian Quarterly, 60*(4), 404–414.

Communist Party of Australia. (CPA). (1977). *Law in disorder.* Brisbane, Australia: Author.

Dickie, P. (1989). *The road to Fitzgerald and beyond.* Brisbane: UQP.

Finn, P. (1994). The significance of the Fitzgerald and the WA Inc Commissions. In P. Weller (Ed.), *Royal Commissions and the making of public policy* (pp. 32–39). Sydney, Australia: Macmillan Education Australia.

Finnane, M. (1987). The Fitzgerald Commission: Uncovering the Lewis years. *Legal Services Bulletin, 12*(5), 210.

Finnane, M. (1994). *Police and government: Histories of policing in Australia.* Melbourne, Australia: Oxford University Press.

Fitzgerald, G. (1989). *Report of a Commission of Inquiry pursuant to Orders in Council.* Brisbane, Australia: Queensland Government.

Fitzgerald, G. (Tony). (2009, 29 July). What went wrong with Queensland? [Edited version of speech]. *The Courier-Mail*. Retrieved 30 July 2009, from http://www.news.com. au/couriermail/story/0,23739,25849996-3102,00.html

Gibbs, H. (1992). Foreword. In A. Hede, S. Prasser & M. Neylan (Eds.), *Keeping them honest: Deocratic reform in Queensland*. Brisbane, Australia: UQP.

Hawker, B. (1981). Police, politics, protest and the press: Queensland 1967–81. *Alternative Criminology Journal, 4,* 57–91.

Herbert, J., & Gilling, T. (2004). *The bagman: Final confessions of Jack Herbert*. Sydney, Australia: ABC Books.

Lewis, C. (1988). *Police accountability Queensland style*. Unpublished honours thesis, Griffith University, Australia.

Lewis, C. (1997). *Civilian oversight of complaints against police: External relationships and their impact on effectiveness*. PhD thesis, Griffith University, Australia.

Lewis, C. (1999). *Complaints against police: The politics of reform*. Sydney, Australia: Hawkins Press.

Lewis, C. (2000). The politics of civilian oversight: Serious commitment or lip service. In A.J. Goldsmith & C. Lewis (Eds.), *Civilian oversight of policing: Governance, democracy and human rights*. Oxford: Hart Publishing

Lucas, G. (1977). *Report of the Committee of Inquiry into the enforcement of Criminal Law in Queensland [Lucas Report]*. Brisbane, Australia: Queensland Government.

Milte, K., & Weber, T. (1977). *Police in Australia: Development, functions and procedures*. Melbourne, Australia: Butterworths.

NSW Ombudsman. (1993). *Annual report*. Sydney, Australia: State Government Printer.

Prasser, S. (1992). The need for reform in Queensland: So what was the problem? In A. Hede, S. Prasser & M. Neylan (Eds.), *Keeping them honest: Democratic reform in Queensland* (pp. 15–29). Brisbane, Australia: University of Queensland Press.

Preston, N., Sampford, C., & Connors, C. (2002). *Encouraging ethics and challenging corruption: Reforming governance in public institutions*. Sydney, Australia: Federation Press.

Proctor, C. (1985). The police. In A. Patience (Ed.), *The Bjelke-Petersen premiership, 1968– 1983: Issues in public policy*. Melbourne: Longman Cheshire.

Queensland Government. (2009). *Integrity and accountability in Queensland discussion paper*. Retrieved September 14, 2009, from http://www.premiers.qld.gov.au/community-issues/open-transparent-gov/assets/integrity-and-accountability-paper.pdf

Queensland Parliament. (1982, April 1). *Queensland Parliamentary Debates* (p. 5519). Brisbane, Australia: Author.

Queensland Parliament. (1990, May 10). *Queensland Parliamentary Debates* (p. 1347). Brisbane, Australia: Author.

Queensland Parliament. (1994, February 9). *Queensland Parliamentary Debates* (p. 1503). Brisbane, Australia: Author.

Ransley, J. (1992). Reform of parliamentary processes: An assessment. In A. Hede, S. Prasser & M. Neylan (Eds.), *Keeping them honest: Democratic reform in Queensland* (pp: 149–164). Brisbane, Australia: UQP.

Ransley, J. (2001). The Queensland Fitzgerald Inquiry and EARC: A case study in political, legal and administrative reform. In C. Sampford (Ed.), *Transparency International Integrity handbook* (pp. 4–17). Brisbane, Australia: Key Centre for Ethics, Law, Justice and Governance, Griffith University.

Ransley, J. (2008). Illusions of reform: Queensland's Legislative Assembly since Fitzgerald. In N. Aroney, S. Prasser & J.R. Nethercote (Eds.), *Restraining elective dictatorship: The upper house solution?* (pp. 240–253). Perth, Australia: University of WA Press.

Reynolds, P. (1990). Problems and prospects for electoral reform after Fitzgerald. In S. Prasser, R. Wear & J. Nethercote (Eds.), *Corruption and reform: The Fitzgerald vision* (pp: 245–249). Brisbane, Australia: UQP.

Tait, S. (1992). Reform of the Cabinet processes. In A. Hede, S. Prasser & M. Neylan (Eds.), *Keeping them honest: Democratic reform in Queensland* (pp: 123–124). Brisbane, Australia: University of Queensland Press.

The Australian. (1988a, 28–29 May), p. 8.

The Australian. (1988b, 7 September), p. 3.

The Australian. (1988c, 21 September), p. 3.

The Courier-Mail. (1977, 3 August), p. 3.

The Courier-Mail. (1981, 3 March), p. 1.

The Courier-Mail. (1987a, 22 October), p. 4.

The Courier-Mail. (1987b, 21 October), p. 4.

The Courier-Mail. (1987c, 4 December), p. 4.

The Courier-Mail. (1987d, 2 September), p. 4.

The Courier-Mail. (1987e, 28 October), p. 4.

The Courier-Mail. (1987f, 21 August), p. 4.

The Courier-Mail. (1988a, 2 September), p. 1.

The Courier-Mail. (1988b, 30 August), p. 4.

The Courier-Mail. (1988c, 27 May), p. 4.

The Courier-Mail. (1988d, 11 September), p. 4.

The Courier-Mail. (1988e, 29 July), p. 1.

The Courier-Mail. (1988f, 3 November), p. 4.

The Courier-Mail. (1988g, 4 March), p. 1.

The Courier-Mail. (1988h, 12 October), p. 4.

Sydney Morning Herald. (1987, 13 October), p. 3.

Whitton, E. (1989). *The hillbilly dictator: Australia's police state.* Sydney, Australia: NSW ABC Enterprises for the Australian Broadcasting Corporation.

2

Fitzgerald:
A Model Investigative Inquiry?

Janet Ransley

Australia has a long tradition of appointing royal commissions and other forms of official inquiry to investigate corruption, crime, and associated police and political misconduct. Unlike many other investigative inquiries, the *Commission of Inquiry into Possible Illegal Activities and Associated Police Misconduct* (hereafter the Fitzgerald Inquiry) has had a lasting effect both from its policy recommendations, as discussed elsewhere in this book, and in the model it has provided for subsequent investigative inquiries. This chapter discusses how Fitzgerald built on and expanded practices already pioneered by the *Royal Commission on the Activities of the Federated Ship Painters' and Dockers' Union* (hereafter the Costigan Commission) to establish this investigative inquiry model.

The chapter begins with a brief overview of why governments appoint inquiries and how they seek to control and limit their investigations. It then examines some prominent examples of less successful inquiries to show how the Fitzgerald Commission was able to overcome similar restrictions to generate real reform. Significant techniques included seeking and obtaining expanded terms of reference and statutory powers, targeted use of witness indemnities in return for incriminating evidence, and the adoption of a proactive law-enforcement approach rather than a traditional, passive judicial form of inquiry. These have since become standard practices not just for ad hoc royal commissions, but also for the subsequently created standing crime and corruption commissions.

Note: Sections of this chapter draw on Ransley, J. (2001). *Inquisitorial Royal Commissions and the Investigation of Political Wrongdoing*. PhD thesis, Griffith University.

In addition to these investigative practices, Fitzgerald also chose to focus on the need for public exposure of the nature and extent of wrongdoing, rather than to maximise prosecutions, and created and sustained a supportive political, media and public environment. While these factors contributed to the lasting impact of the inquiry, they also provided grounds for two major streams of criticism — that the inquiry failed to yield enough prosecutions particularly of major criminals, and that it became too active a political and media player. A third criticism was that the commission lacked understanding of public administration and failed to commission independent social science research on which to base its recommendations.

The chapter concludes that rather than being failings, a focus on continuing reform by new agencies, and strong engagement with the political context were essential factors for Fitzgerald's lasting success. The difficult task for an investigative inquiry is to achieve the right balance between first, the attribution of individual blame and the development of ongoing, systemic reforms; and second, between independence from political processes on the one hand and the maintenance of public and political support on the other. The Fitzgerald Inquiry trod a carefully balanced path between these competing claims, and in doing so provided an enduring model for subsequent investigators.

Investigative Inquiries in Australia

Some royal commissions, commissions of inquiry and other forms of official inquiry[1] are appointed with purely policy functions, such as to make recommendations on difficult economic, health or welfare issues (Hallett, 1982). Investigative inquiries, however, are required to examine wrongdoing of some kind, although this may be accompanied by a responsibility to make policy proposals to prevent a recurrence of the problem. Two distinct types of investigative inquiry have examined police and corruption in Australia, the first focusing specifically on police misconduct, and the second on organised crime and drugs (see Finnane, 1988). The latter category is relevant because almost inevitably organised crime and drug trafficking involve police corruption or ineffectiveness. Notable examples of police, crime and drugs inquiries from various jurisdictions in the last 40 years are listed in Table 2.1. The table illustrates that the problem of police corruption and crime has been persistent and widespread across the larger Australian jurisdictions. While many of these inquiries received considerable attention during their life, few have achieved the lasting impact of the Fitzgerald Inquiry.

Governments appoint inquiries into matters such as these for both pragmatic and political reasons (Gilligan, 2002). Pragmatically, they serve to gather information and investigate issues that the mainstream institutions of government, such as police, prosecutors and public service agencies, cannot or should not address, particularly allegations of their own corruption or inefficiency. Other practical issues may include the need for specialised expertise, a multi disciplinary or cross-jurisdictional approach, or coercive powers. Royal commissions and commissions of inquiry have evolved in Australia in a unique way to meet the need for this type of investigation.[2] Politically, governments appoint such inquiries when public, opposition and media pressure forces them to do so, as a means of crisis management (Gilligan, 2002; Tiffin, 1999), or to deflect potential criticism through the establishment of a process perceived as independent (Prasser, 2006).

Equally, governments resist calls for royal commissions for both practical and political reasons. Practically, commission inquiries can be expensive, legalistic and slow. Politically, once appointed they can be difficult to control and can stray into unanticipated areas (Prasser, 2003). These concerns are overridden only when an issue is perceived as requiring independent investigation, by a body with coercive and intrusive powers, and when significant

---

Table 2.1
Australian Inquiries Into Police, Crime and Drugs Since 1970

Inquiries into police misconduct	
NSW	Lusher Royal Commission into NSW Police Administration (1979)
	Wood Royal Commission into NSW Police (1997)
QLD	Southport betting inquiry (1975)
	Lucas Inquiry (1976)
	Sturgess Inquiry (1984)
	Fitzgerald Commission of Inquiry into Possible Illegal Activities and Associated Police Misconduct (1989)
VIC	Kaye Inquiry into Abortion and Police Involvement (1970)
	Beach Royal Commission into Police Corruption (1975)
SA	Inquiry into the Activities of Police Special Branch (1977)
	Royal Commission into Dismissal of Police Commissioner Salisbury (1978)
WA	Kennedy Royal Commission into Whether There has been Corrupt or Criminal Conduct by any Western Australian Police Officer (2002)
Inquiries into organised crime and drugs	
Cmth	Williams Royal Commission into Drugs (1980 — jointly with NSW)
	Stewart Royal Commission into Drug Trafficking (1983)
NSW	Costigan Royal Commission on the Activities of the Federated Ship Painters' and Dockers' Union (1984 — jointly with Vic)
	Moffit Royal Commission into Organised Crime in Clubs in NSW (1973), Woodward (1977)
WA	Royal Commission into Commercial Activities of Government (WA Inc, 1992)

public pressure supports an inquiry. Even then, some governments remain resistant to the idea (e.g., successive Victorian governments have resisted persistent calls for either a royal commission or permanent corruption commission to examine alleged misconduct, as well as similar calls for a criminal justice research agency such as the New South Wales Bureau of Crime Statistics and Research).

Despite public and media perceptions of them as 'judicial', inquiries are in fact appointed by governments to perform executive functions. Their principal role is to gather information and make reports to support government decision-making (Hallett, 1982). While all of the Australian jurisdictions have enacted statutes giving inquiries a range of coercive powers, they do not exercise an adjudicative function.[3] In particular, they cannot reach conclusions as to criminal guilt or innocence (Hall, 2004). So while their functions are often preparatory or connected to the criminal justice system, such as investigating alleged corruption or misconduct to see if prosecutions should be started, or investigating disasters to see if negligence or other actionable misconduct caused them, properly speaking, inquiries are arms of the executive government of the day which can provide advice and recommendations only.

However, crime and corruption inquiries often look and act like courts, mimicking adversarial process with witnesses examined and cross-examined under oath, and parties represented by counsel. They are almost invariably headed by judges, former judges or senior counsel. The practical reason for this is that senior lawyers are experienced in assessing evidence, and are aware of the legal impact investigations may have on individual rights. The political reason is that generally such appointments attract public confidence as being impartial, non-political and independent. A side effect of their dominance by lawyers is that many inquiries fail to use fully their statutory powers to choose their own procedures, and are cautious about departing from the rules governing courts, such as the non-admissibility of hearsay evidence. So while these inquiries are clearly performing executive not judicial functions, they choose to proceed judicially (Hallett, 1982), in the sense that they comply with the legal system's notions of evidence gathering and appropriate conduct. This limits their capacity for proactive investigation.

Despite this, when governments do appoint inquiries, they seek a degree of lasting control through such measures as the choice of commissioners and their staff, determining their terms of reference, creating legislation that empowers and restricts them, and allocating their resources. These forms of control can enable governments to create an illusion of independent inquiry, while in reality maintaining tight control over an investigation.

A simple recipe for government control over an inquiry involves establishing it with a lack of resources, a compliant or conservative commissioner, and limited terms of reference and powers. As inquiries are external to the bureaucracy and therefore outside the normal budget process, they receive no vote of their own funds, but are instead reliant on whatever the department funding them — usually the Attorney-General's or Premier's department — will allocate. If resources are limited, the inquiry's capacity to hire staff, hold hearings, initiate or commission research and even write reports is clearly and directly affected. This control over resources is vividly illustrated when an incoming government inherits from its predecessor an inquiry which it does not support. For example, the Costigan Commission appointed by the Fraser government was supported by the incoming Hawke government in its inquiries into tax evasion, but when pressing for funding to examine links between unions, drugs and organised crime, it was denied requests for extensions of time and resources (Gilligan, 2002).

Governments also seek to control inquiries through choosing their membership. As discussed in chapter 1, in the period prior to the Fitzgerald Inquiry, Queensland's Police Complaints Tribunal was headed by District Court Judge Eric Pratt, a former police prosecutor whose attitude to investigating complaints against police was well known to the government. When Deputy Premier Bill Gunn announced what was to become the Fitzgerald Inquiry, his initial proposal to appoint Judge Pratt was met with objections from the legal community (Davis & Wanna, 1988). When Gunn was persuaded that a fresh and more independent face would be preferable, he no doubt still felt relatively safe in appointing a former federal court judge with little prior involvement in policing or criminal issues, as Fitzgerald then was (Coaldrake & Wanna, 1988). A decade later, when Queensland's Borbidge-led coalition government established the *Commission of Inquiry into the Future Role, Structure, Powers and Operation of the Criminal Justice Commission*, commonly known as the Connolly-Ryan Inquiry, they could be confident of the views of at least one commissioner, given that Mr Connolly had formerly given legal advice critical of the CJC to a government minister (see Ransley, 2001).

Another technique by which governments control inquiries is through restricting their terms of reference. By focusing inquiries on narrow issues or persons of interest, governments can attempt to minimise their capacity to broaden investigations into unwanted or unexpected areas. No better example can be given of these types of government controls over inquiries then the investigations into police misconduct in Queensland that preceded the Fitzgerald Inquiry, especially the 1963 *Royal Commission into Allegations Made Against Members of the Police Force in Relation to the National Hotel*, commonly known as the National Hotel Inquiry.

An Investigative Inquiry Set Up to Fail

Misconduct allegations against Queensland police had a long history, with some of the same officers investigated by Fitzgerald having been scrutinised by the National Hotel Commission of Inquiry. In 1963 it was alleged in the Queensland Parliament that senior police were drinking after hours and condoning prostitution at the National Hotel. A commission of inquiry headed by then Supreme Court Justice Harry Gibbs was appointed in November 1963. The commission found that while the hotel had breached the rules regarding the serving of liquor after hours, there was no evidence of any misconduct or violation of duty by police. At the Fitzgerald Inquiry, some of the police investigated by Gibbs admitted that they had in fact been corrupt at the time of the inquiry and had been guilty of the offences of which they had been accused in 1963 (including Boulton, Parker and Herbert — see Fitzgerald Report).

The failure of the Gibbs Inquiry has been described as monumental (R. Fitzgerald, 1990), not only because of what it did not uncover, but because it gave tacit encouragement to the continuation and growth of police corruption in Queensland until it reached the endemic proportions revealed by Fitzgerald. However, the inquiry was doomed to failure from the beginning.

First, it was given only a counsel assisting, with no independent investigators or capacity to engage them. It had to rely on the police comrades of those it was investigating. In fact, Don Lane was both a police investigator assisting the Commission, and an officer listed as being represented at the inquiry, presumably because his conduct was encompassed by the allegations (Fitzgerald Report, 1989). He later entered Parliament, became a Cabinet minister, was investigated by the Fitzgerald Inquiry and then jailed for corruption.

Second, the terms of reference were very limited, being constrained to particular conduct, specifically after hours drinking and the condoning of prostitution, at a particular hotel during a particular period. There was no scope to examine broader events and relationships or the general policing of illegal drinking and prostitution. The narrowness of the terms of reference also facilitated the strategy adopted by the corrupt officers of discrediting the allegations. They provided evidence contravening the specific charges, and discredited the witnesses against them, thereby distracting attention from other evidence affecting their own credibility (R. Fitzgerald, 1990).

The Commission also suffered from the defects of the relevant legislation — at that time there was no ability for commissions to compel self-incriminating evidence, no ability to obtain evidence from witnesses who had left the jurisdiction, and no ability to offer indemnities from prosecution to potential witnesses. But additional limits were self-imposed. Gibbs generally would not allow the giving of hearsay evidence at the inquiry, excluded evidence he considered lacking in relevance to his terms of reference, and only accepted evidence given verbally at hearings and subject to cross-examination. In addition, these rules were applied selectively with some witnesses against the police themselves subjected to attacks based on hearsay and irrelevant matters (R. Fitzgerald, 1990).

Finally, the Commission permitted the same senior counsel to represent the cabinet, its ministers, and the police under investigation. Hence any attack on the credibility of police could be interpreted as an attack on the government of the day. Witnesses were understandably reluctant to come forward and the eventual whitewash of police conduct became inevitable.

The failure of the National Hotel Inquiry is by no means unique. In a similar vein, the New South Wales government appointed then chief justice of New South Wales, Sir Laurence Street, to an inquiry as a result of a 1983 Four Corners program, *The Big League*. The program made allegations against, among others, the chief stipendiary magistrate Murray Farquhar, and Premier Neville Wran. This inquiry also suffered from narrow terms of reference focused on particular allegations, but in addition, according to some commentators, Street chose not to pursue evidence that would have uncovered more widespread wrongdoing. This was partly due to his belief that the inquiry should be finalised expeditiously due to the looming state election, and partly to:

> ... a passive approach to gathering pertinent evidence, itself derived from a narrowly and pre-defined legal rather than substantive definition of the investigative task before them. (Tiffin, 1999, p. 101)

Another prominent failed inquiry was the Connolly-Ryan Commission, established by Queensland's coalition government in 1997. It was conceived by the government as a counter attack against the CJC's Carruthers Inquiry, which was inquiring into alleged government misconduct in signing a pre-election memorandum of understanding with the Queensland Police Union. Carruthers resigned his commission in protest, especially after being directed to preserve his records for access by the Connolly-Ryan Commission, and both Carruthers and the CJC initiated legal action against the commissioners. The Supreme Court issued both a declaration that the commissioners were disqualified from continuing with their investigations, and an injunction restraining them from so proceeding. The court found overwhelming evidence of ostensible bias by Connolly in the conduct of the inquiry and that there were reasonable grounds to uphold a suspicion of apprehended bias by Ryan, and thus shut the inquiry down. The Commission had already been the subject of continued public criticism, both by the opposition in Parliament and the local media. It was attacked on the basis of its bias, its costs which by the time it was shut down had exceeded $25 million, and the fact that it was an obvious political device to attack and undermine the CJC. With the support of an independent member of parliament, the opposition was able to achieve a vote of no confidence in the then Attorney-General, Denver Beanland, because of his appointment of the commission (Ransley, 2001).

These commissions are examples of inquiries doomed to failure, from a combination of government-imposed controls on their terms of reference, resources and personnel, and the choices made by the commissioners themselves as to how they conducted their investigations. Therefore, they provide a useful contrast with the much more successful model established by the Costigan and Fitzgerald inquiries, as discussed in the next sections.

Lessons Learned From Costigan

The Costigan Royal Commission was established in 1980, jointly commissioned by the federal coalition government led by Malcolm Fraser and the Liberal state government of Victoria. It had several noteworthy features, some of which, as will be seen, set a pattern for other inquiries, including Fitzgerald, to follow. The first such feature was that it sought and achieved extended terms of reference on seven occasions. Five extensions achieved only extended reporting dates, one triggered the operation of amended legislative powers enacted at the commission's request, and one substantially broadened the ambit of the investigation, particularly to facilitate investigation of tax evasion and other matters extending beyond union misconduct (Costigan, 1984).

Second, the Costigan Commission sought and achieved amendments to existing legislation that greatly enhanced its powers, together with those of subsequent Commonwealth royal commissions. This needs to be considered against the background of the Commonwealth *Royal Commissions Act 1902*, which had not been substantially reviewed since 1933 (Hallett, 1982; Ransley, 2001). In addition, royal commissions were affected by other legislative provisions, particularly secrecy provisions which prevented access to information held by other government agencies. The first recommendation made by the Costigan Commission was for amendment of one of these secrecy provisions contained in tax legislation, to facilitate its investigation of tax evasion. Recommendations were also made for changes to the *Royal Commissions Act* to enable the issue of search warrants during commission inquiries and to extend the provisions dealing with the compulsion of evidence.

The third notable feature of the Costigan Commission, in addition to its success in extending both its terms of reference and legislative powers, was its use of new investigative techniques, particularly its use of computers to keep track of and analyse the large amount of documentary evidence

(Costigan, 1984). The style adopted by the commission was not the passive one of traditional royal commissions such as those headed by Gibbs and Street, depending on relevant information being produced by witnesses, but a more aggressive, law-enforcement type approach which actively sought out evidence from large numbers of sources. The use of computers greatly facilitated this approach, as did the employment of the commission's own investigative and administrative staff, at its height numbering over one hundred people.

The fourth notable feature of the Costigan Commission was also related to its approach, particularly how it dealt with the evidence of wrongdoing it uncovered. The focus was not just on prosecuting identified wrongdoers, but in exposing and preventing criminal behaviour. Costigan justified this approach:

> The maintenance of law in society demands more than mere prosecution of offenders. First it requires the prevention of its breach; and further, where the breach is occurring, it requires it to be stopped ...
>
> The second requirement to maintain law and order where a criminal scheme is identified is to take steps to avoid its repetition in the future. This may be achieved by prosecution but only if it is successful. It is only then that it may have effect as a deterrent. Prosecution takes time and that may not be soon enough to act as a deterrent to others. Other means of deterring recurrence should be explored and employed if they are available. It may be that recurrence of the scheme can be deterred by exposure of its criminality or by changing laws which are being exploited or by changes in administration of public affairs. (Costigan, 1984, vol. 2, pp. 133–135)

Hence, Costigan took the view that while prosecution of wrongdoers was a desirable outcome, it was not the only or even the most desirable of outcomes to achieve from the investigation. The stopping of wrongdoing and the prevention of its recurrence were even more important. As part of this approach, the commission's attitude to the media and publicity was important. While the inquiry was established amidst considerable publicity, this had diffused until the interim report dealing with tax evasion was released. That Report caused intense media and public interest, and:

> ... from that point on publicity was an important part of the political pressure Costigan built to promote policy reform, and to gain the necessary search powers to further pursue organised crime. (Tiffin, 1999, p. 106)

The Commission's relationship with the media and the public then, was its fifth notable feature. This was a two-way relationship. Not only did the inquiry try to maximise public attention and support for its efforts, but it also became an ongoing source for media stories. This was typified at the time of the 'goanna' revelations, when allegations concerning media and gambling magnate and one of Australia's wealthiest men, Kerry Packer, were leaked. The goanna allegations also highlighted criticism of the inquiry, for its impact on individuals' civil liberties (Gilligan, 2002; Tiffin, 1999).

The sixth notable feature of the Costigan Commission was its contribution to the creation of new government agencies or institutions. Costigan recommended in the fourth interim report the creation of a task force to pursue criminal prosecution of those involved in tax frauds. The government responded by passing legislation to create the Office of the Special Prosecutors. In the same report, the creation of a special commission was recommended, to have responsibility for the fight against organised crime (Costigan, 1984). Initially this was met by the appointment of another special prosecutor, to pursue prosecutions other than those related to tax. The Fraser government's proposed but never enacted legislation for a National Crimes Commission, and the subsequent Hawke government legislation establishing the National Crime Authority (NCA), were the ultimate responses to this recommendation, although neither was entirely consistent with Costigan's recommendations.

Finally, the Costigan Commission stands out because of the breadth of its recommendations; it was not content to simply focus on identifying and exposing wrongdoing, but also addressed the reasons why this had not happened before. The inquiry focused to a large extent on the legal, institutional and administrative factors that had allowed misconduct, such as the bottom of the harbour tax evasion schemes, to develop and flourish with seemingly little consequence. Many of the recommendations were directed to removing these factors, and to coordinating and strengthening Commonwealth law enforcement efforts.

The main lasting consequences of the Costigan Commission then, were the broadening and modernisation of powers for all Commonwealth royal commissions, the development of a law-enforcement rather than a judicial model of investigations, a broad focus on structural reform as well as individual prosecutions, and the establishment of a permanent NCA. These features were adopted and further developed by Fitzgerald.

Fitzgerald's Processes

Fitzgerald too transformed his brief from one originally conceived as a narrow investigation of certain individuals to a broad-ranging examination of the whole system of governance in Queensland. The initial terms of reference were expanded and broadened, from a very narrow focus on specific allegations of police corruption to a virtually unlimited probe of police and government impropriety during an unlimited period. As with the Costigan Inquiry, the relevant legislation, the *Commissions of Inquiry Act 1950 (Qld)*, was amended four times to greatly increase and strengthen the powers of all

Queensland inquiries. And the inquiry employed its own independent investigative staff and developed extensive sources of information and intelligence which it managed in its own databases.

A combination of fortunate political circumstances and astute exploitation of those circumstances led to this transformation. Before accepting the commission Fitzgerald sought assurances that he would be allowed to conduct a free and full investigation. After his appointment had been publicly announced, he insisted on the fulfilment of that promise through (see Fitzgerald Report):

- extensions of the initially limited terms of reference;
- government waivers of any claims to Cabinet or parliamentary privilege, or other justifications for non-disclosure of information;
- the right to choose his own staff, including lawyers outside government and 'cleanskin' police;
- generous resourcing to underpin the inquiry;
- separate, partly government funded legal representation of the government, the police department, and individual persons under investigation.

The amendments to the *Commissions of Inquiry Act* gave Fitzgerald and subsequent commissions new or increased power to:

- apply to a judge of the Supreme Court for authority to use listening devices;
- override secrecy oaths and provisions, such as those binding some public servants and ministers;
- summons evidence other than documents including computer files and other electronic media;
- continue inquiries notwithstanding current or proposed court proceedings on related subjects;
- order prisoners to be brought before them (Ransley, 1994).

In addition, other amendments created further offences of contempt against commissions, empowered them to publish recordings of conversations which would otherwise be contrary to the *Invasion of Privacy Act 1971,* and gave greater flexibility by allowing for the appointment of a deputy commissioner, the making of separate and interim reports, and the copying of documents and records (Ransley, 2001). These amendments, modelled in part on changes to the Commonwealth Act spurred by the Costigan Inquiry, both modernised the legislation to take account of changes in technology, and increased substantially the extent of powers of commissions. The amendments broadened commissions' ability to search for, obtain and deal with evidence, and to deal with recalcitrant, fearful or dishonest witnesses.

Next, Fitzgerald began public hearings very early in the life of the inquiry, and managed witnesses so that from the very beginning there were bomb-shells attracting wide public interest. Police Commissioner Lewis appeared first to give evidence that the government, contrary to its public pronounce-ments, had countenanced a policy of not enforcing prostitution laws, aiming instead for containment. Other senior police supported this view, said that brothels served a useful public purpose, and told of taking Police Minister Hinze on guided tour of brothels and illegal gambling dens in Brisbane (Dickie, 1989). Announcements were made that senior police officers had been granted indemnities against prosecution, and soon evidence of police corruption at the highest level emerged, to be followed by evidence of highly suspect conduct by senior government and political figures.

Fitzgerald also insisted on continued fulfilment of early promises even after the inquiry had been established. Before the report was delivered, he gained an unprecedented, public commitment from the leaders of all three major political parties in the State that whomever was in power after the report was delivered would implement it 'lock, stock and barrel' (Lewis, 1997, p. 154). This public commitment to implement a report, sight unseen, was extraordinary, and has not since been repeated.

Evidence to the inquiry was reported extensively in media throughout Australia, and attracted massive levels of public interest and outrage. Reporting of the inquiry was actively encouraged, and national media organ-isations were present at the inquiry on a daily basis. The ABC's *7.30 Report* presented nightly re-enactments of the most sensational evidence. The *Courier-Mail* was given leave to participate in parts of the hearings. Any per-ceived retreat from the inquiry became politically impossible, particularly as members of the government itself began to be implicated by the evidence. This politically unstable environment intensified with the demise of Bjelke-Petersen as Premier in December 1987.

Apart from clever exploitation of the unstable political situation and the media, the other main contributing factor to the inquiry's investigative success was its use of indemnities. In return for giving evidence to the inquiry, key witnesses were guaranteed immunity from prosecution. It was this tactic that resulted in a series of senior police giving public evidence very early in the hearings, of their longstanding corruption and that of their col-leagues (Tiffin, 1999). This had the political effect of enhancing the public legitimacy of the inquiry, and the investigative effect of achieving evidence otherwise very difficult to uncover, because of the clandestine and participa-tory nature of corruption. Very often, people with knowledge of corruption are reluctant to come forward because they too are implicated by the evidence. The use of indemnities for major players, and the legislative guarantee that witnesses' evidence to the inquiry could not be used in prosecutions of them, overcame these inhibitions. In addition, the public revelation of the evidence gained through immunities established the credentials of the inquiry as a real investigation, as opposed to those that had gone before, and this encouraged others to come forward with evidence they might otherwise have feared revealing. For the first time it seemed that witnesses could be and would be protected against retribution.

Finally, and again like the Costigan Inquiry, the Fitzgerald Commission interpreted its mandate widely to deliver recommendations for comprehensive review and reform of policing, government and administration in the State, through the mechanisms of the Criminal Justice Commission (CJC) and the Electoral and Administrative Review Commission (EARC).

In summary then, the Fitzgerald Inquiry followed the model established by the Costigan Commission in several respects. It recognised the need for strengthened terms of reference and statutory powers and used public support for its investigations to achieve both. It also followed Costigan's lead in adopting a pro-active law-enforcement approach to obtaining evidence. However, the Fitzgerald Inquiry refined and improved upon this approach with its use of targeted indemnities which served both to expose the extent of the problem and encourage other witnesses to come forward. Like Costigan, the Fitzgerald Inquiry also chose to focus on the need for public exposure rather than to maximise prosecutions, and to develop broad and systemic recommendations. Again, it improved on the original model with its creation and exploitation of a sustained, supportive political and public environment, particularly with its use of the media.

Of course there were criticisms of Fitzgerald. At the time of the inquiry, there were concerns that this new form of investigative inquiry corroded individual rights and tainted people not proved guilty of any offence (Cooray, 1989). There were also complaints that the focus on recommending law reform had diverted the inquiry from the task of uncovering evidence of corruption and major crime, especially drug crime (Toohey, 1990).

Despite these criticisms, perhaps the major achievement of the Fitzgerald Commission was that majority political and public support for its work continued not only for the duration of its inquiry, unlike the Costigan Commission which had suffered a waning in support, but also long after it had finished. For years after its report, calls on the Fitzgerald vision or the Fitzgerald reforms as support for various policy or administrative changes still held considerable appeal. The inquiry had successfully created a public expectation that all recommendations would be fully acted upon, to the extent that the report was referred to as a 'bible', from which no deviation was possible. The critics had remarkably little impact on this expectation that Fitzgerald's 'vision for reform' would continue to be implemented. And this expectation was at least partly realised with the institutionalisation of the reform agenda via EARC and the CJC.

Twenty years later, this public expectation has been shown to have remarkable durability. Fitzgerald emerged from his self-imposed silence about his inquiry to critique successive governments for their lack of commitment to reform (see Fitzgerald, 2009). This re-emergence launched an intense firestorm of debate and criticism about implementation of the original Fitzgerald vision suggesting an ongoing force that must be virtually unique among similar inquiries. But even prior to this, the Costigan-Fitzgerald model of investigative inquiry has established its enduring influence.

Conclusion: Ongoing Influence?

The techniques pioneered by Costigan and further developed by Fitzgerald have been used to varying extents in subsequent inquiries. The *Report of the Royal Commission into Commercial Activities of Government and Other Matters*, or WA Inc Inquiry in the early 1990s used many of the same strategies. During its life the Western Australian *Royal Commissions Act* was amended twice, updating and expanding the powers of inquiries. However, the focus forced on that inquiry by its terms of reference which required it to fully investigate specific alleged financial wrongdoing not only consumed its attention and many of its resources, but also lacked the sustained fascination of the Fitzgerald revelations of police and politicians' wrongdoing. While the allegations made against the Premier and other leading politicians did attract interest, particularly the bombshell at the first public hearing of a $300,000 personal donation to former Premier Brian Burke, weeks of evidence about corporate responsibilities and auditors were not so compelling (Harman, 1994) and the royal commission's public support waned as a result. Despite this, like Costigan and Fitzgerald, the WA Inc Inquiry did leave a lasting legacy in the form of a permanent corruption and crime commission, the Anti-Corruption Commission, later replaced by the more powerful Corruption and Crime Commission.

The *Royal Commission into the New South Wales Police Service*, or Wood Inquiry, also learnt obvious lessons from Fitzgerald, not least because it recruited key members of his staff (see Tiffin, 1999). It was given general terms of reference enabling it to focus on systemic issues rather than being confined to specific investigations. It interpreted that mandate broadly, reflecting on the inadequacy of traditional forms of ministerial accountability as a means of countering police misconduct, and recommending structural change to overcome that deficiency. It established its own large investigative capacity, and used its powers extensively in pursuit of investigations. The Wood Inquiry was particularly notable for its use of undercover agents and covert surveillance. Those techniques coupled with indemnities persuaded corrupt officers to confess and implicate others in their confessions. The inquiry also made use of the media in this process, releasing covert video recordings of conversations between corrupt officers, which were widely broadcast and had multiple effects. The recordings forced shocked public acceptance of the nature and extent of the problem and pressured other corrupt officers into volunteering to come forward as witnesses. Some officers were confronted in the witness box with film of their own corrupt activities. This also helped to break the solidarity among officers that had previously been a barrier to investigations. A Police Integrity Commission was created as a continuing anti-corruption measure. Finally the Wood Inquiry showed keen understanding of the broader political environment through the focus it gave to its 'tagged-on' paedophilia terms of reference, forced onto an unwilling government by repeated allegations made in Parliament, especially in the Legislative Council.

Inquiries such as Costigan, Fitzgerald, Wood and WA Inc were a new development for Australia. Finn (1994) points out that before the Fitzgerald and WA Inc inquiries, constitutional, governmental and administrative arrangements '… for better or for worse, were in large measure what elected governments wished to make of them — or allowed to be made of them'. In other words, governments were very much in charge of ordering their own business, with little public oversight or input into whatever arrangements they chose to put into place. While the party in government would change from time to time, the business of government continued, largely unreviewed. This was regardless of continuing allegations of political wrongdoing. These inquiries were significant because to varying degrees they went beyond mere inquisitions into wrongdoing, they provided a window of opportunity for external review and comment on the business of government in their jurisdictions. Additionally, they all contributed to the creation of permanent changes to the institutional framework of government, by reforming practices and recommending standing agencies.

The Fitzgerald Inquiry in particular stands out because it chose, despite significant investigative duties, to give prominence to its reform role. As well as forensically uncovering evidence in the face of entrenched obstacles, where previous investigations had failed, it focused on exposing the extent of wrong-doing rather than simply investigating specific allegations, as Costigan had prescribed. And through its selective use of the media it created a sustained momentum for change. This momentum was institutionalised and given longevity in the form of new agencies, the CJC and EARC. The achievements of Fitzgerald were even more notable given they occurred in a state jurisdiction, where police and political corruption are most widespread and entrenched, and in a state where many previous attempts at exposure had failed so dismally.

Endnotes

1   The terms 'royal commission' and 'commission of inquiry' are virtually interchangeable in Australia. The term 'inquiry' is used collectively in this chapter to refer to such commissions along with other forms of official inquiry that lack commission status and therefore some of their legal powers and privileges. For a full discussion of the distinctions, see Ransley (2001).

2   British royal commissions are quite different to those in Australia, in that they lack any statutory basis or coercive powers. The closest equivalent there to the Australian model is established under the *Tribunal of Inquiry (evidence) Act* 1921, which is rarely used. Canadian and New Zealand royal commissions are closer to Australian usages, but there are also some significant differences — see Ransley (2001) for a full discussion.

3   The exception is that in some jurisdictions royal commissions have a limited adjudicative function in relation to some contempts committed against them — see Ransley (2001).

References

Coaldrake, P., & Wanna, J. (1988). 'Not like the good old days': The political impact of the Fitzgerald Inquiry into police corruption in Queensland. *Australian Quarterly, 60*(4), 404–414.

Cooray, M. (1989). Denying a Fair Hearing?. *Quadrant, 33*(12), 16–19.

Costigan, F. (1984). *Final report of the Royal Commission into the activities of the Ship Painters and Dockers Union* (Vol. 1–5). Canberra, Australia: Australian Government Publishing Service.

Davis, G., & Wanna, J. (1988). The Fitzgerald Commission: The politics of inquiries. *Canberra Bulletin of Public Administration, 82.*

Dickie, P. (1989). *The road to Fitzgerald and beyond.* Brisbane, Australia: Queensland University Press.

Finn, P. (1994). The significance of the Fitzgerald and the WA Inc Commissions. In P. Weller (Ed.), *Royal Commissions and the making of public policy* (pp. 32–39). Sydney, Australia: Macmillan Education Australia.

Finnane, M. (1988). The Fitzgerald Commission: Law, politics and state corruption in Queensland. *Australian Journal of Public Administration, 47*(4), 332.

Fitzgerald, G.E. (1989). *Report of the Commission of Inquiry into Possible Illegal Activities and Associated Police Misconduct.* Brisbane, Australia: GoPrint.

Fitzgerald, G.E. (2009, 29 July). What went wrong with Queensland? *The Courier Mail*, p. 4.

Fitzgerald, R. (1990). Judicial culture and the investigation of corruption: A comparison of the Gibbs National Hotel Inquiry 1963–64 and the Fitzgerald Inquiry 1987–89. In S. Prasser, R. Wear & J. Nethercote (Eds.), *Corruption and reform: The Fitzgerald vision* (p. 62). Brisbane, Australia: University of Queensland Press.

Gilligan, G. (2002). Royal commissions of inquiry. *Australian and New Zealand Journal of Criminology, 35*(3), 289–307.

Hall, P. (2004). *Investigating corruption and misconduct on public office: Commissions of inquiry — powers and procedures.* Sydney, Australia: Lawbook Company.

Hallett, L.A. (1982). *Royal commissions and boards of inquiry.* Sydney, Australia: Law Book Company.

Harman, E. (1994). The 1992 WA Inc Royal Commission: Did it make a difference? In P. Weller (Ed.), *Royal commissions and the making of public policy* (pp. 40–60). Sydney, Australia: Macmillan Education Australia.

Lewis, C. (1997). Civilian Oversight of Complaints Against Police: External Relationships and their Impact on Effectiveness. *PhD thesis*, Griffith University.

Prasser, S. (2003). A Study of Commonwealth Public Inquiries. PhD thesis, Griffith University.

Prasser, S. (2006). Royal commissions in Australia: When should governments appoint them? *Australian Journal of Public Administration, 65*(3), 28–47.

Ransley, J. (1994). The Powers of Royal Commissions and Controls Over Them. In P. Weller (Ed.), *Royal Commissions and the Making of Public Policy*. Sydney, Australia: Macmillan Education Australia.

Ransley, J. (2001). *Inquisitorial royal commissions and the investigation of political wrongdoing*. PhD thesis, Griffith University, Australia.

Tiffin, R. (1999). *Scandals: Media, politics and corruption in contemporary Australia*. Sydney, Australia: University of New South Wales Press.

Toohey, B. (1990). Fitzgerald — How the process came unstuck. In S. Prasser, R. Wear & J. Nethercote (Eds.), *Corruption and reform: the Fitzgerald Vision* (pp. 81–88). Brisbane, Australia: University of Queensland Press.

3

Exploring the Limits:
Media as Watchdog in Queensland

Julianne Schultz

During the 1980s the Australian media realised its power in a new way —
different to the influence the press barons had traditionally exercised in
clubby, back-room deals with politicians. Rather, this power came from a
strong story, graphically told. A new breed of vocationally motivated journalists grew up with the beat of Watergate in their heads, determined to
pursue the truths that lay beneath the pub gossip, especially about crime and
corruption (Schultz, 1998). They were supported, to varying degrees, in this
ambition by television network owners who realised that edgy current affairs
programs were the top-rating genre (Schultz, 1998), newspaper owners with
a sense of moral purpose and a reinvigorated public broadcaster with a
policy commitment to speak truth to power.[1] The media barons had always
known that the news business — 'a bastard institution' — was most significant when it married political influence with commercial success: 'one foot
in commerce and the other in politics' (Schultz, 1998, p. 4). Investigative
journalism was its new manifestation — often troublesome for media
owners, as well as the public figures it reported.

Stories about pervasive corruption, especially those broadcast on the
Australian Broadcasting Commission's (ABC) program *Four Corners*,
Channel 9's *60 Minutes* and published in the Fairfax newspapers and *The
Bulletin*, provided an underlying narrative to a decade of rapid economic
and social transformation in Australia. Many old orders were disrupted as
the economy was deregulated and multiculturalism normalised — the face
of power changed. The investigative journalism that flowered during this
period tapped the spirit of these times and gave rise to royal commissions
and other inquiries, and eventually helped to prepare the way for new

monitory and regulatory institutions, and legislation facilitating freedom of information and protecting whistleblowers.

From the mid-1980s to the early 1990s the news media played a more significantly disruptive role in setting and framing the political agenda than it has done since, or did before. The breakthrough reports which triggered the commissions of inquiry were themselves newsworthy, and the official investigations that followed provided fodder for countless news pages and broadcasts. The journalists involved in this investigative journalism were motivated by the desire to have their work noticed and used. But the information the subsequent inquiries uncovered, using more extensive, sophisticated, even coercive, intelligence gathering means than those available to the news media, highlighted the limits of journalistic methods in gathering, marshalling and evaluating complex information. As new independent accountability and monitory agencies became operational, they also demonstrated the limits of the media's role as a watchdog — 'the fourth estate'. At best, the media could, in a considered, fair and comprehensive fashion, 'signal events' (Schultz, 1998, p. 55); at worst, it became a player prepared to amplify the cause of any protagonist with a bag of sensational material in search of an audience.

The high-water mark of the intersection between journalism and politics during this period was the reporting that triggered the establishment of the Fitzgerald Inquiry. In the days preceding the broadcast of the *Moonlight State* on Monday May 11, 1987, the ABC tantalised its viewers with a sexy promo that promised to join the dots between Queensland's sleaze industry and police corruption. The carefully 'legalled' program went further and suggested that corruption extended to the highest political office in the state. Since 1983, when it broadcast *The Big League* an explosive story about judicial corruption in New South Wales, *Four Corners* had become compulsory viewing for anyone interested in Australian public life, with an audience well-prepared for its mix of fearless revelation and graphic story-telling. *Moonlight State* took a step further, juxtaposing images of strippers in sleazy nightclubs with churchgoers singing hymns, incriminating documents of brothel ownership with first-hand stories of abuse of power (Masters, 2008). It laid down a challenge: unanswered questions about police complicity with illegal activities needed to be addressed.

Journalist Chris Masters and his team had come under intense police surveillance (Fitzgerald, 1989; Masters, 1992). During nearly 6 months researching the program, he deliberately crafted it to shock and have an impact in Queensland: 'If journalists believe in anything at all, it seems to me, it should be that people will take notice of what we report' (Schultz, 1998, p. 224). On air Masters adopted a voice that suggested he was telling the story as he had found it, in deep sorrow rather than the breathless anger or the 'snide tone of another smartarse southerner' (Masters, 1992, p. 47). Local audiences had become accustomed to stories about the state's dysfunction, often told with an accusatory or dismissive tone by southern journalists, which suggested Queensland was a lost cause, irretrievably different to the rest of the country. As the Fitzgerald Report noted: 'For many years Queensland has had a corruption problem ... patronage, rather than money was the primary currency exchanged ... as the community grew more affluent a suspicion grew among those in business that dealing with government was not always as open and straightforward as it could be' (Fitzgerald, 1989, p. 30).

Rebutting rumours of corrupt practice was a political narrative Premier Sir Joh Bjelke-Petersen had developed, refined and used to his advantage since the early 1970s. Fortuitously on the evening the program went to air Sir Joh, who had been re-elected premier for the fifth time on November 1, the previous year, was abroad. At that time he was also preoccupied with his bid to move to federal politics, and there were increasing signs that the robustness of the political system which he had created was fraying at the edges. In response to the broadcast Bill Gunn exercised his authority as acting premier to call an inquiry to investigate the questions *Four Corners* had left unanswered about the vice and drugs 'industry', police and political corruption.

Appointing inquiries to investigate such allegations had become part of the political tool kit in the southern states. In Queensland, the premier had been more inclined to swamp any allegations with bluster, or ignore them with a dismissive 'they would say that wouldn't they', than allow a potentially unpredictable independent examination. Masters advocated an inquiry; he recalled being 'interviewed ad nauseum after the program saying as loud as I could, "why don't they for once, for Christ's sake, do a proper inquiry"' (Schultz, 1998, p. 224). Like many of the journalists who had been involved in the 1980s investigative journalism Masters had developed a somewhat jaundiced view of the time-consuming and whitewashing potential of such inquiries. But he cherished what he described as his professional naivety (Schultz, 1998, p. 226), and nursing more information than he had been able to include in the 50-minute program he happily changed hats to an advocate, passing on contacts and information to the inquiry, albeit with modest expectations.

As Mr G.E. (Tony) Fitzgerald noted in his report: 'The general expectation was that the inquiry would be brief and ineffectual, and was primarily a device to ease the political pressure on the Government'. That it was not is a tribute to Fitzgerald and the forces he was able to marshal. Peter Manning, executive producer of *Four Corners*, noted in 1990: 'The Street Royal Commission [which investigated the allegations in *The Big League*] had been a very "cynicising" process for me … you suddenly realised how royal commissions may well not find the truth. Until Fitzgerald I thought royal commissions were forever going to be thus. I think Fitzgerald actually restored some faith' (Schultz, 1998, p. 224).

Success has a thousand fathers so it was scarcely surprising that other journalists were ready to claim credit for provoking the Queensland government into initiating the potentially far-reaching investigation — especially once it became clear it would not be a whitewash. This was not without some justification; the *Moonlight State* was not the first serious attempt to reveal the corruption that lay at the heart of the state. There had been reports prepared with periodic bursts of energy for local and national media. Former Toowoomba teacher, Evan Whitton, a journalist for Fairfax had been a persistent scourge of the government, and for more than a decade Quentin Dempster had reported abuses of political power and examples of corrupt behaviour for Queensland Newspapers and the ABC, including in late 1986 the ground-breaking documentary *Sunshine System*. Three years earlier Allan Hall had prepared a report for the national broadcaster's evening current affairs program *Nationwide* which featured a disgruntled policeman exposing illegal gambling and corruption in the force, allegations to which the corpulent police minister Russ Hinze responded and, 'baldly denied the existence of illegal casinos that some assembled journalists happily frequented … when Hall raised a voice of protest Hinze spat at him, telling him he would be out of a job tomorrow'(Masters, 1992, p. 54). As Masters found when he rang former officers, the legacy was that many were bitterly jaded and could see no point in talking to journalists; the media was unreliable, at best a fair weather ally.

In January 1987, the *Courier-Mail* published a front page story which described in some detail some of the illegal brothels operating in Fortitude Valley. It had been written by Phil Dickie, a dogged young reporter who lived in nearby New Farm. Dickie had spent several months researching the operations of the highly visible sex industry in inner-city Brisbane under the direction of the paper's chief-of-staff Bob Gordon who had been shocked by what he had seen as he passed 'sin triangle' in a bus from the city.[2] Dickie completed his investigations before going on holidays and the story was eventually published (on Monday, January 12) after extensive legal vetting but without a byline or his prior knowledge. The story had grown beyond Gordon's initial expectations but was not the top item of gossip at the newspaper's Bowen Hills' headquarters that week — the Queensland Newspapers' board was preoccupied with its response to a bid by Rupert Murdoch to buy the company.

Like some other earlier stories, Dickie's report scratched the surface and received an official denial that prostitution occurred in the city. Like many of the earlier stories it was not followed up by the newspaper, was not accompanied by demands for an investigation, and did not trigger an official inquiry. As the Report noted: 'There was nothing particularly unusual about this. Similar controversies had surfaced from time to time for many years' (Fitzgerald, 1989, p. 2). This too would have been an aberrant one day wonder if it had not been for Greg Chamberlin who became editor of the paper in March 1987, after it had been acquired by Murdoch. He encouraged Dickie to continue. Their competitive instincts were spurred by the increasingly visible presence of Masters' team in Brisbane (Schultz, 1998). Nigel Powell, a former Licensing Branch police officer who became a whistleblower after the police minister declared there was 'no prostitution in the massage parlours' (Schultz, 1998, p. 221) was a crucial source for both groups of reporters, focused on the nexus between vice and official corruption. Although Dickie won the 1987 Gold Walkley award for outstanding journalism and Fitzgerald acknowledged the role of the *Courier-Mail*, he attributed the origins of his inquiry to the *Moonlight State* (Fitzgerald, 1989).

While the State's media was keen to claim paternity of the inquiry, in truth it had failed to hold an increasingly corrupt political system to account for at least 15 years. In a relatively small city the managers and owners of the news media were significant business leaders and in a state where the government dispensed patronage and was an important part of the economy, there was an understandable caution about causing offence to the dominant political party.

Notably on November 1, 1984, the Premier demonstrated his commercial power when he cancelled the government's multi-million dollar advertising in the *Courier-Mail* in protest against an uncharacteristically critical series of reports in the paper. The Premier also used the law of defamation to chill critical reporting (Fitzgerald, 1989).[3] Most notoriously in 1982, he filed for defamation against Channel 9. When Alan Bond bought the station in 1986, he paid $400,000 to settle the action (Fitzgerald, 1989, p. 92ff) — 'the price of doing business in Queensland' (Barry, 1990, pp. 311–318; Schultz, 1998, p. 103) — a payment which also eventually triggered an inquiry into whether Bond was a 'fit and proper person' to hold a broadcasting license (Schultz, 1998, pp. 103–104).

By the 1980s all the protagonists clearly understood how difficult it was to balance with one foot in commerce and the other in politics — life in the media business was a long way from the idealistic role which Sir Theodore Bray, the editor-in-chief of the *Courier-Mail* described in a major speech in 1965:

At the risk of being called precious, even pompous, I would maintain that to be the Fourth Estate is still one of the main functions of the press ... To survive a newspaper has to serve in a unique way. This is as a guardian of the people's fundamental right to free expression of opinion. It has also to be a watchdog of civil liberties and a protector against the petty tyranny of bureaucrats and all those clothed with or assuming authority against the common man. Readers, praise be, still think of their newspapers as the ordinary man's last court of appeal, as his protector and champion ... Newspapers clearly have a function beyond mere reporting and recording — a function of probing behind the straight news, or interpreting and explaining and sometimes of exposing .... The press lives by disclosure. (Schultz, 1998, pp. 43, 113)

Bray had long ceased direct involvement with Queensland Newspapers by the late 1980s, although in his role as Chancellor of Griffith University he adopted a similarly sceptical view about the exercise of political power and the networks which supported it in Brisbane (Schultz, 2008, pp. 11–41).[4] Over the two decades following his speech there were very few examples of Queensland Newspapers adhering to his dictum. The morning broadsheet *Courier-Mail* and afternoon tabloid *Telegraph* exuded the complacency typical of any monopoly even after Rupert Murdoch launched the *Daily Sun* in 1982.

In the small, clubby world of Brisbane social networks constrained professional practice, a fact which had as much influence in journalism as it did in the law, medicine, business or the public service. Some journalists and editors frequented the illegal brothels and casinos, others played poker with corrupt police, and all were accustomed to a form of political information management which Sir Joh likened to 'feeding the chooks'. 'Leaks', as Fitzgerald noted, were dispensed to 'selected journalists who are able to delude themselves that they are not being used ... should [they] "bite the hand that feeds them" the flow of information would dry up or be diverted to a rival outlet or colleague ... leaks became a way of making the media a mouthpiece for factions in government' (Fitzgerald, 1989, p. 142).[5]

For many of those employed on the major news outlets there was an astonishing level of complicity and lack of shame about this disregard for their professionalism. Russ Hinze's threat following Allan Hall's critical report was not unusual, and had precisely the chilling effect that the government and corrupt police desired — the following day a commercial current affairs program broadcast a 'puff' piece singing the praises of the police minister (Masters, 1992, p. 54). A prominent journalist recalled years later her embarrassment when the *Age's* Michelle Grattan attended one of Sir Joh's Brisbane press conference and asked afterwards, 'do you always let them treat you like children' and realised that the answer was 'yes'.

For anyone who came in contact with its exercise of raw power, there was nothing benign about this paternalism. The muscularity of Sir Joh and the National Party's governing style was illustrated sharply in the 1970s in a series of confrontations, which not only established Terence Lewis as police commissioner, but by challenging traditional civil liberties, both radicalised and traumatised many Queenslanders. From the Springbok protests in 1971 to the marches in response to the 1977 ban on public assembly, thousands of people were arrested. It was arguably one of the most significant periods of protest in Australia, but one which the National Party was able to use for its electoral advantage and to establish the preconditions for corrupt police to assert themselves (Fitzgerald, 1989). Despite the widespread public engagement, this assault on traditional rights, and its consequences for public administration and business, was something the local news media was ill-prepared to report. The protesters were easily tarnished, as radicals' 'street violence' was a dramatic media language which did not encourage examination of the underlying issues or consequences. Some ABC and public radio programs 'became a Government 101 seminar room with discussion about the separation of powers, freedom of speech and assembly ... students of government, law and history could see what happened when democratic theory was not applied' (Schultz, 2008, p. 20). But the government unequivocally prevailed. By the time the bans were lifted, the damage had been done, civil society was significantly weakened and corrupt police found they could operate with impunity.[6] The news media is not well suited to reporting dysfunctional systems until it erupts in blatant hypocrisy and measurable corruption. The eventual legacy permeated the systems of justice, business, media, police and public administration.

This is not something that was unique to Queensland. Similar patterns can be seen in many other major transformative political periods, notably the reporting of the McCarthy period (Bayley, 1981) and the activities of the House of Un-American Activities in the United States in the 1950s, and the coverage of the Vietnam War a decade later. The limits of the routines of objectivity which demanded full coverage of official sources of information meant that some journalists were aware that significant stories and issues were not adequately reported, while others were able to satisfy themselves that by reporting both sides their professional obligations had been satisfied. Those Queensland journalists who recognised the limits of the prevailing methodology of professional journalism — including Masters, Dickie, Chamberlin, Whitton, Dempster — began to exercise increasing autonomy. This approach did not produce a comfortable fit with news organisations accustomed to a certain place in the political and social hierarchy, but where the benefit of increased audiences was not offset by real commercial losses, it was tolerated and at times even encouraged by media owners. As Dan Hallin (1986) documented in relation to American reporting of the Vietnam War, the growing autonomy of journalists within news organisations coincided with the tightening of the bonds with those in positions of official power. This set up a tension between the news agenda and the inchoate underbelly of issues and information which in normal circumstances could not move into the mainstream, blocked by both those in positions of power who dispensed information and set the agenda.

It was not surprising then that delight in the appointment of the Fitzgerald Inquiry was not universally shared, even in those parts of the media which were claiming credit for its establishment. Initially, there was a close working relationship, as Chris Masters and Phil Dickie handed over their research to the Commission, and facilitated introductions to key contacts; both the ABC and Queensland Newspapers were given standing at the Inquiry because of their role in the creation of the Commission. From the outset, steps were taken to ensure that the media was included in the process, had access to key information and was able to report comprehensively. This approach was maintained throughout — indeed journalists were placed in a position of 'special privilege with corresponding responsibilities' (Bayley, 1981).

The relationship between the Inquiry and the media is a richly nuanced tale. In part, no doubt because the Inquiry was triggered by media reports, and also because of a shrewd assessment of the need for news coverage if the investigation was to have widespread public impact and legitimacy, there was an emphasis on openness and inclusiveness from the beginning. In this approach, Tony Fitzgerald facilitated an applied interpretation of Sir Theodore Bray's articulation of the watchdog role of the press 27 years earlier. As the Report noted:

> The Inquiry received intense day to day coverage. The constant controversy made the responsibility of controlling the Inquiry extremely burdensome, but it is undoubtedly the openness of the proceedings and the media coverage which encouraged a flow of information from the community and developed public support. (Fitzgerald, 1989, p. 21)

This was welcomed by the news media, but not uncritically; especially as much of the work of the Commission was necessarily conducted in secret. Despite Fitzgerald's determination to run an open inquiry, this was tested by what he considered deliberately inaccurate reporting in the first week of hearings (Fitzgerald, 1989, p. A215) and as the months rolled on his impatience with the wilfulness of the media became tangible. The self-interested shortcomings which characterised some of the coverage were a harbinger of the limits on the institutional role of the media, limits which became sharply apparent in the following decades.

In an exercise designed to inform the public, clarify matters arising from the investigation, educate journalists about the legal processes and challenge them to reconsider their professional responsibilities, the Chairman occasionally prefaced hearings with what comments the media 'dubbed "the homilies": that is, depending on one's point of view, either statements for the "spiritual edification" of the audience or "tedious moralizing discourses"' (Fitzgerald, 1989, p. 4).

The collected homilies provide a remarkable insight into the limits of the media's capacity to engage with the inquiry as a substantive examination of systemic corruption rather than an ad hoc exposé of random misdemeanours. The increasing exasperation of the Commission is clearly articulated. For instance on 10 August 1987, the Chairman reflected on reports which suggested that coverage would be restricted. He archly commented:

> It seems that some people are extremely fortunate. Not only do they always know what is right, apparently by some special instinct, rather than any process of reason, but by some happy chance what is right always coincides with their own interests. (Fitzgerald, 1989, p. A180)

Over the months his tone became sharper. So on November 4, he reluctantly threatened to recommend contempt charges unless the reporting demonstrated greater respect:

> Surely it is not beyond the media to understand that the task of the commission is both difficult and important to the people of Queensland and that, irrespective of the short term news worthiness of the immediate publication of the views of potential witnesses, the difficulties confronting the commission are immeasurably increased by the interference of journalists. (Fitzgerald, 1989, p. A197)

By May 18 the following year, he suggested that the wilful misunderstanding of hearsay evidence was deliberately discrediting the Inquiry (Fitzgerald, 1989).

A month later, the Deputy Chairman commended a *Sunday Mail* column by Quentin Dempster and pointed out that the inquiry was not:

> ... a competition between a bunch of loveable rogues and a group of narrow-minded prudes ... the demi-monde with which the inquiry is concerned is not a jolly place peopled by happy-go-lucky fun lovers sampling the pleasures provided them by generous benefactors. It is a world of greed, violence, corruption and exploitation, where the weak and immature are preyed upon ... Silence contempt and perjury are not the bonds of mateship, but the machinations of another code based on self-interest and in some case intimidation. (Fitzgerald, 1989, p. A210)

By mid-July, an article undermining a potential witness provocatively placed on the front page of the *Courier-Mail* — considered part of a disinformation campaign engineered by Police Commissioner Lewis (Dickie, 1989) —

provoked the Chairman to question Queensland Newspapers' commitment to honestly reporting the inquiry since the beginning. He accused the company of hypocrisy — boasting of its role in establishing the inquiry while benefitting from advertising for escort agencies and massage parlours. He suggested its approach was tainted by personal relationships with some of those under investigation (Fitzgerald, 1989).[7]

Not all the coverage provoked such admonitions, but that such reprimands should pepper what was an otherwise open investigation was a telling insight into the complex, often adversarial relationship between the self-appointed watchdog and the one which operated with the full authority of the state. In the final Report, the Commission noted:

> With some notable exceptions, there was insufficient careful or reasoned media analysis of the commission's work. Most criticism was ill-considered or based on misconceptions, while the real issues, on which competing views could legitimately be held were neglected. Some damaging reports were blatant propaganda and others were unsubstantiated and recklessly, if not deliberately damaging. Some created unrealistic community expectations, while others eroded essential public support. At the very least controversies raised by such reports distracted commission resources and energies from other pressing tasks. Nevertheless there is no doubt the commission could not have achieved its task in secret. The openness of the hearings and the work of responsible journalists have, it is to be hoped, laid the basis in the public mind for the process of reform to begin. (Fitzgerald, 1989, p. 21)

The ABC had a great deal invested in the inquiry, and as a non-commercial national broadcaster it had less at stake in the commercial and social milieu of Brisbane. It took its role particularly seriously and was assiduous in its reporting. It is worth noting that in 1985 the Corporation's board adopted a policy articulating its role:

> Inherent in the obligation to maintain an independent news and information service is a responsibility to be inquiring and if necessary, controversial; to not be afraid of pursuing the truth ... The ABC cannot simply report; its legislation clearly implies that it should also work within the best traditions of investigative journalism ... While it remains independent of sectional interests it will be well placed systematically to pursue issues of public concern through innovative and reliable journalism to contribute uniquely to the freedom of information that is essential to a democratic society. (ABC, 1985, pp. 12–15; Schultz, 1998, p. 60)

In the context of an inquiry which it had provoked, the national broadcaster was determined to find a way to keep the story interesting for its audience, distil the key evidence and produce engaging television. Realising that the traditional methods of current affairs television were not sufficient for the task at the beginning of 1988 it hired actors to present daily re-enactments of key evidence on the nightly *7.30 Report*. This risked turning the inquiry into a soap opera, but its faithful representations of evidence instead gave it additional gravitas and urgency. Fitzgerald commended the ABC's innovative approach but quipped that he would appreciate it if the actor playing him looked a little more like Robert Redford (who played Bob Woodward in *All the President's Men*; Hayes, 2009).[8] The consistency of the ABC's coverage contrasted with some of its commercial competitors who were more inclined to use selective chunks of evidence, often juxtaposed with voyeuristic images of brothels, and with an emphasis on punishment rather than addressing what was clearly systemic failure of major public institutions (Neilsen, 1989).

The recommendations in the Report delivered with great fanfare on July 3, 1989 did not come as a surprise. The public had been well prepared for the substantial realignment of the regulatory and administrative apparatus of the state, and the major political parties had committed to its implementation, a commitment which gained momentum after the election in December 1989 of Wayne Goss as the first Labor Premier for 33 years. For the media, which had played such an important role in the establishment of the inquiry, the extent of the corruption it uncovered and the nature of systemic failure went well beyond the purview of routine — or even exceptional — journalism. As much of the reporting of the Inquiry had revealed, the news media was a flawed monitory institution — tempted by sensation, accustomed to receiving information dispatches from those in power, distracted by commercial and personal interest, often poorly informed about the rule of law and easy prey for propagandists. As the Report noted:

> The media played a part in exposing corruption, but as one of the powerful institutions in our society it must also share the blame for its growth. Journalists' uncritical dependence on their sources, orchestrated government leaks and the operations of publically-funded government media units and press secretaries have reduced the independent perspective of the media and can lead to it becoming a mouthpiece for vested interests. (Fitzgerald, 1989, p. 359)

In recommending the establishment of the independent Electoral and Administrative Review and Criminal Justice Commissions, Fitzgerald created organisations with a formal and accountable monitory role, but not autonomous organisations which were potentially at risk of being 'infused by an inevitable sense of importance and crusading zeal' (Fitzgerald, 1989, p. 302). These commissions were promptly founded and began the substantial task of reform. Fitzgerald had urged vigilance and openness in the relationship between the media and the government, and in 1991, at the end of the second year of the Goss government, freedom of information legislation was also introduced.

The challenges of grafting new monitory organisations onto the existing political apparatus were considerable. Much of the news coverage of these institutions was preoccupied with issues of personality and other proxies for partisan politics. Similarly the decision to limit the scope of the freedom of information legislation in 1993 produced a major backlash by the media, which saw in this action a corruption of the principle of openness of government central to Fitzgerald's recommendations. Fitzgerald had sought to balance the interests of elected politicians in getting their message out, with the rights of the community to reliable and truthful information, and although he urged vigilance in the relationship between the government and the news media the number of people employed in media management in government continued to increase over the following decades. The media, as a bastard institution, was beyond his regulatory recommendations.

While the incoming government of Wayne Goss maintained a principled commitment to the Fitzgerald institutions, this was not unproblematic and a backlash was building which came to a head with the subsequent government. After he assumed office in 1996 National Party Premier Rob Borbidge was determined to assert the Parliament's authority and limit the institutional reform that Fitzgerald had begun, declaring: 'Let's get away from the idea that Tony Fitgerald is God!' (Schultz, 2008, p. 33). The *Inquiry into the Future, Role, Structure, Powers and Operations of the Criminal Justice Commission* (Connolly-Ryan Inquiry) that Borbidge appointed was widely regarded as an attempt to 'muzzle' the Commission, but in the confusing welter of daily reporting of conflicting evidence, perspective on the underlying issue was easily lost. As one close observer noted: 'The media lacks a corporate memory and a capacity to join the dots to discern a pattern, instead seeing each event as self-contained and transitory' (Barclay, 1999).

A decade after the Fitzgerald Inquiry commenced, the media environment was profoundly different. Not long before the Inquiry commenced, Rupert Murdoch's News Ltd acquired Queensland Newspapers and with it the entire Herald and Weekly Times group. As the new proprietor of the leading daily newspaper, Murdoch personally encouraged the editor of the *Courier-Mail* to foster Dickie's work. But within 10 months competition was reduced when on February 5, 1988, Queensland Newspapers closed the afternoon *Telegraph,* and the *Daily Sun* became an afternoon paper — until it too closed three years later, on December 10, 1991 (Kirkpatrick, 2006). Fairfax ceased publishing its investigative *National Times* in 1986 and on 13 March 1988 its successor paper, the *Times on Sunday,* which had reported extensively on corruption and misconduct in Queensland also closed. News Ltd's national paper *The Australian* circulated widely in Queensland, but at that time did not have an investigative or campaigning focus.

Attempts by various governments to provide incentives to attract new publishers to set up a new newspaper in Brisbane came to nought. As a result, two and a half years after Fitzgerald described the need for greater robustness and accountability of key institutions, Brisbane had become a monopoly newspaper city. Furthermore in response to budget cuts in 1996 the ABC ceased production of state based nightly television current affairs. The commercial appeal of television news and current affairs had also diminished and the networks no longer had state based programs, replaced by generic sensationalist tabloid television current affairs.

In a little over a decade the investigative journalism which had characterised the 1980s had largely dissipated (Schultz, 1998, pp. 233–238). The limited capacity of the media to fulfil a quasi-institutional role was clearly demonstrated in the years leading up to the Fitzgerald Inquiry, but in the new environment there were fewer media outlets and those that remained were constrained by space, time, perceptions of audience and limited staff numbers. The media was the only institution which had not been transformed as a result of the Fitzgerald agenda. Newspaper self-regulation via the industry-funded Australian Press Council remained voluntary, and the regulatory processes of commercial television and radio rarely impinged.

Labor Premier Peter Beattie was elected in 1998 and quickly earned a reputation as the most skilful communicator to hold the office. The media was grateful for his ease and access, but suspiciously branded him a 'media tart' as he sought to neutralise the Opposition and make peace with Sir Joh and his legacy.[9] Like most politicians who depended on the media, he was privately critical of it. On March 25, 2003, he made these views public in a speech in Queensland Parliament:

> I want to talk about a difficult problem — one that all politicians seek to avoid, since it brings them into direct conflict with the media. I want to talk about making the media more accountable ... Just as nineteenth-century democracy relied on independent members of parliament to keep the executive accountable, so it placed great value on a free press to ask the hard questions, to keep a spotlight on ministers and their actions. But who would guard the guardians? Who would keep the media in turn honest? For early advocates of a free press the answer was simple: competition. Just like parliamentary democracy, the idea of a free press has been made part of our institutional fabric even though it no longer exists. For the cut and thrust of a thousand competing voices is long gone. Many Queenslanders live in communities in which there is only a single local daily newspaper deciding what will be news, supplemented by radio and television stations. A near monopoly is not a free press, at least in the traditional political sense of the term. Sure it remains free from government censorship, but there is no mechanism left to expose and correct bias within the media. But in the absence of meaningful competition, how can the public know whether it is getting the truth? What is it not being told?

I do not believe journalists should be responsible to government. But I do argue they should be responsible to the public, in the same way ministers are responsible — through public scrutiny of their actions. And so today I'm calling for a public debate about truth-in-media laws — how can we make the media more accountable? How, given the realities of limited competition, can we use legislative means to ensure effective public scrutiny of the media? Should the principles of freedom of information be extended to journalists, so that the media can be held to the same tests of honesty as other public institutions? (Beattie, 2004, p. 55)

The substantive issues raised by Beattie's speech were not addressed in the local media and the speech was not reprinted — 'the "debate" about Beattie's proposal never moved beyond outright condemnation to contemplate difficulties with applying FOI law' (Sikes, 2004, p. 59). Notwithstanding their reluctance to engage with demands for greater accountability in 2007 the media companies had formed an organisation to advocate for greater media freedom, defamation law reform, liberalisation of laws regulating freedom of information, whistleblowers and protection for journalists from revealing their sources. This demand was not accompanied by an offer by the media companies or journalists to accept greater responsibility, but it coincided with declining profitability and uncertainty about the future of the industry.

The relationship between the government and the media in Queensland remains problematic. The quasi-institutional legitimacy of the media has been found wanting — although the monopoly daily newspaper remains influential, its circulation has fallen despite a growing population. The Fitzgerald recommendations were in keeping with other similar agencies established in other jurisdictions. As John Keane (2009, pp. 81–102) has noted, the creation of these agencies, marked the beginning of a new global model of democracy in which the representative model is supplemented by formal mechanisms of accountability — which Keane has called 'monitory democracy'. In this context the news media is a very limited and partial watchdog.

The notion of the news media as the fourth estate arose at a time of limited franchise, far from universal literacy, in essentially homogeneous societies, where news outlets were unapologetically partisan and sought to provoke public discussion. That this notion lasted into the 20th century was the outcome of a deliberate strategy by influential news media owners and managers to adopt a policy of professional objectivity coupled with a dictum of 'social responsibility' (Schultz, 1998, p. 41). In part this was a defensive mechanism designed to limit external regulation, and in an era of mass audiences and political neutrality, a way of maximising both profits and influence, with one foot in commerce the other in politics.

In the more complex and variegated society of the late 20th century the capacity of the news media to fulfil this role was questionable. It could signal events, but the pressure to maximise sales, provide a congenial environment for advertisers and to analyse complex system failure was increasingly beyond the capacity of the news media to undertake in any systematic fashion. As Quentin Dempster noted at the turn of the century:

> The media can be deeply superficial, ignorant, sensationalist, easily diverted and manipulated, sometimes cowardly, most times pursuing its commercial imperatives … ahead of the more worthy and valuable pursuit of the public interest. Sometimes the media redeems itself with a determined exposure of corruption or wrong doing from which our democratic systems greatly benefits. But these occasions are fewer as a new layer of pressures are applied to journalists and the media. (Dempster, 2001, p. 1)

The high aspirations of the investigative journalists whose work had triggered inquiries, including Fitzgerald, foundered on the weakness of a bastard institution which was ill-equipped to systematically monitor the sources of power in an increasingly complex society in the 21st century. Concurrently, it was losing its commercial resilience in a rapidly evolving media market. The business model that made it possible for media owners to use profits to underwrite the cost of producing quality journalism is under assault. This is coupled with increasingly sophisticated media management by figures in public life which has made journalists and editors acutely aware of their limits.

At its best the news media can shine a light on egregious failings, but it is ill-equipped to address systemic shortcomings in 'democratic system management' (Kunczik, 1989) — instead it has become a captive of routines and processes, and without the financial resources to underwrite the cost of lengthy inquiries. The Fitzgerald process and its aftermath demonstrated both the strengths and limits of the media. In recent times its limits have been more clearly on display.

While it is possible that the non commercial public broadcaster would undertake an investigation similar to that which provoked the Fitzgerald Inquiry, it is unlikely that the commercial media would play a similar role. Neither is well equipped to report and analyse more the more disparate system failure which allowed corruption to flourish in Queensland.

It remains to be seen whether the new forms of internet communication, citizen journalism and social networks will evolve more significant models of democratic scrutiny of complex system failure. If it does, it is likely to do so in conjunction with more robust monitory agencies. As the news media's business model is challenged the bastard institution, which has been reluctant to revise its notions of institutional responsibility while claiming greater rights on the basis of its quasi-institutional status, is finding it increasingly hard to keep its balance.

Endnotes

1   James Fairfax as Chairman of Fairfax from 1977 had a view that newspapers 'no matter who owns them or controls them exist as a service to the public ... not only to record the facts, but to provide a commentary on them ... commentary intended to influence the actions of those who read or hear of it' (Souter, 1991, p. 89). Shawcross (1992, pp. 187–188) noted that Rupert Murdoch found new commercial justifications to assert a more investigative and campaigning approach, urging his editors to pursue stories that touch widespread public concern and have the capacity to increase circulation. See (Schultz, 1998, pp. 59–60).

2   Bob Gordon was of the view that Phil Dickie was the unsung hero of the entire process. Shortly before he retired as editor of the *Gold Coast Bulletin*, he wrote a letter arguing that: 'I have always been bemused that a lawyer should get all the glory. Tony Fitzgerald was an admirable and worthy soul, but he would not have got the gig without pressure from the *Courier-Mail* and *Sunday Mail*. If any name should be enshrined in the history of Queensland it is that of the lead reporter whose series of stories forced the inquiry. He is Phil Dickie, then a very junior reporter and it was a slow news day, as we say in the great game, that led to him being assigned to find out why corruption, prostitution and drug dealing was so blatant in Fortitude Valley and on the Gold Coast. I was his chief of staff at the time ... and I must say his courage and thoroughness were such that our State will always be in his debt. Fitzgerald simply at a rather high cost and operating under privilege gave an official imprimatur to some but not all of the excellent newspaper reporting ... As I said the real hero in all this was Phil Dickie and his editors and the management of Queensland Newspapers who had the courage to back him even when we could have papered the walls with frighteners from assorted lawyers working for the underworld, the police and various politicians ... I have always thought it ironic that Fitzgerald enshrined a nice little earner for lawyers, as the device to protect Queensland from further corruption His Crime and Misconduct Commission has morphed into various forms but a late night stroll through Fortitude Valley or Surfers Paradise gives the proof or how ineffectual it has been'. This letter was displayed in the Fitzgerald Exhibition at Griffith University in August 2009.

3   In 1986, the Cabinet approved public funds to further defamation actions brought by the Premier against the media and numerous defamation writs were issued. After March 1986, 16 publicly funded defamation cases were issues, 13 by the Premier; although most were subsequently discontinued, the Fitzgerald report notes that the state paid more than $100,000 in costs on these actions.

4   Bray took no prisoners when challenged in the closed world of the Brisbane upper middle class. After a Supreme Court judge chided him for running a 'communist uni out there', Bray responded: 'Well if we are that may be a good thing — in contrast to some other universities.' (Schultz, 2008, p. 26)

5   It is also worth noting that the trigger for Cabinet indemnity for the costs of defamation actions by the Premier followed the spectacular fall from grace of his former press secretary Allan Callaghan and his wife in 1986, who were found

guilty of fraud and misappropriation. By 1986 the edifice Sir Joh had built was
beginning to crumble (Fitzgerald, 1989, p. 118).

6   It is worth noting that the corrupt former police officer Jack Herbert began col-
    lecting the $3million he raised in graft in 1979 immediately after this period of
    civil disruption (Fitzgerald, 1989, p. 67).

7   Greg Chamberlin (2007) put the Queensland Newspapers' response to this
    exchange in an article in the *Courier-Mail* on 11 May 2007: 'The *Courier-Mail*
    kept up its work once the inquiry began, as well as covering the inquiry. Almost
    every night [defamation lawyer Doug] Spence would travel from the inquiry to
    the newsroom to provide pre-publication advice. Fitzgerald was uneasy about
    media inquiries continuing once the commission had started. He was concerned
    news reports might canvass potential evidence; there was always the risk of
    contempt. The newspaper, which did not agree its work should cease, sometimes
    consulted with the commission before publishing sensitive material and on occa-
    sions became the subject of a stern Fitzgerald homily. The most serious followed
    a report that a protected inquiry witness was wanted by police over possible unre-
    lated criminal matters but they could not serve the warrant because they did not
    know her whereabouts and their investigations were therefore hampered. To
    describe Fitzgerald as angry was an understatement. But the truth was that the
    material had been run past the Commission. The newspaper had the choice of
    showing its hand, potentially to the detriment of the inquiry's public reputation,
    or taking the rebuke. Although it denied publishing false information it took the
    view that the work of the commission should not be undermined. Documents
    the journalist relied on remained in safe keeping for many years'.

8   This was in a private note presented to Quentin Dempster by a commission
    orderly the morning after the *7.30 Report*'s first re-enactment went to air early in
    1988. Cited by Mark D. Hayes: 'Dear Quentin, I realise the ABC is short of funds
    and please do not take this as a criticism of an otherwise good effort by all con-
    cerned, but I noticed that the actor you have employed to portray me in no way
    bears my uncanny resemblance to either Tom Cruise or Robert Redford. Best
    wishes, Tony Fitzgerald'.

9   Tony Fitzgerald felt that Beattie lacked a commitment to the reform agenda, and
    set out to have the public forget that the state had been governed for many years
    by a corrupt government that distorted elections and used a dysfunctional police
    force to stifle dissent.

References

ABC. (1985). *The role of the national broadcaster in contemporary Australia* (pp. 12–
    15). Sydney, Australia: ABC Corporate Relations.

Barclay, P. (1999). *Background Briefing*. Sydney, Australia: ABC Radio National.

Barry, P. (1990). *The rise and fall of Alan Bond*. Sydney, Australia: Bantam Books.

Bayley, E. (1981). *Joe McCarthy and the press*. New York: Pantheon.

Beattie, P. (2004). Addicted to celebrity: Who guards the guardians? *Griffith Review,*
    5, 55.

Chamberlin, G. (2007, 19 May). No stopping judgement. *The Courier Mail*, pp. 56, 65.

Dempster, Q. (2001, August). *Indecent exposures — The media's corruption role*. Paper presented at the Corruption Prevention Network, Darling Harbour, Sydney, Australia.

Dickie, P. (1989). *Road to Fitzgerald and beyond*. Brisbane, Australia: University of Queensland Press.

Fitzgerald, G.E. (1989). *Report of a Commission of Inquiry pursuant to Orders in Council*. Brisbane, Australia: Queensland Government.

Hallin, D. (1986). *The uncensored war*. New York: OUP.

Hayes, M.D. (2009, March). *Address*. Paper presented at the Journalism after Fitzgerald Symposium, Brisbane, Australia.

Keane, J. (2009). Participation society: Monitory democracy and media-saturated societies. *Griffith Review, 24,* 81–109.

Kirkpatrick, R. (2006). *Select chronology of significant Australian press events from 1951 to 2005*. Retrieved July 31, 2009, from http://www.nla.gov.au/anplan/heritage/1951-2005.html

Kunczik, M. (1989). *Concepts of journalism*. Bonn: FES.

Masters, C. (1992). *Inside story*. Sydney, Australia: Angus and Robertson.

Masters, C. (2008). Moonlight Reflections. *Griffith Review: Hidden Queensland, 21,* 57–68.

Neilsen, P. (1989). Dempster and Carroll Reporting: Television current affairs and the Fitzgerald Inquiry. *Social Alternatives, 8*(2), 62–64.

Schultz, J. (1998). *Reviving the fourth estate*. Melbourne, Australia: Cambridge University Press.

Schultz, J. (2008). Disruptive influences. *Griffith Review: Hidden Queensland, 21,* 11–41.

Shawcross, W. (1992). *Rupert Murdoch*. London: Chatto.

Sikes, N. (2004). Addicted to celebrity: An affront to democracy. *Griffith Review, 5,* 49.

Souter, G. (1991). *Company of heralds*. Melbourne, Australia: Melbourne University Press.

4

Crime and Misconduct Commission: Moving Away From Fitzgerald

Colleen Lewis

One of the principle recommendations of the 1989 *Report of a Commission of Inquiry Pursuant to Orders in Council* (hereafter referred to as the Fitzgerald Report) was the establishment of the independent Criminal Justice Commission (CJC). The CJC was not the result of duplicating or piecing together elements of existing police and public sector anti-corruption models.[1] It was a bold visionary plan that reflected Fitzgerald's deep understanding of how ineffective public sector accountability and the misuse of political power can lead to institutional decay, a feature of many aspects of public life in Queensland prior to the establishment of the 1987 *Commission of Inquiry into Possible Illegal Activities and Associated Police Misconduct* (hereafter referred to as the Fitzgerald Inquiry).

Not wishing to leave the implementation of one of his key recommendations to chance, the Fitzgerald Report laid down a blue print for the structure of the Commission, the roles it should perform and how it should operationalise them, the manner in which it should be held accountable and who should be responsible for monitoring and reviewing the CJC on a regular basis (Fitzgerald, 1989, pp. 308–322; 372–379). The Report also describes the process to be adopted for establishing the Commission (1989, pp. 346–348). The coercive powers Fitzgerald recommended for this independent, anti-corruption body exceed those of the police, and when coupled with the ability of the CJC to conduct public hearings, meant that Fitzgerald recommended the establishment of a standing royal commission.

The unique CJC model established a new benchmark for police and broader public sector accountability institutions and some 20 years later it continues to influence the design of independent police and public sector anti-corruption models in Australia and beyond. Even when those who recommend and formulate anti-corruption policies decide not to replicate the CJC model, they need, at least, to engage with it.[2] This is a testament to the enduring influence of Fitzgerald's far-sighted model.

Since the CJC became operational in 1990 there have been two major government initiated changes to its structure and the roles it performs. In 1998, the Borbidge National–Liberal Party Government removed the organised and major crime function from the CJC and gave it to a newly created Queensland Crime Commission (QCC). In 2002, the Beattie Labor Government 'merged' the CJC and QCC to form the Crime and Misconduct Commission (CMC). This chapter examines those changes.

After briefly describing the structure of the original CJC model and the thinking behind it, the chapter explores the motivations underpinning the 1998 restructure. It then focuses on the purported merger of the QCC and CJC to form the CMC and argues that the CMC is not simply an amalgamation of these two organisations. The *Crime and Misconduct Act 2001* (*CM Act*) establishes a different approach to one of the CJC's key functions: complaints management. This new approach, coupled with the CMC's recent foreshadowing of other changes to the processing of complaints, takes the CMC in a different direction to that recommended by Fitzgerald. There are risks associated with this change as it has the potential to weaken the CMC's reputation as an effective citizens' watchdog body.

The Original CJC Model

The Fitzgerald Inquiry exposed a system in which endemic corruption and abuse of power had, over many years, slowly eaten away at the moral fibre of Queensland public life. The extent of the problem was such that Fitzgerald and his team knew that any reform program, to be effective, would need to adopt a comprehensive, strategic approach. The exceptional CJC formed a vital part of their strategy.

Fitzgerald recommended that the CJC be headed by a full-time chairperson and four part-time commissioners. The chairperson had to be eligible for appointment as a judge (or formerly have been a judge) of the High Court, the Federal Court, or a Supreme Court of Australia. He/she was to be assisted by four part-time commissioners, of which one had to be a practicing legal practitioner with a demonstrated interest in civil liberties. The other three were to have a demonstrated interest in community affairs with one of them being a person with senior managerial experience in a large organisation. The Parliament responded positively to Fitzgerald's recommendation and similar criteria apply in respect of the CMC.[3]

In an attempt to reduce the negative effect party politics had on the administration of criminal justice in Queensland, Fitzgerald (1989, p. 309) recommended the establishment of a standing all-party parliamentary committee, the Parliamentary Criminal Justice Committee (PCJC), to monitor and review how the CJC discharged its functions and exercised its powers. The PCJC was also responsible for receiving complaints made against the Commission and its employees. The Committee was required to conduct three-yearly reviews of the CJC and to report its findings to the Parliament. When the CMC was established, a Parliamentary Crime and Misconduct Committee (PCMC) was created to perform similar functions.

When the CJC became operational in early 1990, it comprised five Divisions: Official Misconduct; Misconduct Tribunals; Intelligence; Witness Protection; and Research and Coordination (CJC, 1990). The following gives a brief overview of the rationale underpinning the creation of these Divisions and their main roles.

Official Misconduct Division

Pointing to the abject failure of the Queensland Police Force (QPF)[4] to investigate and discipline its own (Fitzgerald, 1989, pp. 200–212), and the very low opinion in which the external Police Complaints Tribunal was held by honest police and the Queensland community (Fitzgerald, 1989, p. 292), Fitzgerald recommended that the CJC's Official Misconduct Division (OMD) be given responsibility for receiving, screening and classifying all complaints against police. It was also given responsibility for deciding how complaints would be handled and for investigating all complaints except those classified by the chief officer of the Complaints Section as being frivolous or vexatious. For police, this included behaviour classified as misconduct and official misconduct. The CM Act also draws a similar distinction in terms of its jurisdiction over police and other units of public administration.[5]

The Inquiry revealed that corrupt practices were not confined to QPF personnel and that the (illegal) cooperation of public officials from other public sector organisations was necessary to the success of certain criminal activities. Hence, the OMD was given responsibility for overseeing alleged and suspected official misconduct in other Queensland public sector organisations (Fitzgerald, 1989).

The Inquiry extended to the conduct of elected officials and exposed the disreputable and corrupt conduct of some parliamentarians who had difficulty separating their private interests and public duties. Thus, OMD's role included investigating official misconduct involving members of the Legislative Assembly, the Parliamentary Service and Executive Council. OMD was also given responsibility for carrying on the work of the Fitzgerald Commission of Inquiry, including the investigation of major and organised crime (CJC, 1990). The Fitzgerald team understood that a reactive, investigative approach, on its own, would not change behaviours, hence OMD was assigned a corruption prevention role that included proactive, educative and liaison functions.

Misconduct Tribunals

The Misconduct Tribunals had an original and appellate jurisdiction, to review decisions about disciplinary issues within the QPS and to make original administrative decisions in relation to allegations of official misconduct (Fitzgerald, 1989, pp. 315–316). The Tribunals were originally constituted as part of OMD, which as noted above, also had responsibility for investigating complaints against police and other public servants.

It was quickly apparent to the CJC (1990), that having the quasi-judicial Tribunal responsible for adjudicating decisions undertaken by OMD was contrary to legal principles. The Commission immediately did what it could to establish the Tribunal's independence from OMD. It accommodated Tribunal staff in premises separate from the CJC, the Director of OMD relinquished any active involvement with the Tribunals and the tasks of establishing the infrastructure and procedures for the Tribunals were assigned to the CJC's General Counsel. A Registrar was also appointed (CJC, 1991).

Intelligence Division

The Fitzgerald Inquiry (1989) found that the QPF did not have the capacity to provide an effective intelligence service in relation to major and organised crime and other criminal activity that went beyond the local policing level. Accordingly, the highest level of intelligence information and oversight of the police intelligence system was made the responsibility of the CJC. Its role was to build an intelligence database, secure all intelligence data and records and restrict access to intelligence material on a need-to-know basis, to oversee the performance of the Service's Bureau of Criminal Intelligence and the Queensland Police Service's (QPS) liaison with other law enforcement agencies. Subject to the Commission's approval, the Intelligence Division was to give reports to the premier and police minister on issues of criminal intelligence relevant to government considerations, policies and projects (CJC, 1991).

Witness Protection Division

Witness protection was allocated to the CJC, not because police involved in this function were considered corrupt, but because of the conflict of interest situation that arises when those seeking witness protection are giving evidence against police. Fitzgerald (1989, pp. 318–321) made it clear that the Division should be separate from the QPS and that any police officer seconded to it should only be answerable to their superiors within the (CJC) Division. The Witness Protection Division was established to protect those who the chairperson (in consultation with the director of the Division) deemed in need of protection. To be eligible, a person must have assisted the Commission or a state law enforcement agency in the discharge of its functions and responsibilities (CJC, 1990).

Research and Coordination Division

The Fitzgerald Inquiry uncovered considerable evidence of research into police and criminal justice issues being deliberately buried at police headquarters and in other public sector institutions. To ensure that this did not happen again, and to facilitate the public airing of politically sensitive matters, a Research and Coordination Division responsible for researching and writing publicly available reports and papers was recommended (Fitzgerald, 1989, pp. 316–317). Its role was to conduct research into matters affecting the administration of criminal justice and to review activities with a view to recommending law reform in Queensland.

Understanding that the police reform program could easily unravel at the implementation stage, the independent Research and Co-ordination Division was assigned responsibility for continuous oversight of the QPS reform program, including community policing, crime prevention and the recruitment and training of police officers (CJC, 1991).

Changes to the Original Model

Many of the changes to the original CJC model have been minor and represent modifications designed to achieve a more efficient and/or effective process. Structural change had been necessary to rectify unintended consequences of the reform program. For example, after repeated requests by the CJC, the Misconduct Tribunals finally moved from the CJC to the jurisdiction of the District Court in 1997 (*Misconduct Tribunals Act 1997* (Qld)).

The accountability of the CJC was also changed and those changes have been incorporated into the accountability of the CMC. In 1997, the *Criminal Justice Legislation Amendment Act 1997* (Qld) established the statutory position of Parliamentary Criminal Justice Commissioner to assist the PCJC in its monitor and review role. At the direction of the Committee, the Parliamentary Commissioner investigates complaints against the Commission and audits and reviews its activities. The Commissioner has compulsive powers and can require Commission staff to give evidence at a hearing and to produce records, files and other documentation.

In 1998, the position of Public Interest Monitor (PIM) was established by the Borbidge Government. The PIM monitors the Commission's applications to use surveillance and covert search warrants, appears at any hearing of an application to a judge of the Supreme Court or Magistrate's Court and can test the validity of a Commission's application (CJC, 1998, p. 9).

Other structural changes have been internal. In the first few years of the OMD's existence, it became obvious that reactive matters were taking precedent over proactive issues. To try to remedy the situation, in 1992 the corruption prevention function was taken from OMD and made a separate division within the CJC: the Corruption Prevention Division. In 1998, it was decided to merge the functions of the Research Division and the Corruption Prevention Division to form a new division; Research and Prevention. The amalgamation of the CJC's research and corruption prevention functions into the one division aligns with then part-time Commissioner Ross Homel's view, as a leading corruption prevention expert, that:

> The key to improving effectiveness is to design Commission-wide strategies that focus on specific kinds of misconduct, are built around quantitative measures of performance, and coordinate the activities of the Intelligence, Research, Corruption Prevention and Official Misconduct Divisions. (1997, pp. 46–47)

Homel's 'integrated prevention strategies' inform part of the recommendations of the Parliamentary Criminal Justice Committee's (PCJC) three-yearly review of the CJC (CJC, 1998, p. 56).

Following an organisational review in 1998, the Intelligence Division became the Intelligence and Information Division and incorporated an Information Retrieval Section to provide 'centralised expertise in accessing a wide range of internal and external data from sources available to the CJC' (PCJC, 2001, p. 80).

The first major government initiated change to the Fitzgerald reform program occurred in 1998 when the organised and major crime function was removed from the CJC and given to a crime commission. As discussed below, it appears that the reason underpinning this change had as much to do with party politics as it did with the efficiency and effectiveness of the CJC.

Removing Major and Organised Crime

The newly created QCC had a limited brief to investigate organised and major crime and paedophilia. It was given a 'standing statutory reference' in relation to criminal paedophilia matters but in terms of all other criminal matters its Management Committee had to 'refer the relevant criminal activity for investigation either on its own initiative or at the request of either the Police Commissioner or the Crime Commissioner' (Carmody, 2001, p. 3). The *Crime Commission Act 1997* (Qld) confined the Police Commissioner's requests to matters requiring the use of the extraordinary coercive powers of the QCC or where the issue was such that it could be classified as a matter of public interest (Carmody, 2001, p. 3).

As well as its gatekeeper role, the Management Committee was responsible for overseeing the activities of the QCC, for making the necessary arrangements to establish a police task force to assist the QCC with investigations and for approving operational-related matters. It could also send an investigation to another entity to investigate if it thought it more appropriate or if it considered an investigation did not justify the resources needed to investigate. In addition, the management committee determined the powers that could be exercised in an investigation and had the ability to approve the QCC holding public hearings (QCC, 2001). The management committee dealt with complaints against members of the QCC or the organisation, excluding official misconduct. It had a statutory obligation to refer suspected official misconduct matters to the CJC as it retained carriage over such matters (QCC, 2000).

The powerful management committee was comprised of nine people: Crime Commissioner (Chair); Commissioner of Police; Chair of the Criminal Justice Commission; Chairperson of the National Crime Authority; Commissioner for Children and Young People and two community representative (one had to be female and one a person with proven interest in civil liberty matters). The remaining two members were politicians: the Chairperson of the Parliamentary Criminal Justice Committee (a government member) and the Deputy Chairperson of the Parliamentary Criminal Justice Committee (a member of the opposition; QCC, 2001).

The creation of a management committee added gatekeeper elements to the investigation of organised and major crime that did not exist when the CJC was responsible for the function. Moreover, there is no plausible explanation for having two politicians on the Management Committee. Their appointment to an organisation created to undertake a previous CJC function directly undermines a Fitzgerald reform objective: reducing or excluding party political considerations from criminal justice-related decisions.

The removal of the CJC's major and organised crime function also affected the Intelligence Division. Its focus shifted from a broad intelligence role to one that was more targeted toward official misconduct and the identification of long-term trends and patterns to assist the CJC in its 'more proactive and integrated approach to its responsibilities, including investigations' (PCJC, 2001, p. 79).

The Borbidge National–Liberal Party Government maintained that the establishment of the Crime Commission was about quarantining '… the substantial issues of conflict that arise between the CJC's watchdog role over police and its current direct working relationship with police through the Joint Organised Crime Task Force' (Parliament of Queensland, 20 November 1997, p. 4511). It also argued that the creation of the QCC would allow the CJC 'to concentrate more fully on its very important charter of corruption detection and prevention' (Parliament of Queensland, 20 November 1997, p. 4511).

The CJC voiced its concerns about the transfer of one of its key functions to another body. In the Commission's 1997–1998 Annual Report (1998), the Chair of the CJC Frank Clair, wrote that transferring the CJC's organised and major crime function to a newly created institution:

> ... was not informed by a careful review and rational analysis of the issues but stemmed, rather, from a somewhat precipitate decision to create a crime commission. That decision was made amidst high levels of unwarranted public concern created by allegations of official cover-up of pedophilia and related crime over many years. After a lengthy and exhaustive inquiry, retired district court Judge Jack Kimmins recently found that not one of those allegations had substance in fact.

Clair went so far as to describe the series of events that led to the CJC losing its ability to deal with organised and major crime as 'disturbing and somewhat bizarre', claiming that it was but one example of the 'volatile environment' which had surrounded the CJC in recent times (CJC, 1998, p. iii). The volatility was linked to attempts to wind back many of Fitzgerald's reforms.

The first major attempt concerned a 'secret' Memorandum of Understanding between the National–Liberal Party Opposition and the Queensland Police Union which, if implemented, would have confined the CJC's complaints handling role to 'serious criminal matters only' and returned 'simple offences, misconduct and discipline matters' to the police (Lewis, 1999, pp. 161–163). The second was the National–Liberal Government's establishment in 1997 of the Commission of Inquiry into the Future Role, Structure, Powers and Operation of the Criminal Justice Commission, commonly known as the Connolly-Ryan Inquiry. Before it could make any recommendations, the Queensland Supreme Court closed this Inquiry down for 'ostensible bias' (*Carruthers/CJC & Others v Connolly & Others*, Supreme Court of Queensland, Nos 4924 & 5236 of 1997 per Thomas J).[6]

The Labor Party Opposition saw the removal of the CJC's organised and major crime function as another attempt by the National–Liberal Party coalition to dismantle a core element of the Fitzgerald reform program. In the second reading of the Crime Commission Bill, a member of the opposition (Jim Elder) put forward the argument that the QCC:

> ... was not developed with the primary intention of improving the structure of crime and corruption fighting in Queensland. Its sole purpose — its one and only purpose — and its ultimate purpose is that it was created to get the CJC ... At the end of the day, this Government's view is that the CJC must be steamrolled. (Parliament of Queensland, 1997, 20 November, p. 4509)

Not deterred by the closing of the Connolly-Ryan Inquiry, the Borbidge Government announced changes to the CJC's structure. It removed the organised and major crime function from the Commission.

In a speech to an audience that had come together to commemorate the 20th anniversary of the publication of his landmark Report, Fitzgerald made it clear that, in his opinion, the Borbidge Government was intent on dismantling his key reforms. As he explained:

> ... a coalition of Nationals and so-called Liberals, including relics of the Bjelke-Petersen era, regained power [in 1996] in Queensland with the help of the Police Union.
>
> The Connolly-Ryan Inquiry was soon set up to discredit the reforms which had been introduced on my recommendation so that they could be dismantled with minimum community disquiet, but that exercise failed when the Supreme Court stopped the farce because of (Justice Peter) Connolly's manifest bias. (Fitzgerald, 2009)

In the 1998 State election the Beattie Labor Government won power. It was responsible for 'merging' the QCC and CJC to form the CMC. Obviously, the Beattie Government did not share the Borbidge Government's concerns about the need to remove the major and organised crime function from the CJC, as the merger returned this crime function to the body that replaced the CJC.

Structural Tensions

The Borbidge Government's attempts to dismantle crucial aspects of the Fitzgerald reform program can be explained, in part, by the Commission's capacity to investigate the conduct of politicians and to a lesser degree its jurisdiction over public servants.

The CJC and CMC's power to investigate the conduct of appointed public servants can cause embarrassment to governments, as their findings sometimes call into question a government's superintendence of the public sector. This often creates structural tensions between an independent, anti-corruption body and governments. A reason for this is the somewhat unusual constitutional position many anti-corruption bodies occupy. In the New Zealand, British, Canadian and Australian context, they interfere with the Westminster system of responsible government and its doctrine of ministerial responsibility where, in theory at least, ministers are responsible to the Parliament and hence the people for the actions of their department/agency. Because the independent CMC (and CJC before it) reports to the Parliament through a standing all-party parliamentary committee, it circumvents the authority and influence of the executive. This denies the executive the levers of control usually available to it when misconduct within a government department is publicly exposed. But it is the

Commission's ability to investigate the conduct of elected public officials, of politicians, that has most often put it on a collision course with politicians and governments.

Tense relationships between the CJC and state politicians were evident from the early days of the CJC's existence. The *Report on an Investigation into Possible Misuse of Parliamentary Travel Entitlements by Members of the 1986– 1989 Queensland Legislative Assembly in December 1991* was the first of many clashes. The inaugural chair of the Commission Sir Max Bingham, said that during the investigation into parliamentary travel entitlements 'the message coming from all sides was to pack it in' with some people suggesting that the inquiry was putting the future prospects of the CJC at risk (Walker, 1995, p. 173). The CJC's 'travel rorts' report, as it was commonly known, claimed some high profile political scalps. The reaction to the report's findings was immediate and fierce. It is exemplified in one parliamentarian's public comment that 'the CJC had dished out kangaroo-court style justice in an unprofessional, subjective, sloppy, judgmental and pathetic report' and that it 'had too much power' (*Courier-Mail*, 12 December 1991, p 2). Throughout this period and during other more turbulent times, when relations between the CJC and government were potentially lethal for the Commission, it was the Queensland community's trust in the CJC and its support for the Commission that helped to protect it. The crucial matter of community trust is revisited later in this chapter.

From CJC to CMC

On January 1, 2002, the CMC became operational. Like the CJC, it is a unique anti-corruption body, which in many respects has a similar mandate to its Fitzgerald-inspired predecessor.

However, there have been some significant changes to the CJC model. Two new senior positions have been created, the assistant commissioner crime and assistant commissioner misconduct. They are responsible to the chairperson for the proper performance of the Commission's crime and misconduct functions. Given the size of the Commission (approximately 300 employees) and its complex structure these additional positions help to strengthen the CMC's senior management. Broadening the senior management base may also allow for succession planning, as the two assistant commissioners must have the qualifications and professional experience required for appointment as commissioner (*Crime and Misconduct Act 2001* (Qld), Part 3).

Unlike the CJC, the CMC has a Crime Reference Committee which performs a similar gatekeeper function as the QCC's Management Committee. Its role is to refer major crime matters to the CMC for investigation and to coordinate major crime investigations the Commission undertakes in conjunction with any other law enforcement agency. An important difference concerns the composition of the Committee. In line with Fitzgerald's previously mentioned desire to reduce, as much as possible, the negative effect party politics can have on the administration of criminal justice, there are no parliamentarians on this Committee. It is a seven-member group comprised of the assistant commissioner crime (chair), the chairperson of the CMC, the commissioner of police, the Commissioner for Children and Young People and Child Guardian, the chief executive officer of the Australian Crime Commission and two community representatives appointed by the Governor in Council. At least one of the community representatives must be female and at least one must have a demonstrated interest in civil liberties. Before appointing a community representative to the reference committee, the Minister must consult with the Leader of the Opposition (*Crime and Misconduct Act 2001* (Qld), Part 4, s. 278).

The three principle areas of activity for the CMC are combating major crime; witness protection; and reducing misconduct and improving public sector integrity. To support these activities the CMC is sectioned into 'work areas': crime, witness protection, operations support, research and prevention, intelligence and misconduct. Corporate Services supports all areas of the Commission. The following gives a brief explanation of the principle functions of these work areas before concentrating on the misconduct area that is responsible for the management of complaints.

The crime area, which houses the proceeds of crime unit, works with the QPS and other law enforcement organisations to combat and prevent major and organised crime, including criminal paedophilia, serious crime and since 2002 terrorism.[7] Witness Protection is responsible for protecting eligible witnesses considered to be in danger because they assisted QPS and other law enforcement agencies in their investigations. Operations Support provides specialist operational and investigative assistance to all three of the CMC's principle areas of activity (outlined above). They do this by providing physical and technical surveillance and forensic computer resources. Research and Prevention undertakes research into criminal justice and public policy matters including crime, misconduct, policing and other legislative and policy areas. It also works with the misconduct area to provide misconduct and capacity building services to the QPS and other government departments and agencies. Intelligence is responsible for collecting, collating and analysing information and intelligence, for facilitating the exchange of information between the CMC's crime and misconduct areas, for assisting the investigative teams through the provision of tactical information and for providing intelligence support (PCMC, 2009). The misconduct area focuses on reducing misconduct and improving public sector integrity. When undertaking its misconduct function it is obliged to apply the principles of cooperation, capacity, devolution and public interest as detailed in the *CM Act*.[8]

Moving Away From Fitzgerald

One of the most significant changes to the CJC model relates to the CMC's misconduct function, more particularly to the approach it adopts when dealing with complaints against police and other units of public administration. As will be argued later in this chapter, the devolution strategy, in particular, could have detrimental consequences for community confidence in the public sector complaints process and hence the reputation of the CMC as an effective public sector accountability institution.

In the CMC's first Annual Report then Chair, Brendan Butler, notes that the *CM Act*, 'heralds a departure from the way misconduct matters were handled by the CJC'. The emphasis, he explained, has shifted to one of cooperation, capacity building devolution and public interest that will see the CMC 'engaging public sector managers in the continuing process of preventing and dealing with misconduct in their own agencies'. Butler goes on to assure Queenslanders that the CMC will conduct a large number of investigations each year but that its focus 'will be on the more serious and complex end of the misconduct spectrum ... with less serious matters [being] best dealt with in and by the agency itself' (CMC, 2002, p. 3). Section 34 of the CM Act sets out clearly the approach the CMC is to take when performing its misconduct functions.

Cooperation

The cooperation principle requires the CMC to engage cooperatively 'to the greatest extent practicable' with units of public administration to prevent and deal with misconduct matters (section 34(a)).

Capacity Building

Capacity building obliges the CMC to take the lead role in building a unit of public administration's capacity to attend effectively and appropriately to instances of misconduct and to prevent misconduct from occurring (section 34(b)). The CMC undertakes this function in several ways including:

- through its various publications, which include research reports, research and issues papers, brochures. guides and flyers;
- the delivery of presentations and workshops and the provision of crime prevention advice and support to units of public administration including the police and local governments;
- through continuous liaison with middle and senior management and while conducting its outreach program which includes visits to rural and regional areas;

- by conducting research into misconduct related issues including misconduct prevention; and
- by working with Indigenous communities (PCMC, 2009, p. 28).

In building a unit of public administration's capacity, the CMC focuses on the standard of a department/agency's investigations, its understanding of what constitutes a conflict of interest as well as identifying any specific deficiencies in a particular agency through the CMC's monitoring of complaints (CMC, 2008a, p. 90). Monitoring includes reviews and audits. Reviews focus on specific complaints that are referred to agencies to investigate after the CMC has identified at the assessment/classification stage that a complaint warrants scrutiny because of systemic or public interest issues (CMC, 2008a, p. 88). The review function can take place before any proposed actions, during the investigation process or after it is completed.

Audits, random and targeted, focus on 'compliance with standards', the integrity of agencies' complaints handling practices in general and how they deal with specific alleged misconduct, for example, 'reprisal against whistleblowers'. Audits involve complaints that the CMC has not reviewed (CMC, 2008a, p. 88). The Commission evaluates matters of 'compliance and integrity' according to an assessment scale which rates a unit of public administration's complaints management capacity as 'very limited', 'competent', 'highly developed' or 'advanced'.

In addition to the above monitoring function, the Commission also undertakes quality assurance reviews to ascertain the quality of a unit of public administration's 'integrity framework', which includes its code of conduct, complaints and record management systems, training program and internal monitoring systems (CMC, 2008a, p. 88).

The CMC (2008a, p. 88) maintains that:

> With the various limbs to our monitoring, the agencies are well aware that any matter that is referred to them to deal with may be subject to scrutiny by the CMC. This builds confidence and encourages compliance with the appropriate standards for dealing with matters.

The CMC's review of police investigations for 2006–2007 and 2007–2008 call into question the degree to which its capacity building function has been successful in relation to the QPS. Of the 220 complaints reviewed for this two year period, '21%' or one-fifth of all complaints referred by the CMC to QPS were not, in the CMC's opinion, dealt with satisfactorily (CMC, 2008a, p. 112). It appears that after 7 years of capacity building, there is further work to be done to address persistent shortcomings in the investigative process when police investigate police. Addressing these shortcomings is particularly important given that the QPS 'has primary responsibility' for handling police misconduct matters. While the Commission 'retains a monitoring role' in respect of such complaints it is not, as the CMC explains, 'as strong a role as it has for official misconduct'. (CMC, 2008a, p. 81)

Public Interest

The public interest principle requires the CMC to promote public confidence in the integrity of the public sector and in the way public sector misconduct is handled. In doing so, the CMC must take into account:

- The capacity (including resources) of the unit of public administration to deal effectively with misconduct matters.
- The nature and seriousness of the misconduct (whether it is an isolated matter or a prevalent or systemic issue).
- Whether public confidence in the process and in the unit of public administration is likely to be enhanced if the CMC, and not the unit of public administration, deals with the issue (PCMC, 2009, p. 28).

It is not apparent how the CMC gauges public confidence in the process it has adopted for devolving complaints to police and other units of public administration. The CMC (and the CJC before it) does conduct surveys about public confidence in the complaints system.[9] However, none of the surveys taken since the establishment of the CMC explain the new approach to complaints handling and then asks members of the public to rate their confidence in the system, particularly its emphasis on devolution. Nor is it readily apparent what key performance indicators the CMC uses to ascertain if its capacity building and devolution programs are maintaining public confidence in the new complaints process.

Devolution

The devolution principle stipulates that subject to requirements attached to cooperation, capacity and public interest 'action to prevent and deal with misconduct within a unit of public administration should generally happen within the unit' (PCJC 2009, p. 28). It was the CMC's predecessor, the CJC, which initially championed this approach. While the investigation of suspected police and/or official misconduct was 'a focal activity of the CJC', toward the end of its existence, it started to promote a shift towards 'devolving responsibility for investigating and preventing misconduct back to the relevant public sector agencies', including the police (PCMC, 2009, p. 22).

In its 1999–2000 Annual Report, the CJC advised that it was working with the QPS to move toward a system of managerial resolution for some complaints (2000, pp. 13–14). In the 2000–2001 Annual Report (CJC, 2001, p. 3), the chairperson Brendan Butler acknowledged that over the past 10 years there had been an 'immense improvement in integrity in the Queensland Police Service and the Queensland public sector generally'. He went on to say that in view of this, 'the CJC had realigned itself to work in partnership with agencies to further enhance their capacity to build ethical, corruption-free workplaces'.

Referring to a joint complaints handling initiative commenced in 2000 with the QPS, the chairperson explained that:

> The ultimate goal is to build the capacity of police managers to accept responsibility for promoting ethical conduct in the ranks. True resistance to corruption is dependent upon police supervisors shaping an ethical tone committed to professional and principled conduct. I believe the time is now right to place trust in police managers to provide that leadership. The role of the CJC will be to promote and support the success of this initiative. (CJC, 2001, p. 4)

In what was to be its final three-yearly review of the CJC, the PCJC supported this approach to complaints handling. It recommended that the CJC 'continue with its present policy of gradually devolving responsibility to the Queensland Police Service for the handling of complaints against police officers', with the CJC 'always to retain an oversight role'. The Committee also recommended that the CJC 'should continue to make the initial assessment of how a complaint is to be dealt with' (PCJC, 2001, p. 37).

The shift to capacity building and devolution initiated by the CJC is as strongly supported today by the CMC, as it was when the complaint management principles of cooperation, capacity building, devolution and public interest were codified in 2002.

In its 2008 submission to the PCJC three-yearly review of the CMC, the Commission argued that the devolution of complaints to the unit of public administration in which the misconduct occurred, 'allows the agency to take responsibility for the actions complained of and also frees up the resources of the CMC to concentrate on 'those matters involving the more complex, systemic and contentious allegations of misconduct' (CMC, 2008b, p. 90). It goes on to explain that this allows the Commission to focus its misconduct investigations on matters such as 'major fraud, corruption and sensitive political matters [and] ... high-risk areas involving the police' (CMC, 2008b, p. 90).

In response to criticisms of police investigating police raised after the Commission handed down *Dangerous Liaison: A report arising from a CMC investigation into allegations of police misconduct (Operation Capri)* (CMC, 2009a) in July 2009, Chair Robert Needham reaffirmed the CMC's support for devolution. He explained that:

> I am of the firm belief that the less serious police misconduct should be handled relatively close to the officer against whom the allegation has been made ... It is only through the supervisor taking responsibility for dealing with allegations of misconduct among his officers that high ethical standards and appropriate supervision will be embedded. (Koch and McKenna, 2009)[10]

Needham further argued that 'if a supervisor is able to send a complaint against an officer to an external body, like the CMC, then they will have the attitude that it's not a matter they have to worry about' (Koch and McKenna, 2009).

Chief executive officers, managers and supervisors do have responsibility for the ethical health of an organisation, but they have always had this responsibility. It is part of their role as leaders, managers and supervisors and the creation of the CJC in 1990 did not remove that responsibility. What it did remove was the ability of managers and supervisors to investigate the misconduct of members of the same organisation, particularly a member they are responsible for supervising. The issue is not only about responsibility for an ethical culture or the conduct of members — it is also about public confidence in a complaints process in which it is perceived that a complaint investigation may not be dealt with in an impartial manner. The CMC needs to demonstrate to the community, through its reviews, audits of agency investigations and through its own proactive investigations that it is achieving the right balance between self-regulation and the external, investigatory control approach more prevalent in the CJC model.

This is needed if the public is to feel confident that, when an organisation investigates its own, the outcome is not inappropriately influenced by a desire to protect an individual or by institutional considerations such as the reputation of the department/agency or a division within it. Rightly or wrongly, it seems that the community does not yet, and may never, have confidence in units of public administration, and police in particular, to investigate their own.

The PCMC in its recent three-yearly review of the CMC noted that it 'frequently receives feedback from members of the community expressing concern that their complaints about officers of a public sector agency have been devolved back to that agency for investigation (PCMC, 2009, p. 29).

The Parliamentary Crime and Misconduct Commissioner Mr Alan MacSporran SC, also raises concerns about this matter in his submission to the PCMC. He refers to submissions made in a private capacity by community members to the PCMC review, to two submissions by Queensland MPs expressing the views of their constituents and two further submissions by Queensland academics in which all express their disagreement with the devolution principle.

MacSporran (2009, p. 9) suggests that if the CMC retains devolution 'strategies must be adopted to ensure that it operates effectively and to establish and maintain public confidence in its operations'. As he says, the difficulty that needs to be overcome is a lingering doubt 'that an investigation has not been carried out impartially' when an organisation investigates complaints against its own. To help address this perception, he proposes more extensive monitoring of complaints referred back to public sector organisations to handle and detailed finalisation reports that are checked and noted by the CMC for 'integrity, thoroughness and adequacy of its process'. The Parliamentary Commissioner sees complaints handling as a simple question of 'transparent accountability' (MacSporan, 2009, p. 11).

As outlined above, the CMC does review and audit some of the complaints it refers back to agencies to investigate. However, the Parliamentary Commissioner is calling for the number of reviewed and audited complaints to be increased.

Tony Koch, a journalist with *The Australian* newspaper, who has covered Queensland politics for over 25 years, was recently critical of the Beattie Government's decision to introduce a devolution principle to complaints handling. Koch views it as 'a dismal failure of an experiment' claiming that 'only the foolhardy would ignore the clear warnings spelt out last night by the courageous Tony Fitzgerald' (Koch, 2009). Koch was referring to the speech Fitzgerald gave on 28 July 2009 to mark 20 years since he brought down his report.

Retired Supreme Court Judge Bill Carter, who chaired two investigations into police corruption in the 1990s, has called for an end to the practice of 'cops investigating cops' for misconduct-related matters. He maintains that such matters should be handled by investigators who are independent of the QPS (Koch and McKenna, 2009).[11]

The devolution issue is more acute in relation to the QPS as Fitzgerald found that its handling of complaints against fellow officers was abysmal. While the QPS has undergone considerable reform and the organisation bears little resemblance to the QPF pre Fitzgerald there is still room for improvement in the way it handles complaints against fellow officers. The CMC has identified 'a range of possible factors contributing to a perceived 'slippage" within the Police Service. These factors include management and supervision and performance management, and the disciplinary system' (CMC, 2009a).

The QPS is not only experiencing problems in relation to the quality of its investigations of other police, it is still experiencing difficulties with some police who see rules and procedures as irrelevant. Moreover, the CMC (like the CJC before it) is grappling with the tendency for the police department to impose disciplinary sanctions that do not align with community or CMC expectations. Both these factors are clearly evident in the CMC's *Dangerous Liaisons* report.

Leaving aside the litany of misdeeds by police involved in illegal and/or highly unsavoury conduct revealed in this excellent report, there is clear evidence that supervisors cannot be trusted to investigate complaints against those they supervise and that '... opportunistic officers exploited a lack of ... supervision' for their own personal gain (CMC, 2009a, pp. 14–15). One supervisor, who for three and a half years was in charge of the Armed Robbery Unit 'failed to implement any pertinent standard operating procedures' and 'none of his subordinates were trained in the requirements attaching to the payment of money from the informant funds' (CMC 2009, p. 17). A supervisor with such an attitude could not effectively investigate people that worked in that unit, or create an ethical climate. Nor could another officer mentioned adversely in the report who had 22 years policing experience before he resigned. That experience included time spent working at the CJC (CMC, 2009a, p. 69).

During Operation Capri (see *Dangerous Liaisons Report*), the Commission informed QPS of problems it was uncovering in relation to the police removal of prisoners. The Commissioner of Police Robert Atkinson, immediately directed QPS to undertake an audit of police officers' compliance with their 'statutory and procedural obligations'. With the agreement of the CMC, the QPS Ethical Standards Command (ESC) 'audited a sample of recorded instances of prisoner removals from 1 July 2000 to 17 June 2006' (CMC, 2009a, p. 38). A draft report by ESC concluded 'that while the audit had identified a lack of compliance with policy, it appeared that the removals "were generally for lawful purposes"'. The CMC was dissatisfied with ESC's conclusion. As it explained, 'the audit process had not involved a sufficiently detailed examination of the circumstances of the individual prisoner removals'. Hence, the CMC pointed out, 'it was impossible to form a view as to the legitimacy of any removal unless the particular circumstances were investigated' (CMC, 2009a, p. 40).

The CMC also expressed its concerns with the sanctions the QPS imposed on six officers whose conduct was found wanting by the CMC as a result of the Operation Capri investigation. The Commission recommended that disciplinary actions be taken against these officers; the QPS dealt with five of them 'by way of managerial guidance only' (CMC, 2009a, p. 4).

In its first Annual Report (1990, pp. 20–21), the CJC noted the importance of the Commission's Complaints Section's role (especially in terms of the police) to the operation of the Commission. It cautioned people to remember that:

> ... the widespread corruption that flourished within the Queensland Police Force ... substantially resulted from the failure of those mechanisms whose function it was to monitor, to control and to punish misconduct within the Force. Such functions have been performed ineffectually in Queensland and widely throughout the common law world. For the commission also to fail would irreparably damage its credibility.

The author wants to make it clear that she is *not* arguing that Queensland public life should forever remain in a Fitzgerald time capsule. Nor is she suggesting that there has not been positive change in the behaviour of police officers and other public servants since the Fitzgerald reform program was initiated. Indeed, the conduct of public life in 2009 bears little resemblance to that which occurred in Queensland pre-1989. The CJC and CMC have played a pivotal role in that change and have made highly significant contributions to the integrity of public life in Queensland and beyond. The following is but a tiny sample of their contribution.

The Witness Protection Division, which has protected over 1500 people since it was established has had a 100 percent success rate (CMC, 2008a, p. 2). It is a leader in witness protection training in Australasia and attained national accreditation for its Witness Protection course, the first police course to be awarded such standing (CMC, 2007, p. 45).

The Research and Prevention Division is greatly respected nationally and internationally for the quality of its empirical research and its excellent reports and corruption prevention policies. Its research helps to inform criminal justice policy in Queensland, Australia and internationally. The Manager Misconduct Prevention has been reappointed as one of seven members of the Institute of International Auditors International Ethics Committee, which is responsible for establishing practice standards for the internal auditing profession.

The CJC was selected as co-consultant for a South African Capacity Building Project which assisted the South African Office of the Public Service Commission to develop and present anti-corruption courses for senior managers of the South African public service (CJC, 2001, p. 55). This consultancy was in recognition of the Commission's growing international standing and expertise in the area of corruption prevention (CJC, 2001).

The Intelligence Division's bulletins and digests have been internationally recognised through an award for Excellence in Law Enforcement Intelligence Publications at a State level by the International Association of Law Enforcement Intelligence Analysts (CMC, 2003).

OMD has had many successes in relation to organised and major crime. It has dismantled complex organised crime networks, disrupted significantly the criminal activities of outlaw motorcycle gang chapters in Queensland and has had significant success in relation to paedophilia-related investigations (CMC, 2008b). All 26 crime and criminal paedophilia tactical investigations completed during 2007–2008 resulted in arrests and charges being laid (CMC, 2008a).

The OMD's Complaints Section has managed effectively the vast majority of the tens of thousands of complaints it has dealt with over the past 20 years. It continues to work toward building the ethical capacity of units of public administration. Its misconduct investigations have been fearlessly and impartially conducted against ministers, parliamentarians, local government councillors, the Queensland Police Union, senior public servants and others.

Despite its many successes, the fundamental change in the way complaints against appointed public servants, especially police, are now handled could have a negative effect on the community's confidence in the powerful, independent watchdog body. The CMC is largely responsible for the integrity of the public sector complaints process in Queensland and it is this process, and not other elements of the CMC's functions that largely determine the level of trust the Queensland community has in its watchdog agency.

Another worrying trend in the management of complaints is the CMC's foreshadowing of its intention to streamline the process even further. It is currently exploring ways to reduce the number of complaints it has to process. The Commission (CMC, 2008a, p. 97) is suggesting that it adopt an:

> ... approach that for certain categories of complaints, the complainant must make the complaint direct to the agency concerned in the first instance. The agency would be required to receive, record and notify the CMC of the complaint, so that the CMC could maintain its monitoring role.

If the CMC goes ahead with its streamline plans it would constitute a further rolling out of its 'section 40 directions' which already allows agencies 'to report less significant matters' by way of a schedule to the CMC on a monthly basis (CMC, 2008a, p. 97).

The broadening of its section 40 directions, coupled with the CMC's focus on capacity building and devolution means that a significant element of the Commission's approach to complaints management increasingly resembles a Civilian External Supervisory model (Goldsmith, 1988). This model, based on a post hoc facto review process, is primarily about a paper review of investigations that have been conducted by police and other units of public administration. Such an approach to civilian oversight has repeatedly proved ineffective. Over time, it results in the community losing confidence in the body responsible for dealing with their concerns about the conduct of public sector organisations, particularly the police (Lambert, 1986; Masterman, 1985; Scarman, 1986).

There is a vital difference between the CMC model and the Civilian External Supervisory model and that is the CMC's ability to investigate in its own right and to take over an investigation if it wishes. Nevertheless, more and more complaints by Queenslanders are being subjected to a post hoc facto review and the section 40 directions are diluting a crucial function of any independent anti-corruption commission: the receiving, classification and assigning of all complaints. At the same time the number of complaints the CMC itself is investigating is declining. In 2007–2008 less than 2 percent of all complaints received were retained by the CMC for investigation (CMC, 2008a).

Conclusion

The reactive-proactive approach to the administration of criminal justice recommended by Fitzgerald established a new benchmark for public sector anti-corruption commissions in Australia and internationally. While several such organisations have the coercive powers of the CMC and CJC, and are increasingly focusing on research and prevention as a way of addressing public sector integrity issues, to the best knowledge of the author, the structure of CMC and CJC and these bodies' range of functions continue to be unique. Their uniqueness accounts in large part for their many successes over the past 20 years. Nevertheless, it is the way in which the complaints handling function is performed that largely determines the level of community trust in citizens' watchdog bodies like the CMC. It is crucial to the credibility of the Commission that it maintains public confidence in its complaints management process as this confidence translates into the community's level of trust for the organisation as a whole. Fitzgerald (1989, p. 6) warned that 'if the community is complacent, future leaders will revert to former practices'. The CJC experienced those practices first-hand. It was, on more than one occasion, encircled by powerful, hostile and persistent opponents. It was public support that helped it to survive.

In Queensland and other Australian States, and in Britain, Northern Ireland, New Zealand and Canada, history has shown that once an oversight body loses the community's trust it is all but impossible to regain. When that happens it has inevitably led to the demise of the oversight body.

Endnotes

1 Anti-corruption bodies are also referred to as civilian oversight bodies and integrity agencies.
2 See the 1996 Royal Commission into the New South Wales Police Service Interim Report; the Royal Commission into whether there has been any Corrupt or Criminal Conduct by Western Australian Police Officers, Interim Report.
3 The *Crime and Misconduct Act 2001* (Qld) stipulates that one part-time commissioner must be a practicing lawyer with a demonstrated interest in civil liberties and one or more of the remaining three part-time commissioners must have '(1) qualifications or expertise in public sector management and review, or criminology, or sociology, or research related to crime or crime prevention; and (2) community service experience, or experience of community standards and expectations, relating to public sector officials and public sector administration' (CMC, 2002, p. 6). In 2008, the *CM Act* was changed to overcome the difficulty in finding a 'practising' lawyer with an interest in civil liberties to take on the role of part-time commissioner. Few practising lawyers

have time to be a part-time commissioner. The Act now requires the 'civil liberties' commissioner to have 'at least five years total of actual practice as a lawyer' (PCMC, 2009, p. 4).

4   In 1990 the Queensland Police Force changed its name to the Queensland Police Service.

5   According to the *Crime and Misconduct Act*, 'misconduct' refers to official misconduct or police misconduct, defined as follows. Official misconduct which applies to all public sector officials, including police, is conduct relating to the performance of a public sector officer's duties or exercise of powers that is dishonest or lacks impartiality, or involves a breach of the trust placed in a person by virtue of their position, or is a misuse of officially obtained information. To amount to official misconduct, the conduct must be a criminal offence or serious enough to justify dismissal. Official misconduct includes conduct by anyone who seeks to corrupt a police officer. Police misconduct (which relates only to police officers), is any conduct — other than official misconduct — that is disgraceful, improper or unbecoming a police officer, or demonstrates that person's unfitness to be or continue as an officer, or does not meet the standard of conduct that the community reasonably expects of a police officer' (CMC, 2008a, p. 9). These are similar to the definitions in the *Criminal Justice Act 1989* (Qld).

6   For a full account of these issues, see Lewis (1999, ch. 9).

7   In 2002, the CMC's Crime Reference Committee approved an 'umbrella organised crime reference' that allowed the CMC, at the request of the Police Service, to use its coercive powers to assist the QPS investigate suspected terrorism-related activity in Queensland. In 2004, the *CM Act* was amended to 'refer legislative responsibility for investigating terrorism-linked major crime to the CMC'. In effect, this gave statutory endorsement to the umbrella referral given by the Crime Reference Committee in 2002 (PCMC, 2006, p. 23).

8   A detailed account of each of these areas can be found in the PCMC's 7th — three-yearly review of the CMC, Report No 79, April 2009 (CMC, 2009a). Crime area pp. 7–25; Misconduct area pp. 26–50; Intelligence pp. 71–74; Research and Prevention pp. 75–90; Witness Protection pp. 91–97; Corporate Services & Governance pp. 105–110. An overview of the Commission's coercive powers can be found on pp. 51–70; Whistleblower Support on pp. 98–104 and an explanation for the way in which the CMC is held externally accountable for its actions on pp. 111–123. The three-yearly review was referenced as it is the latest publication in relation to these matters and therefore reflects the most recent changes to the role, functions and accountability of the CMC.

9   See, for example, the CMC reports *Public Perceptions of the Queensland Police Service: Findings from the 2008 Public Attitude Survey 2009* and the *Public Perceptions of the Queensland Public Service and Local Government: Findings from the 2005 Public Attitude Survey Report 2007* (CMC, 2006, 2009b).

10   'The appropriate manager is the one closest, as the circumstances of the complaint permit, in the chain of responsibility to the business unit or workplace in which the issue arises' (CMC, 2008b, p. 96).

11   The difficulty with Carter's suggestion is that the solution to having no police investigating police is unachievable in the short to medium term. All anti-corruption bodies in Australia that investigate complaints against police use police officers as investigators. Police are either seconded to the oversight body from the police organisation being overseen, which is the case with the CMC, or officers are seconded from other police organizations in Australia, which is the process adopted by the Police Integrity Commission in New South Wales. In addition, nearly all anti-corruption bodies hire former police as investigators. Until oversight bodies themselves train civilians as investigators or hire civilian investigators that have completed investigation courses at tertiary institutions, the situation of 'cops investigating cops' will not change.

Case

Carruthers/CJC & Others v Connolly & Others, per Thomas J, Nos 4924 and 5236 (Supreme Courts of Queensland 1997).

Legislation

Crime and Misconduct Act 2001 (Qld).
Crime Commission Act 1997 (Qld).
Criminal Justice Act 1989 (Qld).
Criminal Justice Legislative Amendment Act 1997 (Qld).
Misconduct Tribunals Act 1997 (Qld).

References

Carmody, T. (2001). *The Role of the Queensland Crime Commission in the Investigation of Organised and Major Criminal Activity.* Paper presented at the 4th National Outlook Symposium on Crime in Australia, New Crimes or New Responses, from www.aic.gov.au/en/events/2001/aic20%upcoming%20event2001/media/conference/o utlook/carmody.ashx.

Criminal Justice Commission. (CJC). (1990). *1989–1990 Annual Report.* Brisbane, Australia: Author.

Criminal Justice Commission. (CJC). (1991). *1990–1991 Annual Report.* Brisbane, Australia: Author.

Criminal Justice Commission. (CJC). (1998). *1997–1998 Annual Report.* Brisbane, Australia: Author.

Criminal Justice Commission. (CJC). (2000). *1999–2000 Annual Report.* Brisbane, Australia: Author.

Criminal Justice Commission. (CJC). (2001). *2000–2001 Annual Report.* Brisbane, Australia: Author.

Crime and Misconduct Commission. (CMC). (2002). *2001–2002 Annual Report.* Brisbane, Australia: Author.

Crime and Misconduct Commission. (CMC). (2003). *2002–2003 Annual Report.* Brisbane, Australia: Author.

Crime and Misconduct Commission. (CMC). (2006). *Public perceptions of the Queensland Public Service and Local Government: Findings from the 2005 Public Attitude Survey report.* Brisbane, Australia: Author.

Crime and Misconduct Commission. (CMC). (2007). *2006–2007 Annual Report.* Brisbane, Australia: Author.

Crime and Misconduct Commission. (CMC). (2008a). *2007–2008 Annual Report.* Brisbane, Australia: Author.

Crime and Misconduct Commission. (CMC). (2008b). *Submission to the Three-Yearly Review of the Crime and Misconduct Commission.* Brisbane, Australia: Author.

Crime and Misconduct Commission. (CMC). (2009a). *Dangerous liaison: A report arising from a CMC investigation into allegations of police misconduct (Operation Capri).* Brisbane, Australia: Author.

Crime and Misconduct Commission. (CMC). (2009b). *Public perceptions of the Queensland Police Service: Findings from the 2008 Public Attitude Survey 2009.* Brisbane, Australia: Author.

Fitzgerald, G.E. (1989). *Report of a Commission of Inquiry Pursuant to Orders in Council.* Brisbane, Australia: Government Printer.

Fitzgerald, G.E. (Tony). (2009, July 29). What went wrong with Queensland?[Edited version of speech]. *The Courier-Mail.* Retrieved July 30, 2009, from http://www.news.com.au/couriermail/story/0,23739,25849996-3102,00.html

Goldsmith, A. (1988). New directions in police complaints procedures: Some conceptual and comparative departures. *Police Studies, 11*(1), 60–71.

Homel, R. (1997). Integrating investigation and prevention: Managing the transformation of the Queensland Criminal Justice Commission. *Queensland Review, 4*(2), 37–49.

Koch, T. (2009, 29 July). Fitzgerald watchdog defanged by Beattie. *The Australian.* Retrieved August 12, 2009, from http://www.theaustralian.news.com.au/story/0,25197,25850854-5006786,00.html

Koch, T., & McKenna, M. (2009, 24 July). Bill Carter QC calls for ban on cops investigating cops. *The Australian.* Retrieved August 12, 2009, from http://www.theaustralian.news.com.au/story/0,25197,25826889-601,00.html

Lambert, J. (1986). *Police powers and accountability.* Kent, United Kingdom: Croom Helm.

Lewis, C. (1999). *Complaints against police: The politics of reform.* Sydney, Australia: Hawkins.

MacSporan, A. (2009). *Submission to the Parliamentary Crime and Misconduct Commission.* Brisbane, Australia: Office of the Parliamentary Crime & Misconduct Commissioner

Masterman, G. (1985). *Keynote address.* Paper presented at the First International Conference on Civilian Oversight of Law Enforcement, Toronto, Canada.

Parliament of Queensland. (1997, November 20). Queensland Parliamentary Debates. Brisbane, Australia: Author.

Parliamentary Criminal Justice Committee. (PCJC). (2001). *Three Yearly Review of the Criminal Justice Commission: Report No. 55.* Brisbane, Australia: Author.

Parliamentary Criminal Justice Committee. (PCJC). (2006). *Three Yearly Review of Crime & Misconduct Commission: Report No. 71.* Brisbane, Australia: Author.

Parliamentary Criminal Justice Committee. (PCJC). (2009). *Three Yearly Review of the Crime and Misconduct Commission: Report No. 79.* Brisbane, Australia: Parliamentary Crime & Misconduct Committee.

Queensland Crime Commission. (QCC). (2000). *1999–2000 annual report.* Brisbane, Australia: Author.

Queensland Crime Commission. (QCC). (2001). *2000–2001 annual report.* Brisbane, Australia: Author.

Scarman, L. (1986). *The Scarman Report: The Brixton disorders, 10–12 April 1981.* Middlesex, United Kingdom: Penguin.

The Courier-Mail. (1991, December 12). p. 2.

Walker, J. (1995). *Goss: A political biography.* Brisbane, Australia: University of Queensland Press.

5

EARC: A Short-Term Experiment in Permanent Reform?

Janet Ransley

The Fitzgerald Inquiry began as an investigation of police misconduct, but as discussed in chapter 1, quickly expanded to examine the political, electoral and bureaucratic context in which corruption had flourished. The Report was concerned with achieving enduring reforms to what it saw as institutional deficiencies, with its first recommendation being that a:

> properly authorised and satisfactorily resourced Electoral and Administrative Review Commission ... which reports directly to a Parliamentary Select Committee on Electoral and Administrative Review ... be established by legislation to provide independent and comprehensive review of administrative and electoral laws and processes. (Fitzgerald, 1989, p. 370)

The *Electoral and Administrative Review Act* (Qld) was passed in 1989 and the Electoral and Administrative Review Commission (EARC) effectively began work in March 1990. In July 1992 the Parliamentary Committee for Electoral and Administrative Review (PCEAR) recommended EARC's abolition when it had completed its then current review program (PCEAR, 1992, p. 67). Cabinet adopted that recommendation in January 1993 and EARC ceased in September that year (PCEAR, 1994).

This chapter reviews what EARC achieved in the nearly four years that it existed, and the lasting benefits that derived from its work. Exercises in improving police accountability had been attempted in various other jurisdictions, but the EARC concept was novel, involving an extra-parliamentary, non-political body undertaking public and inclusive reviews of some of the fundamental political processes, such as electoral systems and the operation of Parliament. Further, EARC reviewed administrative and organisational practices that directly impinged on the incoming Goss government's own reform agenda, creating inevitable tension and conflict about its proper role and limits (Prasser, 2004; Preston, Sampford, & Connors, 2002; Ransley, 1993).

The chapter argues that EARC's greatest success was in recognising that the window of opportunity for reform might be brief. It focused enormous energy on advancing its work from the beginning, while making that work as open and consultative as possible. This approach was justified as the window quickly closed and attention diverted to other issues. The other strength of EARC was that it answered to a parliamentary committee and not directly to government. This guaranteed a public forum for its reports and an advocate for its independence and resources, while enabling democratic oversight of its findings. These factors combined to create a strong public perception of EARC's independence and a confidence in the value of its recommendations that outlasted the Commission itself.

The chapter concludes by asking whether Fitzgerald's vision of *enduring* reform has been achieved, given EARC's short tenure. It argues that while there is considerable merit in the model of a limited term public reform body such as EARC, continuing cycles of scandal and integrity failure suggest that the imperative for reform fades over time, and reform models need revisiting.

Why EARC?

The Fitzgerald Report recognised the political context to corruption and in chapter 3 discussed a range of electoral, institutional and administrative issues that it found had contributed to this context as well as to the ensuing police and ministerial corruption. These issues included: a weak parliament dominated by the executive that failed to exercise any scrutiny over the government as required by Westminster theory; a poorly resourced and ineffective Opposition; inadequate financial processes and a weak Auditor-General; a politicised and compliant public service; cronyism in government appointments, tendering and funds allocation; excessive secrecy and large-scale media manipulation; and a partisan, biased and distorted electoral system.

However, the Fitzgerald Report did not prescribe particular solutions. Its aim, it stated, was 'to ventilate problems — recommend approaches and mechanisms rather than make unsound attempts to prescribe solutions to complex problems' (Fitzgerald, 1989, p. 5). Instead, it recommended the creation of EARC and the Criminal Justice Commission (CJC) to address these issues and to restore confidence in public administration and government conduct in Queensland. EARC and the CJC were to be 'the catalysts ... for continuing reform (Fitzgerald, 1989, p. 357).

Fitzgerald's understanding and depth of analysis of the political and public administration issues has been criticised (see Nethercote, 1990; Prasser, 1992; Toohey, 1990), but the recommendation to establish EARC was seen generally as appropriate and worthwhile. As a response to the familiar Australian themes of corruption, integrity and accountability (Brown and Head, 2005), EARC was seen as a post-inquiry continuation of Fitzgerald's work (Finn, 1994) that removed important electoral, constitutional and administrative issues from an inquisitorial context and placed them into one more conducive to research and review. EARC would be less hindered by the restrictions of time, expertise and legitimacy that would have faced Fitzgerald had he pursued these issues.

The EARC Act closely reflected the Fitzgerald Inquiry's recommendations on strengthening and reforming the operation of government in Queensland — the rationale being that systematic misconduct would be less likely in the presence of open and fair political processes and public debate. EARC was to be a properly authorised and satisfactorily resourced, independent review body, reporting not to government but to an all-party parliamentary committee. It was to comprise members drawn from a balance of academic, public and private administration, legal and industrial backgrounds, supported by professional staff and consultants. PCEAR was also established under the EARC Act. It comprised members of all political parties represented in Parliament. Its statutory role was to monitor and review the work of EARC. It also reviewed EARC's outcomes, reports and recommendations, and often critiqued them or suggested modifications. The parliamentary committee tabled its reports in Parliament and held public hearings at which EARC members were questioned on reviews, processes, priorities and resources.

The Reform Agenda

EARC's first tasks as stipulated under its Act (ss. 2.10–2.11) were to conduct and report upon independent and consultative reviews of the State's electoral system, particularly its system of establishing boundaries and weighing votes according to zones, along with a similar mandate to review the system of local government. It was also to examine a broad mix of other political, legal and administrative matters set out in a Schedule to the Act, including the:

- preservation and enhancement of individuals' rights and freedoms;
- practices and procedures of Parliament;
- expenditure of public moneys;
- activities of ministerial press secretaries and public service media units;
- functions and powers of parliamentary committees;
- functions, powers, practices and resources of the Auditor-General;
- registration of financial interests of members of Parliament, ministers and senior public servants;

- registration of political donations;
- elimination of inappropriate considerations from government decision making and administration;
- freedom of information;
- public notification of personal or political connections of people who benefit from government decisions or activities;
- distribution of functions of units of public administration;
- independence of statutory tribunals;
- administrative appeals and judicial review of administrative decisions and actions;
- public sector employment including the creation of positions, appointments, promotions, transfers, discipline and dismissals and independent review of employment matters; and
- protection of whistleblowers.

Other matters for EARC's attention mentioned in the recommendations of the Fitzgerald Report included the resourcing of non-government members of Parliament, laws relating to public assembly, roles of the offices of Attorney-General and Minister for Justice, administrative independence of the judiciary and the resourcing of the Law Reform Commission (Fitzgerald, 1989).

This extensive agenda was complicated by factors arising even before EARC began work. One of the most significant of these was that the incoming Goss government's existing policy platform included the establishment of a Public Sector Management Commission (PSMC) with specific responsibilities for reviewing:

- the purpose, structure, functions and management of public sector agencies;
- management and personnel standards and systems; and
- the application of merit and equity principles in the public sector (Coaldrake, 1992).

The functions of the PSMC therefore considerably overlapped with those given to EARC in relation to the organisation and staffing of public sector agencies (see 12 and 15 from the list above). Similarly, in 1991 the new government introduced the *Supreme Court of Queensland Act*, which vested substantial administrative powers relating to judicial functions with the President of the new Court of Appeal and Senior Judge Administrator. That Act also created the Litigation Reform Commission with functions to review court structures, practices and procedures and consider issues of law reform (Preston et al., 2002). These actions were reversed when the government changed in 1996 (see the *Courts Reform Amendment Act 1997* (Qld)), after

EARC's demise. But from 1991 until EARC ceased, the Litigation Reform Commission also had overlapping functions with EARC in relation to the administrative independence of the judiciary and law reform more generally.

In addition, some reforms had already been introduced by Premier Ahern when he took office in December 1987 (Preston et al., 2002). These centred on reforming and streamlining Cabinet processes, by introducing systems already operating in many other jurisdictions such as a cabinet handbook, and a system of Cabinet committees to help process the workload. The effect was to shift the concentration of power in the premier as leader to a model where Cabinet exercised control over decision-making. Ahern also appointed Queensland's first Public Accounts Committee to report to Parliament on the government's financial issues. The subsequent Australian Labor Party (ALP) government headed by Premier Goss continued and expanded this shift in decision-making authority, by establishing the Office of Cabinet as a central coordinating agency, and a network of departmental policy and liaison officers to broaden and coordinate advice and input.

So EARC's policy review mandate was significantly affected by already occurring institutional changes within government and the creation of both the PSMC and the Litigation Reform Commission. It was also affected by other aspects of ALP policy, such as its commitment to electoral reform and particularly to a one vote-one value system, notwithstanding EARC's brief to review all electoral matters. In effect then, by the time EARC started work in early 1990, the reform agenda was already fragmented between different review mechanisms, with the government forced, because of its commitment to implement the Fitzgerald reforms, to cede control of significant parts of this agenda to independent or semi-independent agencies (Ransley, 1993). This situation created the potential for resistance and conflict between government and the more independent reform agencies, EARC and the CJC.

The EARC Model

EARC was established as a statutory corporation independent of the public service, consisting of a full-time Chairman and four part-time members. The initial chair was Tom Sherman, who ran EARC from January 1990, in its establishment phase, until his departure in February 1992. He had come from a senior management position in the Commonwealth public service, and left to take up the position of Chair of the National Crime Authority (PCEAR, 1992). He was replaced by journalist and academic David Solomon. Professor Colin Hughes was deputy chair throughout EARC's existence, and other members included community and academic representatives. Most of EARC's staff, which peaked at around 40 positions in mid-1991, was seconded from Queensland public sector positions.

Consultants were also employed to work on various projects (see PCEAR, 1992, p. 8 for a full list). The total cost of EARC over its life was $10.952 million (PCEAR, 1994, p. 8).

Its Act required EARC to carry out reviews of electoral and administrative issues in an open, impartial and accountable manner (s. 2.23(2)). EARC established a review model based on these principles and a considerable attempt at public consultation. This involved, for each review:

- initial research to clarify issues and possible approaches;
- publication and dissemination of an issues paper and advertising call for comments;
- receipt and publication of written submissions and comments in response to those submissions;
- free public hearings or seminars, of which a transcript was made public;
- opportunity for further public comment or submission;
- consideration of the issues including further research and employment of consultants;
- report, including draft legislation, publicly presented to government and tabled in Parliament (see PCEAR, 1992, p. 12).

Public access and scrutiny were maximised through the free provision of issues papers and reports to public agencies, the media, libraries and universities, and the establishment of a public reading room at EARC's offices at which nearly all research materials were made publicly available (PCEAR, 1992). Specific consultation processes were developed for Indigenous communities where reviews had a specific impact upon them, such as those to do with local governments. For most of its existence EARC employed a media officer to facilitate journalists' access to and interest in the review processes.

Each EARC report was subsequently reviewed by the PCEAR. This review involved a revisiting of the issues by calling for submissions and holding hearings relating to the adequacy of EARC's research and the appropriateness of its recommendations (PCEAR, 1992). PCEAR then reported its own findings to Parliament, recommending the adoption, or adoption with some amendment, of EARC's findings.

Taken together, the EARC and PCEAR processes were relatively exhaustive, public and involved a mix of specialist expertise and community input. Along with the CJC and its oversight parliamentary committee which followed similar processes in reviewing areas of criminal justice and police practice and law, they helped create a new public expectation about the way in which policy should be informed and made (Preston et al., 2002; Ransley, 1993), with the expectation being one of openness, public contribution and comprehensiveness. A side effect was that some reviews attracted a degree of public controversy, such as the CJC inquiries into prostitution and gambling, and EARC's review of local government boundaries and electoral systems, which attracted thousands of public submissions.

After this process, suggested reforms became the responsibility of the government, and a contrasting approach to the policy process was quickly evident. For much of EARC's life, consideration of its reports was controlled centrally by the Office of Cabinet rather than the Attorney General's Department or other line agency. Compared to the EARC processes, this consideration was centralist, closed and secretive, with little public input or scrutiny (Prasser, 2004; Ransley, 1993). The end result, as discussed further below, often led to substantial changes to proposed reforms, or to them simply being ignored. There was little requirement for the government to explain or defend these positions, especially given its dominance of the parliament, the lack of an upper house, and a disorganised and ineffective Opposition (Preston et al., 2002; Ransley, 1993).

Outcomes

In total, EARC released 23 reports which addressed all of the matters stipulated for review in both the Fitzgerald Report recommendations for EARC and the Act, except for the independence of the judiciary and resources of the Law Reform Commission, and aspects of public sector administration. The PCEAR review of the closure of EARC found those matters to have been assumed by the Litigation Reform Commission and PSMC respectively (PCEAR, 1994). These reports provide an enduring benefit of the EARC process in the form of a body of research on governance and public administration. Of itself, this is a valuable outcome as there was little prior history or culture of such research in Queensland; however, the reports have also provided valuable models for other jurisdictions.

Another important outcome for Queensland was the precedent that EARC established for review processes and open consultation, as discussed above. Similar consultation processes to those pioneered by EARC, including issues papers, seminars and submissions have been adopted by subsequent review bodies such as parliamentary committees.

The most concrete evidence of EARC's performance is the extent to which its recommendations were adopted and implemented. This was particularly so for electoral reform. For decades, political parties had manipulated electoral boundaries for their own benefit and, during its 32 years in office, the National Party had refined a system of zonal weightage and boundaries that helped ensure it retained office. The Fitzgerald Report made this review a priority for EARC, on the basis that fair and open public administration could not be achieved within the context of an unfair electoral system. While the EARC review of the electoral system received many opposing submissions on what the system should be, its eventual report recommended a compromise that appeased none of the major interests. Eventually, the parliamentary committee in its review found the recommendations to be a probable breach of Australia's obligations under international law. Yet, many years later, EARC's system incorporating weighted seats for remote areas, continues. Electoral administration has been de-politicised, and major issues are now decided by an independent Electoral Commission, rather than by the government. This alone, given Queensland's electoral history over the second half of the 1900s, is a considerable achievement.

Other early-phase EARC recommendations were also implemented quickly. These include:

- a register of interests of members of Parliament;
- a legislated right to peaceful assembly;
- freedom of information (FOI) legislation;
- fundamental legislative standards;
- interim whistleblowers' protection laws;
- reform of judicial review; and
- a reformed electoral system for Local Government.

EARC produced reports on these issues by early 1991, the parliamentary committee reviewed them, and the new laws were in place by early 1992, so the process of reform was rapid — although it must be said that EARC's recommendations were not always accepted absolutely, and most of the resultant laws varied to some extent from what had been suggested. In most cases however, the overall tenor of the majority of recommendations was accepted, with the variations aimed at workability, cost and practicality rather than issues of substance. A significant exception was in relation to FOI laws, where both EARC and PCEAR had recommended the laws extend to government business enterprises. The law as introduced however exempted such agencies entirely from FOI. None of these bodies had made submissions to this effect to either EARC or PCEAR, and the government gave no justification when introducing the law. Clearly, the exemption resulted from behind closed doors lobbying. Further, both EARC and PCEAR had recommended against allowing further exemption of agencies by regulation, instead suggesting openness required such decisions to be justified in Parliament. The FOI Act, however, allowed for exemption by regulation (Ransley, 1993).

Despite the problems with FOI, which were to continue to be problematic well into the future (see chapter 12), most of the other reforms proved successful. The *Judicial Review Act 1991* (Qld) and *Legislative Standards Act*

1992 (Qld) in particular have had pronounced and sustained effects on public administration in Queensland. The requirement to give reasons for administrative decisions and a simplified procedure for seeking review brought the State's system up to date with those operating in most other Australian jurisdictions, and enabled citizens to challenge the way in which decisions were made. Of particular significance was the groundbreaking development of fundamental principles that legislators were required to take into account when developing new laws.

After mid-1992, reform slowed, due mainly to an impending election. The return of the ALP government after the 1992 election signalled a new, more conservative approach to EARC's recommendations.

Furthermore, some of the earlier reforms were significantly watered down. For example, in reviewing public service integrity and codes of conduct, EARC recommended an extensive regime of ethics standards, education and reporting, supported by an independent integrity agency. The *Public Sector Ethics Act 1994* (Qld) however, lacked this supporting mechanism, and subsequent implementation saw minimal budget and resources devoted to the new regime (Preston et al., 2002). A subsequent review found that implementation of the Act was patchy, due to the lack of coordination and central advice and inconsistent training (Ransley, 2001). Preston et al. (2002) describe the overall picture as disappointing. Since then, however, the government has introduced the office of the Integrity Commissioner, initially as a voluntary mechanism by which ministers could seek advice on ethical issues. More recently, the role of the office has been expanded and given some statutory functions (Queensland Integrity Commissioner, 2009).

Similarly, FOI legislation was amended to further restrict its operation. The most significant change was the expansion of the Cabinet document exemption. The end result of this was that the government was able to ensure the secrecy of any document simply by ensuring it was brought into the Cabinet room, without any requirement for the document to be discussed or even read. This clearly undermined completely the stated objective of the Act which was to provide a prima facie right in the public to access government information (see chapter 12 this volume, Solomon). It took another cycle of scandal, inquiry and reform, this time into medical malpractice at the Bundaberg Hospital, to highlight the lack of availability of public interest information and shortcomings of the freedom of information regime. The appointment of the Solomon Review has led to new legislation being introduced in 2009 to improve FOI in Queensland (Queensland Government, 2009).

Some EARC recommendations remain completely or substantially unaddressed. These include the establishment of a comprehensive administrative appeal system (although this is being addressed in part only with the introduction at the time of writing of the Queensland *Civil and Administrative Tribunals Act 2009*), regulation of public sector media units, and the protection of individual rights and freedoms. Others have not achieved their full potential. Reforms to the Parliament and its committees, addressed in chapter 11 of this book, have fallen well short of what was intended (see also Ransley, 2008). The reforms introduced to public sector auditing strengthened the position of the Auditor-General, but did not establish the complete independence of the office and nor did it give it the right to conduct efficiency or performance reviews such as are done in many other jurisdictions (Prasser, 2004).

The other areas of little reform are those which EARC chose not to pursue, because of the overlapping jurisdiction with the PSMC and Litigation Reform Commission. Endorsed at the time as a sensible way of conserving limited resources (PCEAR, 1992), in retrospect these omissions can be seen as a lost opportunity to address significant areas of concern to the Fitzgerald Inquiry. Both the PSMC and Litigation Reform Commission were abolished when the ALP lost government in 1996. While the PSMC had caused significant, extensive, disruptive change to the public sector, its focus was on improving efficiency and political responsiveness rather than integrity, merit and accountability. The demise of EARC coupled with the failure of successive governments to appoint an institutional champion for public sector integrity has meant limited overall reform in this area (Preston et al., 2002). Similarly, while Fitzgerald had expressed concern for the administrative independence of the judiciary, the short tenure of the Litigation Reform Commission and its relative lack of public outputs while it did exist, did little to address this. Instead, the judiciary have remained dependent on the strength of their leadership and their own lobbying ability to secure their freedom from inappropriate government intervention. And while the Queensland Law Reform Commission continues to exist and to review aspects of law reform, it has a low public profile and the issue of its resourcing remains unaddressed.

Enduring Reform?

The process which began with the appointment of the Fitzgerald Inquiry in May 1987 focused on two areas — the Queensland police service, and the political and administrative processes. While this chapter has not canvassed the reforms to the police service, it is clear that the service is now a very different organisation to that of 1987 (see chapters 7 and 8 of this volume).[1]

However, as Fitzgerald noted, the most fundamental issue is the political and administrative climate, and the extent to which it is supported by the institutionalisation of fair, open and accountable processes. The Inquiry had the insight and modesty to perceive its own institutional limitations – that an investigative body heavily dominated by private sector lawyers may not be the best vehicle for finding the answers to the political and administrative problems it had identified. Hence, it recommended the creation of other bodies with different tasks and expertise to carry on this work, in the form of the CJC and EARC.

How successful was EARC? According to one commentator, it was extremely successful, being:

> A model organisation in terms of administrative reform. It has been completely open in all of its work. It has been highly efficient, having processed just about all of the agenda which Fitzgerald laid down for it in only two years ... it has been a cornerstone of the reform process giving exceptional value for money to the citizens and taxpayers of Queensland, and one of the most successful innovations introduced into Westminster systems during the twentieth century (Wiltshire, 2001, p. 265).

EARC's major contribution has undoubtedly been the establishment of new and enduring electoral systems that are fundamentally fair, open and free of political manipulation, at both state and local levels. Further, those systems have been overwhelmingly accepted across the political spectrum and by the public. Several important legal reforms were also achieved, such as those to the judicial review system and the introduction of fundamental legislative standards.

The goals of achieving administrative reform and improved parliamentary performance have generally been much more problematic. While the initial commitment was strong and much was achieved, other priorities developed and the urgency receded, especially as changes to electoral systems and police accountability assuaged the early, pressing public demand for action. The administrative reform process lost momentum and political support.

There have been other enduring aspects of the EARC process. As part of the implementation of EARC's recommendations, a number of other independent agencies were established to fulfil various functions. These included an electoral commission to oversee boundaries and the conduct of elections, an information commissioner to oversee freedom of information laws, and offices of parliamentary counsel (to draft new laws) and an auditor-general (to audit government agencies) with strengthened independence. These agencies continue to operate and perform significant functions many years after the demise of EARC. In addition, EARC research continues to form a starting point for policy problems, even where the recommendations were not introduced fully or at all. For example, some 15 years after EARC's recommendation for a comprehensive administrative appeals tribunal, many of its suggestions have emerged in the government's new Queensland *Civil and*

Administrative Tribunal Act 2009, although the scheme is not as comprehensive as EARC suggested.

As discussed above and elsewhere in this book, however, the areas of parliamentary and public service reform are those where EARC's reforms have had least traction. This can be explained by two main factors. Firstly, these areas are central to the day-to-day functioning of executive governments. Parliamentary control is essential to ensure passage of the legislative and budgetary programs. Control of the public service is essential to secure implementation of government policy. It is not unusual for governments to strongly resist any loss or diminution of their control over these areas.

Secondly, much of EARC's early success was directly attributable to the ongoing impact of the Fitzgerald Report. Public support for reform was high, as was interest in the reform process, as evidenced by the significant numbers of submissions made to early reviews. Many of the measures introduced by the first Goss government exceeded the scope of ALP policy and were a direct result instead of the Fitzgerald-created commissions, EARC and the CJC.

By the end of its first term, however, it was clear that the government was back in control of the agenda, and resistance was growing. Another cycle of scandal and review may be needed before the momentum for reform is regained. For FOI, this occurred in the form of the 2005 *Queensland Public Hospitals Commission of Inquiry*, often referred to as the Davies Commission, which exposed shortcomings in public access to information and led to the Solomon FOI review, and then new legislation. More recently, Tony Fitzgerald's highly publicised critique of reform in Queensland (Fitzgerald 2009) led directly to the government's green paper on *Integrity and Accountability in Queensland*, which seems likely in turn to lead to new laws regarding political donations and electoral funding.

Should then EARC have been retained? New administrative and political reforms have been relatively rare since EARC was disbanded, certainly when compared to the rush of reform in 1990–1991, but they have occurred. This chapter has mentioned already four such reforms introduced or begun in 2009 — the significant expansion of FOI, the comprehensive parliamentary committee system, the unified administrative tribunal system and the review of integrity and accountability. The germination periods for these reforms have admittedly been long and slow, given they all relate back to EARC recommendations from the early 1990s. But it is open to debate as to whether they would have occurred more quickly even if EARC had remained, given the change in political focus that occurred from late 1992 onwards. As discussed, after the return of the Goss government in 1992, the impetus for Fitzgerald-inspired reforms had diminished, and was not regained under subsequent Coalition or ALP governments. A permanent EARC could have been a frustrated agency putting out more reports that were not adopted. It may only have been able to achieve a meaningful role by becoming a monitoring and advocacy body to try and force implementation of its suggestions. In doing this, it would have lost the perception that had been so carefully created of independence and removal from the bureaucratic process. In turn, this would have risked diminishing support for its proposals.

Instead, it is the cycle of scandal and inquiry that shows the best capacity for lasting reform, as the EARC experiment, and the Fitzgerald Inquiry itself, both demonstrate. The best guarantees for enduring reform are likely to be an active and inquiring media and parliamentary Opposition, to investigate and reveal scandal and problems, and a strong judicial and legal system to provide for the type of inquiry conducted from 1987–1989. Unfortunately, these are the very areas where EARC achieved least enduring success. The principal lesson to be learned is that, like the Fitzgerald Inquiry, EARC too recognised its own limitations which, in its case, were that the opportunity open to it was limited and that any reform, even if limited and imperfect, was better than nothing. On those terms, it was a clear success, but that success was over by the end of 1992 and probably would not have been maintained had EARC continued longer.

Endnote

1 In brief, there has been a significant change in personnel, new entrants are better educated and from more diverse backgrounds and the administration of the service has been professionalised. Independent scrutiny of police activity does not prevent all police misconduct, but it has helped to marginalise it and render it unacceptable to most police officers.

References

Brown, A.J., & Head, B. (2005). Institutional Capacity and Choice in Australia's Integrity Systems. *Australian Journal of Public Administration, 64*(2), 84–95.

Coaldrake, P. (1992). Reforming the System of Government: Overview. In S. Prasser, R. Wear & J. Nethercote (Eds.), *Corruption and Reform: The Fitzgerald vision* (pp. 157–159). Brisbane, Australia: University of Queensland Press.

Finn, P. (1994). The Significance of the Fitzgerald and the WA Inc Commissions. In P. Weller (Ed.), *Royal Commissions and the making of public policy* (pp. 32–39). Sydney, Australia: Macmillan Education Australia.

Fitzgerald, G.E. (1989). *Report of the Commission of Inquiry into Possible Illegal Activities and Associated Police Misconduct.* Brisbane, Australia: GoPrint.

Fitzgerald, G.E. (2009, July 29). What went wrong with Queensland?. *The Courier Mail,* p. 4.

Nethercote, J. (1990). Reform of the Bureaucracy — An Overview. In S. Prasser, R. Wear & J. Nethercote (Eds.), *Corruption and reform: The Fitzgerald vision* (pp. 212–219). Brisbane, Australia: University of Queensland Press.

Parliamentary Committee for Electoral and Administrative Review (PCEAR). (1992). *Review of the Electoral and Administrative Review Act.* Brisbane, Australia: Legislative Assembly of Queensland.

Parliamentary Committee for Electoral and Administrative Review. (PCEAR). (1994). *Review of closure of the Electoral and Administrative Review Commission.* Brisbane, Australia: Legislative Assembly of Queensland.

Prasser, S. (1992). The need for reform in Queensland: So what was the problem? In A. Hede, S. Prasser & M. Neylan (Eds.), *Keeping them honest: Democratic reform in Queensland* (pp. 15–29). Brisbane, Australia: University of Queensland Press.

Prasser, S. (2004). Post corruption cleanups: Government reform or putting in a new political 'fix'. *University of the Sunshine Coast, Faculty of Business Working Paper Series,* 7(2).

Preston, N., Sampford, C., & Connors, C. (2002). *Encouraging ethics and challenging corruption.* Sydney, Australia: Federation Press.

Queensland Government. (2009). *FOI Review.* Retrieved July 4, 2009, from http://www.foireview.qld.gov.au/

Queensland Government. (2009b). *Integrity and accountability in Queensland.* Retrieved August 31, 2009, from http://www.premiers.qld. gov.au/community-issues/open-transparent-gov/integrity-and-acountability-review.aspx

Queensland Integrity Commissioner. (2009). Queensland Integrity Commissioner web site. Retrieved July 4, 2009, from, http://www.integrity.qld.gov.au/

Ransley, J. (1993). Legal and Administrative Law Reform. In B. Stevens & J. Wanna (Eds.), *The Goss Government: Promise and performance of Labor in Queensland* (pp. 106–132). South Melbourne: MacMillan.

Ransley, J. (2001). The Queensland Fitzgerald Inquiry and EARC: A case study in political, legal and administrative reform. In C. Sampford (Ed.), *Transparency International Integrity Handbook* (pp. 4–17). Brisbane, Australia: Key Centre for Ethics, Law, Justice and Governance, Griffith University.

Ransley, J. (2008). Illusions of Reform: Queensland's Legislative Assembly since Fitzgerald. In N. Aroney, S. Prasser & J. R. Nethercote (Eds.), *Restraining Elective Dictatorship: The upper house solution?* (pp. 248–261). Crawley, Australia: University of Western Australia Press.

Toohey, B. (1990). Fitzgerald – how the process came unstuck'. In S. Prasser, R. Wear & J. Nethercote (Eds.), *Corruption and reform: the Fitzgerald vision.* Brisbane, Australia: University of Queensland Press.

Wiltshire, K. (2001). Reform of the Bureaucracy: An assessment. In A. Hede, S. Prasser & M. Neylan (Eds.), *Keeping them honest: Democratic reform in Queensland* (pp. 261–275). Brisbane, Australia: University of Queensland Press.

6

Depoliticising Policing: Reviewing and Registering Police Reforms

Colleen Lewis

Queensland's *Commission of Inquiry into Possible Illegal Activities and Associated Police Misconduct* (hereafter the Fitzgerald Inquiry 1987), unlike many other inquiries into policing in Australia and beyond, revealed a highly politicised police force and the destructive effect this had on nearly every aspect of policing, including police behaviour, the police culture, police accountability and police-community relations.

According to noted policing scholar Mark Finnane (1994, p. 33), a police force is politicised when 'policing decisions have been improperly influenced by government ministers or that police themselves have improperly played a role in policy-making and law making'. Both were a feature of policing in Queensland when Sir Joh Bjelke-Petersen was Premier and Terence Lewis Commissioner of Police. As Fitzgerald (1989, p. 82) notes:

> There was little evidence that conventional restraints inhibited the involve-
> ment of Lewis in political matters, the exclusion of the political considera-
> tions from his superintendence and control of the police force, or the
> involvement of Bjelke-Petersen and other influential members of govern-
> ment in policing matters with which they had no legitimate concern.

The politicisation of the Queensland Police Force (QPF)[1] began in earnest in 1971 when Bjelke-Petersen declared a state of emergency in response to threatened protests over a South African Springbok Rugby Union game. Football matches played by this team had been the subject of violent demonstrations in other Australian states (Procter, 1985). When then Police Commissioner Ray Whitrod tried to ensure police respected citizens' democratic rights whilst enforcing the law, the Queensland Police Union (QPU) accused him of being too soft on demonstrators. The Premier's response to allegations that officers had used unreasonable force while policing a demonstration against the Springbok team was to grant police an extra week's leave. In what had become a contest between senior police management and government, rank-and-file officers and the QPU sided with the premier against Commissioner Whitrod. Police union members passed a vote of no confidence in Whitrod and a vote of confidence in Bjelke-Petersen (Dickie, 1989, p. 29; Procter, 1985, pp. 169–170; Whitrod, 2001, pp. 178–179).

The politicisation of the Force was taken to new heights in November 1976 when Terence Lewis was promoted from inspector to assistant commissioner and some three weeks later to commissioner. Lewis's meteoric rise meant that, in contrast to Whitrod, the government now had an acquiescent person in charge of the Force (Finnane, 1994, p. 40). The implied trade-off for Commissioner Lewis's active participation in the politicisation process was the government's unquestioning support of the QPF, which included wilful blindness in relation to police misconduct. By the time the Fitzgerald Inquiry was established in May 1987, the extent of the politicisation was so severe that Queensland was referred to as a police state (Whitton, 1989).

This chapter is interested in the effectiveness of three reforms recommended by Fitzgerald and passed by the parliament to restructure the relationship between police and government thereby preventing a return to politicised policing in Queensland. The first focuses on the procedures for the appointment and dismissal of the police commissioner. The second relates to Fitzgerald's recommendation to make the police commissioner answerable to the head of the Criminal Justice Commission (CJC) and the minister for police. While this decision was intended, in part, to depoliticise the on-going police reform program (Fleming and Lewis, 2002), it resulted in the police commissioner serving two masters, an unsatisfactory situation that took ten years to resolve. The third reform relates to the *Register of Reports and Recommendations to the Police Minister, Ministerial Directions and Tabled Ministerial Reasons* (Queensland Parliament, 1997–2008). Very little has been written about the Register and to the best knowledge of the author, this is the first time a comprehensive explanation and analysis of this important Fitzgerald-inspired reform has been undertaken.

Before examining these reforms, the chapter briefly discusses the doctrine of constabulary independence. It does so because adherence to this doctrine is central to fostering and maintaining an appropriate arms length relationship between police and government in Australia and in other liberal democratic societies such as New Zealand, Canada and Britain. Unfortunately, for the Queensland Police Force and the citizens of Queensland, neither Premier Bjelke-Petersen nor Commissioner Lewis attempted to respect the boundaries the doctrine sets or indeed, appeared even to understand them.

Undermining Constabulary Independence

Since the establishment in England in 1829 of Sir Robert Peel's 'New Police' there have been debates about how to ensure that the considerable power police exercise over citizens' freedoms is not abused by democratic governments for party political advantage (Lustgarten, 1986; Marshal, 1965; Oliver, 1987; Stenning, 2006). Much of the debate has focused on the *obiter dicta* (not essential to the decision therefore not a binding principle) in celebrated court cases in England and Australia (Stenning, 2006). While these cases do not directly address the constitutional status of police, they reinforce the idea that police occupy an unusual position in that they exercise an original and not a delegated power when enforcing the law. This original power is commonly referred to as the 'doctrine of constabulary independence'. Theoretically, Australian police do not have constitutional independence but as Finnane (1994, p. 30) points out, in terms of operational policing they do so in practice.

Constabulary independence requires that the commissioner of police and government make a distinction between matters that require police to exercise operational independence and broader policy issues that are the responsibility of an elected government. For at least 15 years prior to the Fitzgerald Inquiry no such distinction existed in Queensland. Indeed, as Milte and Weber (1977, p. 218) explain, the Bjelke-Petersen Government did 'not even pretend' that aspects of the policing function should be 'independent from its control'.

Ray Whitrod was Commissioner of the QPF between 1970 and 1976. Despite his best efforts, he was unable to protect the Force's operational independence or enforce police accountability. The reason for this was his inability to get Bjelke-Petersen to accept that all police, including the commissioner, exercise constabulary independence. As Whitrod writes in his memoirs, the premier treated him as if he was '... another of his clerks, there to carry out his instructions while not impeding his plans' (2001, p. 142). During his term as police commissioner, the premier also publicly countermanded Whitrod's police accountability directives (Dickie, 1989, p. 45; Hawker, 1984, p. 74) relating to officers' use of force. This in turn undermined the 'rule of law' requirement that police should abide by the law when enforcing the law.

When Terence Lewis became police commissioner in 1976, he was not interested in establishing an arms length relationship with the government. Indeed, the reverse was the case. As an inspector in the remote Charleville police district of Queensland, Lewis spent a great deal of time writing to the premier. His letters, which were exhibits at the Fitzgerald Inquiry, refer to what Lewis claims were promotions denied him by Whitrod, his (Lewis's) many managerial talents and his suitability to head the QPF.

Lewis's diaries, also exhibits at the Fitzgerald Inquiry, suggest that he was an 'intuitive politician' who used every opportunity 'to advance his own cause' (Fitzgerald, 1989, p. 43). In his correspondence to the premier, he went beyond merely criticising Commissioner Whitrod's leadership, claiming that Whitrod had links to the Labor Party and warning the Premier that: 'If Mr. Whitrod hears that I have spoken to you he will immediately engage in the character assassination he learnt so well from his A.L.P. friends in Canberra' (Fitzgerald, 1989, p. 43). Bjelke-Petersen has been described by Walter and Dickie (1985, p. 39) as a politician of the 'radical right' who associated '"the socialist menace" and beyond it the communist bogey' with the Australian Labor Party. In his personal diaries, Lewis described Bjelke-Petersen as a 'bigot'. As an 'intuitive politician' he would have been acutely aware of the impact his suggestion about Whitrod's links to the Labor Party would have on the very right wing premier (Fitzgerald, 1989, p. 45).[2]

Lewis's cultivation of Bjelke-Petersen paid off. His promotion from inspector to assistant commissioner in 1976 occurred even though his name did not appear on the list of recommendations put forward by Commissioner Whitrod or the Commissioned Officers' Association (Roberts, 1988). The promotion also took effect despite Whitrod expressing his concerns to the Police Minister about allegations (known to Cabinet) that Lewis was corrupt (Dickie, 1989, p. 46; Whitton, 1988). The government did not advertise the commissioner's position, nor call for expressions of interest; it chose instead to promote Assistant Commissioner Lewis to the top job. In the space of a month, he went from inspector to commissioner, a promotion that is exceptional in Australian policing history. Interestingly, the Fitzgerald Report (1989, p. 46) notes that the only Cabinet papers missing for a period of some years were those relating to the Cabinet meeting that dealt with Lewis's appointment to commissioner of the QPF.

Commissioner Whitrod resigned over Lewis's promotion to assistant commissioner, which he perceived as an attempt by the premier to take control of the Force. In announcing his resignation, Whitrod stated his belief in the doctrine of constabulary independence, explaining that:

> I am not claiming that there ought to be a complete independence of action for the Commissioner. All I assert is that there ought to be a minimum of interference by the political authority. This is essential if members of the community are to believe that the enforcement of the law is being carried out in a manifestly impartial manner. It needs therefore to be shielded from even the appearance of politically motivated interference. (R.W. Whitrod statement to a press conference, Brisbane, 29 November 1976, quoted in Wettenhall, 1977, pp. 20–21)

In situations where operational independence was a factor, Whitrod did not see himself as answerable to the executive but rather to the law. As he said:

> I kept trying to get through to him [Bjelke-Petersen] that I had a responsibility to maintain the law, that I had taken an oath to this effect and that I was responsible for my own actions as a constable. I said I would implement any legal instruction given to me by him or by my minister, but how I did this was my decision. (Whitrod, 2001, pp. 141–142)

At the press conference to announce publicly his resignation, a journalist asked Whitrod if he thought Queensland was turning into a 'police state'. His 'ominously prescient' reply was 'I think there are signs of that development' (Walker, 1995, p. 54).

The nature of the relationship that developed between the National-Liberal Party Government, the National Party Government and the QPF during Lewis's time as commissioner is exemplified in a remarkably political speech Lewis gave at a swearing in ceremony at the Queensland Police Academy in August 1983. He declared that:

> The people of Queensland and the Police Force owe the Premier a very deep gratitude. The free enterprise policy of the Bjelke-Petersen government has been responsible for Queensland's tremendous growth. Irrespective of whether some people agree with the politics, statements or stands, there is a universal respect, even admiration, for the total loyalty he and his colleagues show for what they believe is in the best interests of Queensland. (Fitzgerald, 1989, p. 85)

This public endorsement of a political party by a commissioner of police highlights just how unhealthy the relationship between police and government had become. This is further confirmed by Lewis's diaries that reveal not only the degree to which the Bjelke-Petersen government had become involved in the day-to-day operations of the Queensland Police Force but also the extent of the police commissioner's involvement with the parliamentary and administrative wings of the National Party. By the time the Fitzgerald Inquiry was established in 1987, a significant number of police had come to see accountability as being almost exclusively to the government and were disregarding their responsibilities to the law, parliament and the citizens of Queensland. As a result, an unaccountable police force, often acting as if the law did not apply to them, was protected from being held accountable for their actions by the premier and a succession of police ministers.

The Fitzgerald Report clearly demonstrates the crucial role a premier, a police minister and police commissioner play in destabilising the delicate balance that separates politicised and non-politicised police forces; a balance in which the doctrine of constabulary independence plays a critical role. It also highlights the problems that can arise when there is no check on the misuse of executive power in the appointment of the commissioner of police.

Safeguarding the Position of Commissioner

Describing the extent of the 'problems' uncovered in the QPF as 'dreadful' (Fitzgerald, 1989, p. 336); Fitzgerald sought to minimise the possibility of the Force again being used for base party political advantage. It appears that he did not trust either the police or politicians to take carriage of the police reform program. Instead, he recommended the establishment of an independent external oversight body: the CJC that was replaced in January 2002 by the Crime and Misconduct Commission (CMC). Both organisations were given responsibility for ongoing carriage of the police reform process (see Lewis, chapter 4, this volume). Making the point that selecting new leaders and the process for doing so was '… of the greatest importance' to the reform program (Fitzgerald, 1989, p. 336), Fitzgerald recommended that the independent chair of the CJC play a role in the hiring and firing of future police commissioners, a responsibility that has since been transferred to the CMC.

The Fitzgerald Report pays considerable attention to the procedures for appointing interim leaders and to the processes that should follow on a more permanent basis (Fitzgerald, 1989, pp. 336–346). It refers to the unsatisfactory nature of the system then in place, including the arrangement whereby the commissioner of police (subject to good behaviour) enjoyed tenure until the age of 65 (Fitzgerald, 1989, p. 278). While making the point that a police commissioner needed 'secure tenure' so that the office is protected from 'potential political interference', the Report noted that tenure until 65 was unsatisfactory and contrary to arrangements for other statutory office holders in the Queensland Public Sector (Fitzgerald, 1989, p. 278). Fitzgerald recommended a fixed term contract of three to five years and police commissioners' contracts now reflect that recommendation.[3]

The Fitzgerald Report (1989, pp. 278–279) recommended procedures to be followed for the appointment and dismissal of the commissioner of police and the need for there to be independent input into both processes.[4] In contrast to the pre-Fitzgerald arrangement, where the Governor in Council, on the advice of the executive, had the power to appoint and dismiss, the appointment of commissioner now requires agreement between the police minister and the independent head of the CMC (the same arrangement applied in respect of the CJC). The removal and suspension of a police commissioner, on grounds prescribed in Part 4 of the *Police Service Administration Act 1990* (Qld) requires that the chair of the CMC concur with the recommendation of the Governor in Council to dismiss. These changes guard against attempts to politicise the office of police commissioner through an inappropriate, politically motivated appointment process, such as that which surrounded Lewis's appointment to assistant commissioner and then commissioner. It also acts as protection against a politically motivated dismissal.

In 1996, there was an attempt to undermine this important reform and to wind back other significant Fitzgerald-inspired improvements to police accountability. In February of that year, a crucial by-election was held for the North Queensland seat of Mundingburra. This was no ordinary by-election for the ability to form government depended on the outcome. While the Queensland Police Union did not openly campaign for the Liberal Party, it did campaign vigorously against the Labor Party Government. The Liberal Party won the seat and with the support of an independent, the National-Liberal Party coalition formed government. Some three weeks later, the *Courier-Mail* newspaper broke the story that the President of the Queensland Police Union Gary Wilkinson, the incoming National Party Premier Rob Borbidge and incoming National Party Police Minister Russell Cooper, had signed a 'secret' memorandum of understanding (MOU). The MOU was designed to curtail significantly the role and functions of the CJC, weaken considerably Fitzgerald-inspired police accountability measures and deliver unprecedented power to the conservative Queensland Police Union, particularly in terms of senior Queensland Police Service appointments (Lewis, 1999, pp. 160–163). For example, item 27 in the MOU, which was 'agreed' to by Borbidge and Cooper states that:

> The Government shall take advice from the QPUE [Queensland Police Union Executive] when selecting the next Commissioner of Police and shall not select an individual for this position that the Union has a genuine reason for opposing.

Had the *Courier-Mail* newspaper not exposed the MOU, thereby forcing Police Minister Cooper to admit to signing the 'secret' agreement some three weeks prior to the by-election, there is every possibility that it would have become government policy. Had this eventuated, policing in Queensland would have returned to the bad old pre-Fitzgerald days where the office of police commissioner and the Queensland Police Force was politicised.

The entrenched nature of politicised policing in Queensland caused Fitzgerald to warn that there could be attempts to undermine the reform program. His report (Fitzgerald, 1989) outlines some of the forms those attempts might take. Several of these are recognisable in the drawing up and signing of the MOU. The Fitzgerald Report (1989, p. 6) also predicts that 'if the community is complacent future leaders will revert to former practices'. This section highlights just such an attempt by the National Party, its coalition partner the Liberal Party and by the Queensland Police Union. However, it also shows that seven years after Fitzgerald bought down his report its findings still resonated with the Queensland community. It was not prepared to stand by and allow crucial Fitzgerald reforms to be unravelled. The immediate and impassioned response by the media and the Queensland community to the existence of the MOU protected the office of commissioner from an inappropriate appointment process and acted as a barrier against attempts to politicise policing again in Queensland. One can only speculate on what the government would have done had the MOU been implemented and the head of the CJC and the Queensland Police Union disagreed about who should be appointed to the position of commissioner.

Unintended Outcome

As the reforms of the Fitzgerald Report were implemented, the difficulties inherent in codifying the relationship between police and government became apparent. The *Criminal Justice Act 1989* (Qld), s. 2.15(h), gave the CJC responsibility for providing the commissioner of police with policy directions in relation to law enforcement priorities, education and training, revised methods of police operations and the optimum use of law enforcement resources. At the same time, the *Police Service Administration Act 1990* (Qld), s. 4.6 (2) (a) (b), stated that the commissioner of police was to comply with all directions given by the police minister in relation to the overall administration, management and superintendence of the Queensland Police Service (QPS) and the policies and priorities to be followed. Through these two Acts the commissioner of police was simultaneously serving two masters: the chair of the CJC and the police minister. Both had the ability to direct him in relation to the same issues (Lewis, 1992, pp. 89–90).

This potentially problematic arrangement was raised in the 1996 report on the *Review of the Queensland Police Service* (Bingham, 1996, pp. 32–33), where the recommendation was made that the *Criminal Justice Act 1989* (Qld) and the *Police Service Administration Act 1990* (Qld) should be amended so that the CJC could no longer exercise its right to direct without first consulting with the police minister, and the minister could not issue directions under the *Police Service Administration Act*, without first consulting with the chair of the CJC. However, it was not until the CJC was replaced by the CMC in 2002 that the matter was finally resolved.

The ability of the CMC to issue directives to the police commissioner has been removed. At first glance, this appears to lessen the CMC's independent powers in respect of ongoing carriage of the police reform program. However, directions are still able to be given by the head of the CMC to the commissioner of police. The difference now is that they must pass through the police minister rather than go directly from the head of the CMC to the police commissioner. This solution aligns with notions of ministerial responsibility, an important element of the Westminster system of responsible government that is a cornerstone of Australia's political system.

Section 64 of the *Crime and Misconduct Act 2001* (Qld) allows the chair of the CMC, after consulting with the police commissioner, to recommend to the police minister that the minister give a direction to the police commissioner. A safeguard against the minister refusing to do so for inappropriate reasons, such as party political advantage, is the requirement that the minister must provide the CMC with his/her reasons and those reasons have to be tabled in parliament. The vehicle for doing so is the *Register of Reports and Recommendations to the Police Minister, Ministerial Directions and Tabled Ministerial Reasons* (Queensland Parliament, 1991–2008), which is discussed in some detail in the following section.

This solution is a convoluted way around rectifying the problems associated with the police commissioner serving two masters. However, it does remove the potential for conflicting directives to be given. While there is no evidence of this having happened prior to the introduction of the *Crime and Misconduct Act,* in the turbulent and highly charged world of politics it is wise not to leave such matters to chance or to the good will of individuals.

Requiring the minister to table his/her reasons for not complying with a directive of the independent head of the CMC is an important way of protecting the force from being politicised or from perceptions that it is occurring, as any difference of opinion and the reason for it are in the public domain.

The Register was initially established to enhance accountability and transparency at the point where it involves directives from the minister to the commissioner and theoretically it still exists for that purpose. However, as the following section reveals, it no longer does so in practice.

The Register

Fitzgerald was well aware of the need for police in democratic societies to exercise operational independence. His report (1989, p. 279) makes it clear that the police commissioner is to have independent discretion to act or not act against an offender and that the police minister should not have the power to direct the commissioner in relation to operational policing matters. However, Fitzgerald also took into account that Queensland operates according to the Westminster system of responsible government and that the concept of ministerial responsibility is central to notions of political accountability within that system. Hence, his report (1989, pp. 278–279, pp. 383–394) states that the commissioner of police is to remain answerable to the police minister for the overall running of the police force.

Understanding that there are grey areas between constabulary independence and ministerial responsibility that could be exploited by future governments wishing to again use the police for party political advantage, the Fitzgerald Report (1989, p. 279) recommends that:

> In the interest of open and accountable government and the proper independence of the police department a register should be kept of policy directions given by the minister to the commissioner and recommendations provided by the Commissioner to the Minister. In the case of staff appointments, the register would also record the instances where the Minister or Cabinet chooses not to follow recommendations put forward. The register would be tabled in Parliament annually by referral through the Chairman of the Criminal Justice Commission to the [Parliamentary] Criminal Justice Committee.

Sections 4.6 and 4.7 of the *Police Service Administration Act 1990* (Qld) relates to the Register. Section 4.6(1)(a) states that the commissioner is to give the minister reports and recommendations in relation to the administration and functioning of QPS when the minister requires the commissioner to do so. Section 4.6(2) notes that the minister, having regard to the commissioner's advice first obtained, may give written directions to the commissioner in relation to the overall administration, management and superintendence of the QPS, the policy and priorities the QPS is to pursue, the number and deployment of sworn and unsworn staff and the number and location of police establishments and police stations. The commissioner is obliged to comply with all such written directions, s. 4.6(3).

The recording and publication of communications is addressed in Section 4.7 of the *Police Service Administration Act.* Section 4.7(1) states that the commissioner of police is to keep a Register which records all reports and recommendations made to the police minster under s. 4.6(1)(a) and all ministerial directions given in writing to the police commissioner under s. 4.6(2). As noted in the previous section of this chapter, the commissioner must also record in the Register all reasons tabled by the minister for not complying with a directive of the independent head of the CMC in respect of police reform policy matters (*Crime and Misconduct Act 2001* (Qld) s. 64).

The Register itself is an uncomplicated document that allows information to be placed under the following headings:

- Subject/file Ref
- Commissioner's Recommendation/Report, s. 4.6.(1)(a)
- Minister's Directions, s. 4.6 (2)
- Commissioner's Comments.

The *Police Service Administration Act 1990* (Qld) s. 4.7(2)(3)(4) outlines the process to be followed for the tabling of the Register in parliament. Within 28 days after 31 December each year, the commissioner of police has to prepare and certify the Register and forward it to the chair of the CMC. Within 28 days of receiving it, the CMC chairperson must forward it to the chair of the PCMC together with any relevant comments of the police commissioner and with or without further comment by the chair of the CMC. The PCMC, which monitors and reviews the CMC, is obliged to table the certified copy of the Register and all comments that relate to it within 14 sitting days after receiving it.

In order to evaluate the effectiveness or otherwise of this under-researched Fitzgerald recommendation, the author examined every Register tabled in the Queensland Parliament. This research covers the period 1991 to 2008.[5]

The first Register, tabled in 1991, reveals a disagreement between Police Commissioner Newnham and the Chair of the CJC Sir Max Bingham over the form the Register should take. The matter was the subject of several letters between Newnham and Bingham with Newnham maintaining he was only obliged to note the topics covered in any reports, recommendations or directions. Bingham disagreed and made it clear that '... full copies of the reports and recommendations and directions are required to enable the provision of the Act to be fulfilled'. Further correspondence between the two failed to resolve the matter (correspondence between the CJC and QPS that forms part of the 1991 Register).

Bingham forwarded Newnham's version of the 1991 Register (at that stage virtually a list) to the chair of the Parliamentary Criminal Justice Committee (PCJC) and included the correspondence that had passed between him and Newnham. The (PCJC) sought legal advice on the interpretation of ss. 4.6 and 4.7 of the *Police Service Administration Act*. The opinion of Kerry Copley QC (5 March 1992), which forms part of the 1991 Register, agreed with the chair of the Criminal Justice Commission's reading of the Act. Copely expressed the view that:

> Parliament, in providing that the Commissioner is '... to keep a register in which are to be recorded ... all reports and recommendations ... and all directions given in writing ...' has prescribed not merely that a list or index of the stipulated material is to form the register, but that the register is to be and to contain the stipulated reports, recommendations, and directions.
>
> If the register is to be merely a list or index it would clearly be unintelligible and could not properly be said to be a 'register in which are to be recorded' relevant documents.

Copely's view was accepted and from 1991 to 1996 the Register includes correspondence between the minister and commissioner and other parties and, where appropriate, supporting documentation.

The following section describes several of the topics that form part of the 1991 to 1996 Registers. While it may appear overly descriptive, it is necessary to show the type of matters referred to during the first six years of the Register's existence, as these Registers stand in stark contrast to those covering the period 1997 to 2008, which do not even constitute an index or list.[5]

For reasons that are perplexing, not a single matter has been recorded in the Registers for the past 12 years. The only remark is found in the Commissioner's Comment column. From 1997 to 2000, it repeatedly states that:

> Criteria developed by the Criminal Justice Commission are used for identifying communications required to be recorded in the register kept by the commissioner of the Queensland Police Service pursuant to section 4.7 of the *Police Service Administration Act 1990*. During the year (relevant year stated), no communications were made which qualify under those criteria for recording in the register.

The comment varies only slightly from 2001 to 2008. For those years the Section begins by stating that 'Criteria developed in 1993 by the then General Counsel for the Criminal Justice Commission', the remainder of the paragraph is the same as that noted above in respect of the 1997 to 2000 Registers.

From 2001, an additional paragraph has been added to the Commissioner's Comment that states that:

> In addition, during (relevant year stated) no 'reasons' were tabled in Parliament under s. 64 of the *Crime and Misconduct Act 2001* (Qld).

This paragraph reflects changes made to remedy the unintended consequence of the police commissioner serving two masters addressed in the previous section of this chapter.

The agreed-to criteria does not excuse the commissioner of police or police minister from any obligations set out in ss. 4.6 and 4.7 of the *Police Service Administration Act*. Rather, it is an agreement about the form compliance with the *Police Service Administration Act* should take (Appendix A outlines the criteria document).

To try to understand the dramatic change of approach from 1997 onwards, the author analysed those Registers that for several years actually contain information. The following is a chronological, descriptive account, which serves to highlight the type of matters referred to in the 1991–1996 Registers.

Registers 1991–1996

Of the 29 matters which form the 1991 Register, by far the most recorded in any one year, topics covered include: staffing requirements at the Police Academy; the tender for computers; the dismissal of a police officer; community lobby and interest groups; Electoral and Administrative Review of street marches and associated legislation; the effective policing of prostitution; and the closure of a police station.

Police Minister Mackenroth issued seven directives to Police Commissioner Newnham in relation to the recruitment of senior staff at the Police Academy; the computer tender; closure of a police station (not approved); requirement that the Minister be notified of an intended dismissal from the Service prior to reports appearing in newspapers; the composition of police personnel strength that the minister directed was to be referred to him; the 'Booze Buses' tender; and the need for compliance by QPS with government policy on the implementation of the standard financial management system. This Register does imply a tense relationship between Newnham and Mackenroth;[6] however, there is no evidence to suggest an attempt to politicise the policing function by either party.

In 1992, 17 matters were noted in the Register. They included: the reimbursement of legal expenses incurred in the defence of police officers; Queensland Police Service delays regarding coronial inquests; the engagement of an external consultant to conduct a survey on public awareness and confidence in police; the future of police education and training; and the operations of the Police Media Unit. In this year, the Minister gave two directions. The first said there were to be no appointments or changes to staffing in the Police Media Unit prior to the Public Sector Management Review without the joint approval of the commissioner and minister. The second covered two issues: changes in police hours and the closure of police stations. In respect of the first, the commissioner was directed to advise the minister of any changes and in relation to the second, the direction was given that no police station was to be closed without ministerial consent.

In 1992, when forwarding the Register to the PCJC, the chair of the CJC Rob O'Regan raised concerns about 'a number of difficulties of interpretation' in relation to ss. 4.6 & 4.7 of the *Police Service Administration Act* which address the form the Register should take. O'Regan believed that the Register 'necessitated an undue commitment of resources by both the Police Service and the Commission in identifying the actual documents required for inclusion in the Register' (covering letter from Criminal Justice Commission to chair of the Parliamentary Criminal Justice Commission January 29 1993, in respect of the 1992 Register which forms a part of that Register). When tabling the Register in Parliament in February 1993, the chair of the PCJC noted O'Regan's concerns. In an attempt to address the issue, 'criteria to be satisfied for inclusion in the Register' was developed in 1993 by the General Counsel of the Criminal Justice Commission. The criteria referred to previously were agreed to by the police commissioner and police minister and took effect in May 1993. These include Copely's advice that the Register must include actual reports, recommendations and directions and not be simply an index or list.

Seven matters were recorded in 1993 including recommendations of the Parliamentary Travel Safe Committee concerning speed limits; strategies to reduce the road toll; and steps to reduce armed hold-ups at service stations, convenience stores and fast food outlets. There were no ministerial directives.

In 1994 and 1995, six matters were noted in each of the two years covering issues, such as police-security industry liaison, social community crime prevention initiatives, motor vehicle theft, review of the police response to domestic violence, and the use of force by police. There were no ministerial directives in 1994. In 1995, three directives were given in relation to increasing the number of recruits from the Aboriginal and Torres Strait Islander community, trials to be conducted and evaluated in relation to face-to-face community conferencing and the requirement that the QPS implement its implementation plans for election commitments regarding *Strengthening the Blue Line and Toward the 21st Century: Resource Priorities for the QPS.*

Two matters were recorded in the 1996 Register concerning the employment details, contracts and performance agreements and evaluation reports of senior officers and a system for furnishing the minister with advice. The latter was a ministerial directive that a system be put in place to provide the minister with quality, timely advice on matters of concern.

What is evident from the 1991 to 1996 Registers is a willingness on the part of police ministers and police commissioners to interpret sections 4.6 and 4.7 of the *Police Service Administration Act* in the way intended by Fitzgerald: to help safeguard the 'operational independence' of the police and 'in the interest of open and accountable government'. During this period sixty-seven matters were recorded in the Registers. As mentioned previously, from 1997 onwards not a single matter has been recorded in any Register.

Register 1997 to 2008

The criteria developed by the CJC in 1993 do not explain the content-free nature of the Registers for a 12-year period, as the agreed-to criteria were introduced in 1993 and, as outlined above, the 1994, 1995 and 1996 Registers all contain information.

As the commissioner of police is the person responsible for keeping the annual Register and because the current commissioner has never recorded one matter in the Register in the eight-plus years he has been commissioner, the author sought an explanation from the Queensland Police Service as to why nothing had been recorded for 12 years.[7] She was advised that:

> ... the Register was never intended to be a full record of all communications between the Minister and the Commissioner. Rather it was intended primarily as an accountability mechanism for those situations where the Minister intervenes in the administration or functioning of the Police Service through the giving of a binding requirement (for a report/recommendation) or direction.
>
> ... there has been regular correspondence and discussion between the Minister of the day and the respective Commissioners since 1997. However, as there have been no requirements for reports/recommendations, or directions, in accordance with the Act and the approved criteria, no entries have been made in the Register since that time.

The QPS is correct in saying that it was not Fitzgerald's or the parliament's intention that the Register include every communication between a police commissioner and police minister in any one year. Given the volume of correspondence that would pass between the two annually, it would be an impractical and onerous request. However, it is highly unlikely that either envisaged that nothing would be recorded for twelve consecutive years.

The QPS explanation suggests, that in accordance with the *Police Service Administration Act*, there has been no written communication whatsoever between the minister and the commissioner from 1997 to 2008 that warrants recording in the Register, while for the previous six years there were 67 such matters.

Given the range of matters that the Register captures and the complex and at times political nature of the policing functions this is indeed remarkable. It means that the commissioner has not been requested by the police minister to provide reports and recommendations in relation to the administration and functioning of the QPS and that the minister, after first taking into account the advice of the commissioner has not directed the commissioner in writing on any matter concerning:

- the overall administration, management, and superintendence of, or in the police service; and
- policy and priorities to be pursued in performing the functions of the police service; and
- the number and deployment of officers and staff members and the number and location of police establishments and police stations' (*Police Service Administration Act 1990* (Qld) s. 4.6 (2)).

If this is the case, it suggests that a series of police ministers may have neglected their ministerial obligation in relation to the QPS, for according to the Westminster system, police ministers are accountable to the parliament for all policy matters in relation to the police department.

Perhaps the absence of any material in the 1997–2008 Registers is the result of the police commissioner adopting a very strict and perhaps too narrow an interpretation of what constitutes a 'requirement' of the police minister and how a 'report' and/or 'recommendation' is being defined.

In essence, if the minister asks for a report or recommendation or issues a directive on matters outlined in ss. 4.6 and 4.7 of the Police Services Administration Act, however the request/directive is worded, he/she is requiring the commissioner to furnish same. If that is the case, it is not unreasonable to expect that such requests, and directives and (as per Copley's advice) any relevant documentation, would be recorded in the Register.

The QPS explanation for the content-free nature of the 1997–2008 Registers goes on to say that:

> It should also be understood that other initiatives have been progressed since 1997 to ensure public accountability. For example, the Parliamentary

> Estimates hearings provide an opportunity for the public examination of the management of the Police portfolio. Similarly reporting to the Queensland Parliament through the Service's Annual Report and Statistical Review has been enhanced progressively over time. (Correspondence from the Queensland Police Service, August 4, 2009)

The initiatives referred to above do help, to varying degrees, to enhance public accountability but individually and collectively they serve a different purpose to the Register.

Fitzgerald and the Queensland parliament considered there was a need for an annual Register and for a period of six years it formed part of the police reform mosaic. The type of information that was on the public record during this time, allowed the CJC, the Parliamentary Criminal Justice Committee (which monitored and reviewed the CJC), and the citizens of Queensland to examine and evaluate certain written communications between the police commissioner and police minister. They also made public the nature of the directives given to the commissioner by the police minister and the reasons for those directives. The Registers also allowed the community to gain some insight into the relationship between police commissioner and police minister and the matters that were of particular concern to both.

The Register is central to highlighting the inevitable grey areas that exist between constabulary independence and ministerial responsibility and between politicised and nonpoliticised policing. No light has been shed on these critical grey areas since 1996.

At the July 2009 Australian Public Sector Anti-corruption Conference, Police Commissioner Robert Atkinson spoke about the relationship between police and government which he said is primarily between the police minister and police commissioner. Commissioner Atkinson explained that during the eight years he has been commissioner of police, he has never been told by government at any level that a police officer should be promoted or not promoted; that the government wanted a person transferred to remote Queensland areas such as Mt Isa, Longreach or Charleville; that the government would like the police to investigate a particular person or stop an investigation or that the government was not happy with a particular officer and would like the commissioner to commence an investigation. He explained that 'there has not been any interference or involvement whatsoever' in relation to such matters. Atkinson also referred to the Register saying that 'Post Fitzgerald there is a Register where if the police minister gives the police commissioner a directive then it has to be recorded'.

It is reassuring to be told that the crude, amoral directions given to the QPF pre-Fitzgerald by members of government have ceased post-Fitzgerald. However, the absence of such abhorrent behaviour does not help to explain the 1997–2008 Register or the fact that for 12 years the minister has never given the police commissioner a directive as outlined in s. 4.6(2)(a)(b)(c) of the *Police Service Administration Act*.

Some may believe that the circumstances that led to the politicisation of policing in Queensland could not occur again. Such thinking implies that history cannot and/or will not repeat itself. Fitzgerald was not so optimistic. He warned that 'superficially innocent modifications' can obstruct reform. He also pointed to a recurring theme in his Report which was 'the need for a free flow of ... information within a society'. This he said was 'needed if public opinion is to be informed (Fitzgerald, 1989, p. 6). For 12 years the Registers have not informed public opinion. Indeed, the reverse is the case.

Fitzgerald also appreciated that Queensland could not stay trapped in a Fitzgerald time-lock. Thus, he noted that while recommendations in his report are 'aimed at allowing permanent institutions and systems to work properly' solutions should also be 'improved and reviewed through the democratic process' (Fitzgerald, 1989, p. 5). It may be time for the 1997–2008 Registers to be reviewed. If it is found that their content-free nature reflects the intent of the Fitzgerald recommendation it may be time to reconsider the Register's usefulness. If, however, it is discovered that a too rigid and narrow interpretation of the Act accounts for the lack of information, then it may be time to amend ss. 4.6 and 4.7 of the *Police Service Administration Act*. In the spirit of Fitzgerald, any review would need to be open, transparent, allow for community input and its findings tabled in the Parliament.

Conclusion: Fitzgerald's Legacy

The extent of the problems associated with a politicised police force revealed by the Fitzgerald Inquiry have not been prevalent in subsequent inquiries into policing in Australia or in relation to major inquiries into police and policing in other liberal democratic societies. For this reason, the suite of Fitzgerald reforms discussed in this chapter and the events that led to them have not been a feature in other inquiries into police malfeasance. However, that does not mean that Fitzgerald's findings on the politicised nature of policing in Queensland have not had influence in other Australian states and beyond. His Report acts as a warning to governments and police organisations of the dangers for both of ignoring the principles underpinning constabulary independence and the thorny overlap in responsibility that arises between ministerial responsibility and constabulary independence. The Report also serves as a constant reminder to the community of the consequences of inappropriate police-government relations.

Ten years after the Fitzgerald Report was tabled in the Queensland Parliament, then Premier Peter Beattie described it is as 'the single most important catalyst for improved behaviour in this State since we became a

State in 1859 … It was a blueprint for rebuilding confidence in the police, the parliament and the bureaucracy'. Former Premier, Wayne Goss described the Report as 'a courageous and a perceptive document'. He went on to say that 'I think we owe a great debt of gratitude to Mr Fitzgerald' (ABC, 1999).

Twenty years after Tony Fitzgerald QC brought down his report, the lasting impact of the Fitzgerald Inquiry and the high personal regard in which Fitzgerald is held in Queensland and other Australian states was evident when he broke his 20-year silence on the state of public sector reform in Queensland.

Fitzgerald warned that:

> Unfortunately, cynical shortsighted political attitudes adopted for the benefit of particular politicians and their parties commonly have adverse consequences for the general community. The current concerns about political and police misconduct are a predictable result of attitudes adopted in Queensland since the mid 1990s. (ABC, 2009)

The response was immediate. The following day Queensland Premier Anna Bligh announced that:

> Cabinet has approved the preparation of a green paper for a widespread public consultation on a range of reforms. Sweeping reforms that will address issues around political fundraising, around the pecuniary interests' of members of Parliament, as well as the internal investigation mechanisms of the public service including the police. (ABC, 2009)

The extraordinary impact the Fitzgerald Inquiry had on policing and public life more generally 20 years ago continues today. But as the events that led to the announcement of the green paper show, without continual scrutiny at all levels, it is possible that the protections put in place by Fitzgerald to prevent a return to a pre-Fitzgerald culture could be dismantled and forgotten. Those protections include having external, independent input into the appointment and dismissal of the police commissioner and, in the interest of transparent relations between police and government, using the Register in the way Fitzgerald intended.

Endnotes

1 The Queensland Police Force changed its name to the Queensland Police Service in 1990.

2 Whitrod strenuously denies Lewis's claims that he had close links to the Australian Labor Party, describing them as 'lies' (Whitrod, 2001, p. 186).

3 Commissioner's fixed term contracts are renewable.

4 The Fitzgerald recommendations are taken up in Part 4 of the *Police Service Administration Act 1990*.

5 More recent copies of the Register (1997–2008) were obtained from the Queensland Parliament web site: www.parliament.qld.gov.au. Copies of the Register from 1990–1996 were obtained through the Bills and Papers Office of the Queensland Parliament.

6   It was strongly rumoured that the two men did not like each other and this was confirmed when their tense relationship spilled out into the public arena (Walker, 1995, pp. 184–185).

7   Jim O'Sullivan was police commissioner from 1992 until October 2000. Robert Atkinson was appointed police commissioner on 1 November 2000 and continues to hold that position.

Legislation

Crime and Misconduct Act 2001 (Qld).

Criminal Justice Act 1989 (Qld).

Police Service Administration Act 1990 (Qld).

References

Australian Broadcasting Corporation (ABC). (1999, May 16). Queensland ten years after Fitzgerald. *Background Briefing*. Available at http://www.abc.net.au/backgroundbriefing

Australian Broadcasting Corporation (ABC). (2009, July 29). Queensland returning to dark corrupt past. *The 7.30 Report*. Available at http://www.abc.net.au/7.30/2009/s2640320.htm

Bingham, Sir Max. (1996). *Report on the review of the Queensland Police Service*. Brisbane, Australia: Queensland Police Service.

Dickie, P. (1989). *The road to Fitzgerald and beyond*. Brisbane, Australia: University of Queensland Press.

Finnane, M. (1994). *Police and government: Histories of policing in Australia*. Melbourne, Australia: Oxford University Press.

Fitzgerald, G.E. (1989). *Report of a Commission of Inquiry Pursuant to Orders in Council*. Brisbane, Australia: Queensland Government.

Fleming, J., & Lewis, C. (2002). The politics of police reform. In T. Prenzler & J. Ransley (Eds.), *Police reform: Building integrity* (pp. 83–96). Sydney and London: Federation Press.

Hawker, B. (1984). Police, politics, protest and the press: Queensland 1967–1981. *Alternative Criminology Journal, 4*(July), 57–91.

Lewis, C. (1992). Police accountability: Unintended consequences of the reform process. In A. Hede, S. Prasser & M. Neylan (Eds.), *Keeping them honest: Democratic reform in Queensland*. Brisbane, Australia: University of Queensland Press.

Lewis, C. (1999). *Complaints against police: The politics of reform*. Sydney, Australia: Hawkins Press.

Lustgarten, L. (1986). *The governance of police*. London: Sweet-Maxwell.

Marshal, G. (1965). *Police and government*. London: Methuen.

Milte, K., & Weber, T. (1977). *Police in Australia: Development, functions and procedures*. Melbourne, Australia: Butterworths.

Oliver, I. (1987). Police, government and accountability. London: Macmillan.

Procter, C. (1985). The police. In A. Patience (Ed.), *The Bjelke-Petersen Premiership 1968–1983: Issues in public policy*. Melbourne, Australia: Longman Cheshire.

Queensland Parliament. (1991–2008). *Register of reports and recommendations to the Police Minister, Ministerial directions and tabled Ministerial reasons, 1991–2008*. Brisbane, Australia: Parliament of Queensland.

Roberts, G. (1988, March 4). Lewis post gave Sir Joh 'control' of the police. *Sydney Morning Herald*, p. 2,

Queensland Police Service. (2009). E-mail correspondence with author.

Stenning, P. (2006). The idea of the political 'independence' of the police: International interpretations and experiences. In M. Beare & T. Murray (Eds.), *Police and government relations: Who's calling the shots.* Toronto: University of Toronto Press.

Walker, J. (1995). *Goss: A political biography.* Brisbane, Australia: University of Queensland Press.

Walter, J.D., & Dickie, K. (1985). Johannes Bjelke-Petersen: A political profile. In A. Patience (Ed.), *The Bjelke-Petersen Premiership 1968–1983: Issues in public policy.* Sydney, Australia: Longman Cheshire.

Wettenhall, R. (1977, March). Government and the police. *Current Affairs Bulletin,* 12–23.

Whitrod, R. (2001). *Before I sleep: Memoirs of a modern police commissioner.* Brisbane, Australia: University of Queensland Press.

Whitton, E. (1988, November 7). Crucial question await Sir Joh. *Sydney Morning Herald,* p. 7,

Whitton, E. (1989). *The hillbilly dictator: Australia's police state.* Sydney, Australia: ABC Enterprises for the Australian Broadcasting Corporation.

APPENDIX A
REGISTER

Police Service Administration Act 1990

Section 4.7(1)

CRITERIA

1. Introduction

1.1 Section 4.7(1) of the Police Service Administration Act 1990 (the PSA Act) provides that:

'The Commissioner is to keep a register in which are to be recorded —

* all reports and recommendations made to the Minister under section 4.6(1)(a);

and

* all directions given in writing to the Commissioner under section 4.6(2).'

Section 4.6(1)(a) provides:

'The Commissioner —

(a) is to furnish to the Minister reports and recommendations in relation to the administration and functioning of the Police Service, when required by the Minister to do so;'

1.3 Section 4.6(2) provides:

'The Minister, having regard to advice of the Commissioner first obtained, may give, in writing, direction to the Commissioner concerning —

(a) the overall administration, management, and superintendence of, or in the Police Service;

and

(b) policy and priorities to be pursued in performing the functions of the Police Service;

and

(c) the number and deployment of officers and staff members and the number and location of police establishments and police stations.'

2. Contents of Register

2.1 Section 4.7(1) permits only the inclusion in the register of the reports and recommendations made to the Minister under section 4.6(1)(a) and all directions given in writing to the Commissioner under section 4.6(2), together with an index or list of contents.

2.2 The register must include the actual reports, recommendations and directions specified in section 4.7(1) and not a mere index or list thereof.

2.3 The register does not have to be in a single volume, e.g. it may comprise an index volume, a volume containing the section 4.6(1)(a) material and another volume containing the section 4.6(2) material.

2.4 Section 4.7(1) does not permit the inclusion of additional material, such as that furnished under section 4.6(1)(b).

3. Criteria to be satisfied for inclusion in register as section 4.6(1)(a) material

3.1 There must be a requirement by the Minister to the Commissioner to be furnished with a report/recommendation in relation to the administration and functioning of the Police Service.

3.2 The Minister's requirement must be made by a formal notice to this effect.

3.3 The formal notice must be in prescribed form I.

3.4 Provided the Minister's requirement is in the prescribed form, it may impose a standing/continuing requirement of the Commissioner to furnish reports/recommendations in relation to a particular aspect of the administration and functioning of the Police Service.

3.5 The Minister's requirement must be in relation to policy and not operational issues, e.g. without limiting the scope of the policy issues to which section 4.6(1) applies, these would include the matters listed in section 4.6(2).

3.6 The Commissioner must furnish a report/recommendation to the Minister in response to such a requirement.

3.7 The report/recommendation furnished by the Commissioner may be prepared by another person on behalf of the Commissioner.

3.8 It is not necessary that the report/recommendation furnished by the Commissioner be in writing, however it is desirable that this is the case.

3.9 A written report/recommendation must state on its face that it is made pursuant to a requirement made by the Minister under section 4.6(1)(a).

3.10 A verbal report/recommendation must forthwith be reduced to writing, with reference to the fact that it is made pursuant to a requirement by the Minister under section 4.6(1)(a), for inclusion in the register.

3.11 Draft Ministerial replies, Cabinet and Executive Council documents, are <u>not</u> to be included in the register.

4. Criteria to be satisfied for inclusion in register as section 4.6(2) material

4.1 The Minister must first have obtained, but not necessarily sought, the written or verbal advice of the Commissioner.

4.2 The Commissioner's advice may be prepared by another person on behalf of the Commissioner.

4.3 The Minister must give a <u>written</u> direction.

4.4 The Minister's direction must concern one of the following matters:
   (a) the overall administration, management, and superintendence of, or in the Police Service;

    (b) policy and priorities to be pursued in performing the functions of the Police Service;

    (c) the number and deployment of officers and staff members and the number and location of police establishments and police stations.

4.5 Any communication by the Minister to the Commissioner in relation to any of the matters referred to in paragraph 4.4 are directions for the purpose of section 4.6(2) if it has the effect of binding the Commissioner to take or not take (or to cause another person to take or not take) action in relation to any of those matters.

4.6 A requirement by the Minister to the Commissioner under section 4.6(1)(a) to be furnished with a report/recommendation in relation to the administration and functioning of the Police Service is not to be classed as a direction given under section 4.6(2),

4.7 The Minister's direction must be made by a formal notice to this effect.

4.8 The formal notice must be in the prescribed form II.

Changing the Approach: Structural Reform in the Queensland Police Force

Jenny Fleming

The *Commission of Inquiry into Possible Illegal Activities and Associated Police Misconduct* (hereafter referred to as the Fitzgerald Inquiry) had its genesis in public controversy that uncovered misconduct and illegal activities in Queensland's police force. Yet one of Fitzgerald's primary legacies has been the way in which the Commission and its subsequent report provided the framework for a series of public sector reforms in the Queensland state government. If we are to talk about the ways in which Fitzgerald had an impact, we can state that his report fundamentally changed the way in which state government departments and their agencies did business. As Finn has noted in his discussion of the Fitzgerald and WA Inc. Commissions:

> ... [Commissions] put governments and thereby, more tellingly, their state's system of government on trial. In this lies their uniqueness. (1994, p. 33)

The Fitzgerald Inquiry was initially concerned with police misconduct, gambling, prostitution and payment to political parties (Fitzgerald, 1989, Appendix 6). The focus broadened when, as Finn observed:

> the nature of the investigation ... [brought] into focus and question the structural and cultural features of the environment in which the events, etc. to be inquired into occurred ... Where an environment is perceived to be merely a part or product of a wider system that influences or affects it, that system (or at least aspects of its principal parts) may itself become the appropriate object of appraisal. (1994, p. 34)

In the end it was the 'wider system' that became the 'object of appraisal' and would ultimately provide the context and political will for public sector reform and 'a change of approach' in the state's police force.

This chapter is in three sections — the first looks briefly at the impact of Fitzgerald's report on state public sector reform. The second section notes Fitzgerald's organisational assessment of the Queensland Police Force (QPF). The chapter focuses particularly on regionalisation, civilianisation and the introduction of community policing as examples of change proposals. It shows that Fitzgerald's enthusiasm for community policing and 'a change of approach' in the QPF was very much part of his thinking for the organisational restructure of the organisation. The third section looks at some of the early reviews and assessment of the QPF's attempts to implement Fitzgerald's reform agenda. This section of the chapter demonstrates that there were clearly expectations that the implementation of Fitzgerald's reforms would be realised earlier and more effectively than was the case. The chapter concludes with the observation that the criticisms and misgivings of the QPF's reform process (and indeed progress) were largely informed by misconceived expectations of the reform process. Despite these early misgivings, it is argued that public sector reform has been embedded in the state government and the QPF and that the impact of Fitzgerald has been the influence of his report and recommendations that has allowed the process of reform to be a continuing process over twenty years. The following section looks at the way in which the Fitzgerald Report provided the final impetus to a new government committed to public sector structural and administrative reform.

Public Sector Reform

The public sector reform agenda had not been embraced as enthusiastically in Queensland as it had in other Australian states (Selth, 1991), although by the late 1980s there was some government acknowledgment of the rapidly changing administrative changes that were occurring elsewhere. In 1988, the National Party Queensland government enacted the *Public Service Management and Employment Act* incorporating many of the structural and administrative reform recommendations from the Savage Report (Savage, 1987) that had been established the previous year to review the state's public sector. The changes sought to ensure that state government departments would comply with government directives and legislative mandates, account for all expenditure and strive to meet community needs and expectations.

Fitzgerald's report was formally submitted to government on 3 July 1989. As Davis (1995) has noted, while it focused primarily on police misconduct and corruption, it was necessary for Fitzgerald to 'formulate recommendations to found the process of reform'. Fitzgerald's observations and recommendations, which went well beyond reform of the QPF, were directly related to accountability and honesty in public life and his observations would be a 'contingent political factor' in shaping the state's broader administrative reform program. So, while Fitzgerald's report did not provide a detailed plan for comprehensive public sector reform, the report 'sparked an unprecedented debate about modernising the Queensland public sector' and in particular, the police force (Davis, 1995, p. 95). Fitzgerald had provided whichever party that won government in the 1989 State election with a mandate to effect reforms in government departments other than the QPF. Armed with its own reform agenda, the incoming Goss Labor government acted swiftly on the blueprint Fitzgerald had provided. It tied its administrative reform aspirations to the Fitzgerald Inquiry revelations and combined its own policy statements, initiated in *Making Government Work (MGW)* (Australian Labor Party, Qld Branch, 1989) and realised in the *Public Sector Management Commission Act*, 1990, with Fitzgerald's blueprint.

The Labor government's public sector reform program was driven largely by ideas drawn from interstate and overseas that emphasised the need for 'the executive and public sector to be linked and coordinated in the interests of consistency and coherence'. Its official policy statement on public sector reform, *Making Government Work (MGW)* would become 'a variation on a national theme, a local expression of a wider trend' (Davis, 1995, p. 128). MGW committed the Labor Party to procedures that would enhance accountability in the Public Service, giving 'effect to the full package of Fitzgerald reforms'. But as Davis has noted, 'Much of the rhetoric [of *MGW*] echoes Fitzgerald, promising to implement, and expand, his agenda' (1995, p. 95). Indeed, Labor's first term was 'marked by the rapid implementation of much of the Fitzgerald package', particularly as it related to administrative reform (Prenzler, 1997, p. 14). The MGW document was, at times, specific. The Attorney-General, Justice and Police Departments would all be restructured to allow for the implementation of Fitzgerald's suggested reforms (Australian Labor Party, Qld Branch, 1989). Thus Fitzgerald's recommendations about the restructuring of the QPF were formally endorsed and subsequently supported by the government through significant increased budget allocations from 1990 (PSMC, 1993).

To ensure the restructuring of departments and related principles were adhered to, Labor proposed a Public Sector Management Commission (PSMC) that would replace the Public Sector Board. The PSMC, in addition to supervising personnel recruitment, training and promotion, would 'overhaul the whole machinery of government in Queensland to ensure complete accountability' (Australian Labor Party, Qld Branch, 1989, p. 1). It would be the new government's first legislative initiative. In recommending the *Public Sector Management Commission Bill* to Parliament in March 1990, Premier Wayne Goss clearly used the Fitzgerald reform agenda to sell the initiative:

> In line with the spirit of Fitzgerald, the Public Sector Management Commission will provide the coordinated management that the public sector, broadly, and the public sector more specifically, require. With the Electoral and Administrative Review Commission and the Criminal Justice Commission, it will complete the trilogy of reform in Queensland. (cited in Davis, 1995, p. 107)

The PSMC would be the first government agency to review and assess the progress of the Queensland Police Service (QPS) in the post-Fitzgerald era. Before discussing the PSMC review and two subsequent reviews of the QPF, the following section looks at Fitzgerald's findings in the context of structural reform and the related recommendations he made to encourage 'changing the approach' to Queensland policing.

Changing the Approach

In his report, Fitzgerald acknowledged the broader public sector reform efforts that had taken place at the state level in the 1980s but insisted that in the context of the police bureaucracy and its decision-making processes, there were major limitations to those reforms. The QPF's 'rigid structure' was essentially 'limit[ing] its capacity to adapt' (1989, p. 273). As Fitzgerald pointed out:

> Although there may be a need for resources, there are changes in emphasis and organization which can be made to the Queensland Police Force which are equally important for the development of a stable, efficient criminal law enforcement body. (1989, p. 230)

Fitzgerald identified 'parallel hierarchies' that were not integrated and noted the 'overlap and duplication of tasks and duties' particularly across specialist functions and squads. The organisational structure was criticised for its 'unnecessary concentration of authority and decision-making in head office' making it difficult for management to hold officers accountable for defined areas of responsibility. Fitzgerald concluded that the centralised management and decision-making systems were 'unwieldy', hierarchical, and 'characterized by complexities which mask inefficiencies, misconduct and corrupt practices' and argued that the organisation 'needs to be thoroughly re-organized' (1989, pp. 218, 224, 273). Fitzgerald recommended that the QPF under the supervision of the Criminal Justice Commission (CJC):

> … restructure its organisation over regional lines with increased levels of authority and responsibility, matched with commensurate accountability for commanding officers at the regional, district and divisional levels. (1989, p. 380)

Fitzgerald's report identified the organisation's highly centralised, rigid and hierarchical structure as a major factor in police corruption, obscuring lines of communication between ranks and hindering decision-making processes

(1989, pp. 363–364). According to Fitzgerald, a flatter structure with 'few organisational levels as possible between the Commissioner and operational police officers' would ensure better communication, observable lines of authority, strengthen accountability and improve efficiency. Regional commanders would have greater levels of authority and more responsibility for staffing and resource allocation, local operational policing services, initiation of criminal investigations and the design of community projects. The report's recommendations would incorporate 'a package of reforms intended to restructure the QPF in line with contemporary theories of public administration' (Fleming and Lafferty, 2000, p. 157).

If public sector reform provided the context within which Fitzgerald viewed the QPF, he was also influenced by the early enthusiasm for community policing in Australia and elsewhere (see Jarratt, 1990 for a contemporary example). In the 1980s, community policing was being hailed by many police organisations around the world as a major paradigm shift from the 'professional' model of policing. Traditional crime-fighting and enforcement-oriented policing with its accompanying centralised, bureaucratic command structure was apparently giving way to an inclusive philosophy based on encouraging partnerships between the police and communities in a collaborative effort to solve crime and disorder (Fleming & O'Reilly, 2008). Fitzgerald would come to recommend that 'community policing be adopted as the primary policing strategy' in the state and argued for structural changes particularly in this context (1989, pp. 381, 230–236). Fitzgerald's observations on structural and administrative practices and the recommendations he made in the context of 'changing the approach' to Queensland policing 'provided further impetus for change' (Fleming and Lafferty, 2000, p. 165) and arguably laid the foundation for the continued development of the QPF over the ensuing years.

In looking at the QPF's structure and practices, the process of regionalisation and civilianisation were two areas that Fitzgerald suggested needed a 'change of emphasis' if the 'change of approach' was to be realised. Such organisational arrangements, regional command processes and an emphasis on the 'local', would, Fitzgerald argued, provide the flexibility needed to achieve the introduction of community policing strategies that would emphasise preventative policing, community inclusion and the trialling of community programs at the regional and district levels (1989, pp. 233–234, 381). The process of regionalisation was emphasised in the context of community policing:

> The establishment of community policing must be accompanied by an increased emphasis upon regional arrangements. If regional Commanders are to respond to the needs of communities which they serve, they must have control over, authority and responsibility for resources, including money, staff and equipment. (Fitzgerald, 1989, p. 233)

Recognising that such structural arrangements were not going to happen overnight, Fitzgerald suggested that regions and districts that had 'excess staff levels' should design community initiatives, programs and various projects on a trial basis. This, he said, 'would be advantageous in the introduction of community policing strategies' (1989, p. 234), as would the recruitment of potential police officers from the wider community with an emphasis on maturity, improved educational standards and those with special skills. Restrictions on women joining the QPF 'should be abandoned' (Fitzgerald, 1989, pp. 363–365).

In line with his concern about the efficient allocation of resources, Fitzgerald also noted that many police officers in the QPF occupied positions that did not require police skills 'and for which, in many instances, they are unsuited' (1989, p. 234). The Report recommended civilianisation whereby sworn police officers are replaced with 'civilian' staff who have either no police powers or limited police powers and who provide either administrative or specialist support to policing. This process would assist in abolishing hierarchical specialist units and squads in line with the regionalisation process and maximise the number of police available for duties 'requiring the exercise of police authority' (Fitzgerald, 1989, pp. 382, 235–237). As the report noted, 'effective policing is dependent upon as many members of the Police Force as possible considering themselves parts of local teams and so identifying themselves with their local areas' (Fitzgerald, 1989, p. 233). Civilianisation would assist in:

> … developing the new community emphasis within the Force. Community policing initiatives will be carried out by civilians and police officers working together. (Fitzgerald, 1989, p. 236)

In his recommendations, Fitzgerald emphasised the need for a 'change of approach' and that restructuring the organisation on a regional basis with its accompanying devolution and local responsibilities would provide the environment within which this could be encouraged. A policy of civilianisation would consolidate this process allowing for the maximum number of police officers available for police duties including community engagement (Fitzgerald, 1989, pp. 380–382). In hindsight, Fitzgerald was overly optimistic in relation to the time it would take to implement such reforms. Two years previously, the New South Wales police had begun the shift to community-based operational strategies involving a 'decentralized multi-skilled, service delivery model'. In 1990, reflecting on the progress made by NSW police, Jarratt concluded that despite major restructuring to bring about regionalisation, 'there remains much to be done' (Jarratt, 1990, p. 143):

> … reform takes much longer than you think. Change in the law and other events must be supported by processes sustained over a long period. (Jarratt, 1990, p. 152)

If Fitzgerald expected the process to be quicker and more efficient in Queensland, he was to be disappointed. The following section looks briefly at three reviews that assessed the extent of the reform progress in the QPS in the post-Fitzgerald period. The reviews by the Public Sector Management Commission (1993), the Criminal Justice Commission (1994) and the Queensland Police Service Review (the Bingham Review 1996), all irrevocably tied to the Fitzgerald Report recommendations, provide some indication of the impact of Fitzgerald's report and suggest that there were a number of expectations at the state level about what could be accomplished in a relatively short time.

Public Sector Management Commission — 1993

The PSMC's purpose was to scrutinise the progress of the QPS in the context of corporate and operational policing issues. This would include progress made in organisational restructuring, civilianisation, and the regionalisation process (PSMC, 1993). The review would be grounded in the context of the Fitzgerald Report. As the PSMC pointed out:

> … the PSMC Review has to be seen in the context of the Fitzgerald recommendations. While the primary function of the Review was not to monitor the implementation of the Fitzgerald report, it is inevitable that many of the issues covered in the terms of reference were either recommended by the Fitzgerald report recommendations or were significantly affected by them. (1993, p. 34)

In the first three years after Fitzgerald, the QPS underwent significant reforms. Structural changes included the introduction of a flatter organisational structure, a process of regionalisation, greater integration of support functions and the inclusion of civilian managers in decision-making processes. Despite what looked like a promising start, the PSMC found there was a lack of clarification around areas of responsibility and areas of accountability across the various arms of the Service (PSMC, 1993, p. 50). The regionalisation process, for example by 1992 had been implemented, but not well — the process of delegation to regions was described as 'inappropriate and piecemeal'. The absence of specific policies and guidelines had led to confusion. An efficient devolution process had not been put in place and accountability, consistency and single-mindedness on the part of Commanders had raised serious questions about the viability of the process. The PSMC observed that the QPS was now operating as 'eight different services rather than an integrated whole' and identifying a 'feudal' mentality across the regions (1993, p. 52).

In 1994, the PSMC revisited the regionalisation process and while observing ongoing difficulties with the devolvement of authority, duplication, burgeoning of regional bureaucracies and lack of effective central guidelines, the report did note some progress and was positive about some of the benefits regionalisation would offer (1994). Perhaps notably, the 1994 report identified some of the unintended consequences of implementing regionalisation, consequences that would perhaps explain the slow process of implementation. For example, there had been a significant growth in administration positions resulting from Fitzgerald's recommendation that regional offices should sit organisationally separate from district level management (1994).

On the policy of civilianisation, the PSMC noted in 1993, that although up to 200 police positions had been 'civilianised' in the period 1990–1992, it didn't necessarily follow that police officers were moving more swiftly into operational roles. As with the regionalisation process, there had been no attempt to put in place a formal civilianisation policy or any guidelines at all. The PSMC noted the formation of the Community Policing Support Branch in 1990, but argued forcefully that the Branch was located outside central headquarters, thus reinforcing the notion that 'community policing is something removed from normal police duties' and 'the sole responsibility of one small branch'. In an implicit criticism of Fitzgerald's insistence that community policing become the QPS's primary policing strategy, the PSMC suggested:

> A new operational philosophy for the Queensland Police Service needs to be stated in terms for striving for improved methods of operational policing generally, incorporating both preventative policing and community policing initiatives wherever possible into traditional policing methods. This is a far more inclusive and realistic approach than to say community policing must become the new primary philosophy of the Police Service. (1993, p. 127)

The PSMC concluded that, in the QPS, 'community policing [was] the subject of confusion, apathy and alienation within the Queensland Police Service ... a result of widespread misconception of community policing, its status within the Service and exaggerated claims made on its behalf' (1993, p. 128). Several recommendations were made in relation to tightening up understandings of what community policing actually meant and the importance of integrating the community policing support branch into the Policy and Strategy branch where it could 'form part of overall policing strategies' (PSMC, 1993, p. 126). Ensuing reviews into this aspect of Fitzgerald's reforms would not be any more encouraging.

Criminal Justice Commission — 1994

At the same time that the PSMC was assessing progress in the QPS, the CJC was conducting a more specific review of 'the implementation of the recommendations of the Report of the Commission of Inquiry so far as they relate to the Police Service' (CJC, 1994, p. iii). Given the proximity of the reports to each other, the CJC incorporated the PSMC's recommendations and noted progress where applicable. For example, the CJC review observed that following the PSMC's recommendation to develop a devolution process for the delegation of responsibilities to the regions (1993, p. 83), this action had 'been deferred pending the outcome of a general PSMC review of regionalization in the Queensland public sector'. However, the PSMC's recommendation to implement a revised organisational structure with clearly defined management streams (1993) was acted upon almost immediately with 'almost all of this restructuring' in place by November 1993 (CJC, 1994, p. 30). Following its assessment, the CJC concluded that the regionalisation process in 1994, with its lack of clarity over roles and responsibilities and problems associated with staffing, devolution of authority, financial management and costs generally had not delivered the benefits that Fitzgerald had prophesied. However, it argued for the retention of decentralisation processes 'subject to periodic reviews', noting that the QPS was 'taking steps to address' the 'shortcomings' (CJC, 1994, p. 40).

The CJC's observations relating to civilianisation were in line with the PSMC's observations the previous year. Progress had been made, with 353 new civilian positions being created since 1990 and a newly created funding basis to support civilianisation processes established. However, it was still the case that more police were not available for operational duties. The CJC cited implementation problems, unresolved industrial issues, government policy, inadequate funding, inadequate human resource practices and the status of civilians within the QPS as 'obstacles to civilianisation'. Just as it had argued for the retention of regionalisation, the CJC argued that civilianisation should 'remain a priority' (1994, pp. 110–116).

The CJC devoted a whole chapter of its report to Fitzgerald's vision of 'community involvement [as] essential to successful police work' (Fitzgerald, 1989, p. 231). It concluded that despite the implementation of a range of structures and processes into the QPS to develop and manage police–community interaction, there had been 'relatively little change to the basic operational policing strategies employed in the organisation' (CJC, 1994, pp. 59, 69). The report argued that unless the concept of community policing was better communicated to police and that the importance of police-community liaison was emphasised and 'integrated into operational policing practices', little would be achieved. The report also recommended 'greater encouragement of innovation and the use of problem-solving strategies' and more resources and autonomy to local areas to develop community initiatives. It recommended significant change to 'training, incentive structures, performance measures, information systems, management styles and authority relationships' if community policing were to be fully implemented. The CJC appeared to agree with the PSMC that Fitzgerald's community policing aspirations were 'unrealistic' and 'overly optimistic about the speed with which changes of this magnitude can be made ... Structural reform of this magnitude cannot be achieved quickly and will require a long-term implementation strategy' (1994, pp. 69–72).

In a 1996 submission to the Queensland Police Service Review, the CJC observed that despite some 'limited initiatives' its concerns relating to community policing 'remain[ed] an issue' (1996, pp. 2–4). The same update also identified regionalisation as an issue where some initiatives had been taken but that overall it also 'remain[ed] an issue' (CJC, 1996, pp. 1–2). The move to civilianisation over two years was looking better with 'some progress being made' in the areas of training and plans to accelerate the process in the ensuing years (CJC, 1996, p. 6). Both the PSMC and the CJC reports discussed here had based their reviews on assumptions and expectations that the Fitzgerald reforms could be implemented quickly and without significant upheaval. There was little concession in the respective reports about the kind of changes that would be required in an organisation that traditionally (in Australia and elsewhere) was renowned for its resistance to organisational change (Chan, 1997, p. 1)). In Queensland, where not every police officer was committed to the Fitzgerald reforms, it was always going to be a challenge (Fleming and Lafferty, 2000, p. 165).

As the reform process moved forward, albeit slowly, political events in Queensland were once again about to take centre stage. Six years after Fitzgerald had passed his report to parliament and the Labor government had taken office in Queensland, the political 'fairy tale' was in disarray. A series of political crises including, the 'Travel Rorts Affair', and the Mundingburra by-election (Lewis, 1999, pp. 152–154, 160–163) apparently, according to some commentators, provided substantial examples of the 'failure' of Fitzgerald's blueprint for reform (Prenzler, 1997). Labor lost office in 1996 paving the way for a third review of the QPS.

Queensland Police Service Review 1996
Under the purview of the incoming National–Liberal Party Coalition government, and taking into 'account the findings and recommendations of earlier relevant inquiries and evaluations' (Lewis, 1999, p. 163), Max Bingham, the inaugural chairperson of the CJC and his Review Committee once again sat down to examine the QPS in order to gauge its efficiency, effectiveness and accountability in terms of service delivery and in the context of the recommendations that had been made for the QPS since Fitzgerald's report. The Committee's 'main goal' was perceived as estab-

lishing 'a clear direction which will give operational police the best possible environment in which to deliver the best possible service to the people of Queensland' (CJC, 1996, pp. 1–2).

Much of the report was given over to summaries of previous reviews, and given the short time frame between the CJC reviews and the current investigation, the report did not add much to the existing knowledge of structural reform in the QPS. Bingham concurred with the CJC on the QPS' lack of progress with the regionalisation process. As the report noted, 'no real progress has been made in delineating separate roles for Headquarters, regional offices and district offices, with resultant duplication of activity and excess bureaucratic staff at every level'(Bingham, 1996, p. 70). On civilianisation, Bingham commended the policy in place but recommended 'continuing oversight' and 'an ongoing process of assessing further positions for civilianization (1996, pp. 78–81).

In line with previous reviews and reports, Bingham noted that the QPS had been 'slow to embrace the community policing philosophy' and recommended that the 'Commissioner develop a clear policy statement about policing in partnership'. As Bingham noted, 'the challenge for the QPS therefore is to mobilize the community to identify problems and assist in solving those problems'(1996, p. 198). Bingham, like Fitzgerald before him, was optimistic. As scholars have argued over time, community policing in Australia, at best, has been 'small-scale' and 20 years on few Australian police jurisdictions have succeeded in integrating a community policing philosophy into organisational and operational activities (Bayley, 1989; Beyer, 1991; Fleming & O'Reilly, 2008). However, Queensland has been cited in recent years as one jurisdiction that does manage some of its community policing initiatives well (Fleming & O'Reilly, 2008).

Some commentators at the time described Bingham's report as essentially 'negative', citing the Report's concerns with morale, corporate vision and professional autonomy for example, as evidence of the failure of Fitzgerald's 'blueprint' for reform (Prenzler, 1997, p. 22). This, despite the fact that Bingham had specifically said that his Committee would only be looking at issues 'that warranted attention'(Bingham, 1996, p. 5). These criticisms and others were arguably based on specific expectations (and misconceptions) of what a reform program of this magnitude could achieve in the time that had elapsed. After all, Fitzgerald provided the blueprint for reform but not the implementation guidance as to how the findings might be realised.[2] Yet it was not just the reviews that had high expectations of what the Fitzgerald reforms could accomplish in a few years in an organisation like the QPS.

The Response to Fitzgerald

Almost before the ink was dry on Fitzgerald's report, the criticisms of his approach were being formulated and by 1990 it was 'becoming fashionable to belittle the contribution made by Tony Fitzgerald QC to Queensland public life' (Coaldrake, 1990, p. 157). The scholarly community were quick to assess the progress of Fitzgerald's recommendations that had supposedly been accepted by the National Party government (and all other major political parties) 'lock, stock and barrel' a year before its release (Prasser, 1990, p. 101). So for some, the reform process with respect to police matters was not being 'carried out exactly as prescribed' by Fitzgerald (Dann & Wilson, 1992, p. 208); Fitzgerald was criticised for only having 'a tenuous grasp of the nature of public administration' (Nethercote, 1990, p. 217); for Toohey, Fitzgerald's 'comments in his final report did not rise above the trite' (1990, p. 85) while Vickery argued that Fitzgerald 'had gone too far' (1990, pp. 89–97). Clem Lloyd considered Fitzgerald 'naïve' and lacking in analysis and assessment. He also perceived Fitzgerald's summary as 'useless for inculcating into the public mind the basis for the transfiguring of the political and administrative culture of Queensland' (Lloyd, 1989, p. 129). Not all commentary on Fitzgerald's blueprint for reform was negative, but these comments serve to illustrate the considerable expectations and optimism that had accompanied the delivery of the Fitzgerald Report and the announcement that the recommendations would be implemented. These criticisms coupled with the review assessments discussed above suggest misplaced optimism and disappointment; an early indication perhaps that high expectations regarding the police reform agenda (and indeed public sector reform generally) would become a significant pressure point in the ensuing years for those committed to Fitzgerald's reform agenda and recommendations.

The media hype and personal community interest taken in the Inquiry and the subsequent report ensured a level of expectation that few would be able to meet. As Prasser has noted, the implications of the 'lock, stock and barrel' promise, its 'open door policy and the expectations it raised concerning the acceptance and implementation of all aspects of the Fitzgerald Report regardless of their suitability needs to be appreciated' (1990, p. 101). Given the lack of 'theoretically informed, empirical studies' (Dixon & Chan, 2007, p. 447) available to Fitzgerald while writing his report, it was perhaps inevitable that Fitzgerald's 'understanding' of what could be achieved and how quickly, was based on the 'unknowable' in many ways. It would be many years before many of the recommendations would be realised.

Discussion

This chapter has considered the impact of some of Fitzgerald's recommendations relating to structural change in the QPS, in particular regionalisation, civilianisation and community policing. We have seen that Fitzgerald's recommendations relating to public sector reform were in line with contemporary administrative theory and provided a sympathetic framework for the Goss Labor Party's public sector reform agenda. On being elected to government in December 1989, Labor was able to implement much of its *Making Government Work* agenda with little opposition partly by linking it explicitly to Fitzgerald's recommendations pertaining to institutional reform.

The chapter has also demonstrated that Fitzgerald's recommendations for structural reform in the QPS were consistent with his vision for community policy as a primary operational policing strategy. Structural reform in the QPS began quickly but proceeded slowly. For some, this pace was disappointing. Formal reviews of the reforms found the process wanting in many ways and when we look back in hindsight we can see that few realised just what organisational change in a traditional police organisation, and particularly change of this magnitude, would take (see Chan, 1997, pp. 1–3). Managing expectations across the government's reforms generally (Stevens & Wanna, 1992) and those in the QPF proved to be difficult.

Prasser has suggested that the 'inevitable test of an inquiry's success is whether its recommendations have been implemented or perceived to be implemented' (1990, p. 88). He does not suggest a time frame within which such perceptions should be examined. At what point do we say implementation has taken place? Certainly the reviews discussed here suggested that some progress was being made in the early 1990s and annual reports of the QPS since that time have suggested incremental and structural change.

If it was once the Australian jurisdiction that had failed to catch up administratively with its interstate counterparts, the Queensland public sector in 2009 is now a fully paid up member of Australian public administration principles. A cursory glance at Queensland Government department web pages, those of the CMC and that of the newly established Public Sector Commission demonstrates that 20 years after Fitzgerald, Queensland does have state institutions that are subject to public scrutiny, comment and accountability. Twenty years ago this was not the case.

In the context of the QPS, its recent annual report (QPS, 2009) suggests that it is a police organisation of the 21st century. Run essentially as a corporate entity with strategic planning, performance management and a strong commitment to community engagement and local partnerships, the organisation reflects the structural vision Fitzgerald had painted in his report. The QPS now has a strong regionalisation structure with flatter managerial structures that allow for local responsibility for planning, projects and budget management. The QPS has systematic accountability measures in place, recruitment processes that seek to reflect the broader community, employment practices that are in line with public sector practice and higher education is encouraged. Demonstrating the agency's commitment to progressing women in the workplace, the organisation's Deputy Commissioner is a woman. Civilianisation policy is now commonplace despite the early difficulties in implementing such radical change. There is a strong commitment to community policing with Queensland having a number of award-winning community initiatives to its credit (Fleming & O'Reilly, 2008). Its online 'compliance check' and 'statement of affairs document' provides the Queensland community with opportunities to evaluate 'the functions of the Queensland Police Service and the effect of its operation on the community' (QPS, 2009). This is not to say that the organisation does not have its critics nor is it meant to imply that the QPS now mirrors Fitzgerald's aspirations. It is true that at times the corporate culture 'does not adapt readily to the police context' and that there have been problems in introducing change and implementing reform processes (Fleming & Lafferty, 2000, p. 166). However, it is self-evident that what has changed is that the organisation now at least seeks to reflect and align itself with the Queensland community. What has changed is that the QPS is now a very different organisation to the one that Fitzgerald scrutinised in 1989; an organisation whose organisational chart and operational strategies reflect the structural changes that have taken place over time (QPS, 2009). Perhaps importantly, the community appears to believe this is the case. The Crime and Misconduct Commission (CMC) (previously the CJC) has been surveying the Queensland community on its attitudes to police since 1991. Its most recent survey suggests that public confidence in the QPS is 'increasingly positive' with dissatisfaction with police generally showing a decline over the years (CMC, 2009).

In 1990, Fitzgerald was criticised for his naivety in believing 'that a remedy is to be found in organizational and management changes' (Nethercote, 1990, p. 217). Perhaps this observation was based on the fact that there 'have been few systematic attempts internationally to eliminate police corruption through the introduction of new management techniques' (Fleming and Lafferty, 2000, p. 165). Twenty years after Fitzgerald, perhaps on reflection, such an observation would be tempered. As Dickie (2004) observed, one of the 'far-reaching consequences' of the Inquiry has been that 'every subsequent royal commission or equivalent inquiry now ha[s] a much higher bar to jump'. Many of the reforms that have been instituted in the QPS in the years since Fitzgerald have been built on the organisational changes advocated by Fitzgerald. Organisational change both in the machinery of government and its state police force was always going to be a long process. In 1983, Paterson reflected on bureaucratic reform:

> ... it can be a long and costly process, but change by osmosis, by absorption of environmental influences appears to be overwhelmingly the predominant source of organizational reform. (cited in Jarratt, 1990, p. 152)

Had commentators considered this in the early 1990s, perhaps the somewhat premature assessments of Fitzgerald's report and recommendations may have been tempered with patience. Twenty years on, it is evident (especially to those us who lived in Queensland during this time) that the state and its organisations have changed — for the better. It is also evident that Fitzgerald's observations played a significant part in that change and provided the framework within which others would implement their own reform agendas and change their approach.

References
1   The Queensland Police Force was renamed the Queensland Police Service in 1990.
2   Fitzgerald did, however, provide such guidance for the CJC.

References

Australian Labor Party, Queensland Branch, Transition to Government Committee. (1989). *Making government work: Public sector reform under a Goss government.* Brisbane, Australia: Australian Labor Party, Queensland Branch.

Bayley, D.H. (1989). Community policing in Australia: An appraisal. In D. Chappell & P. Wilson (Eds.), *Australian policing contemporary issues* (pp. 63–82). Australia: Butterworths.

Beyer, L. (1991). The logic and the possibilities of 'wholistic' community policing. In J. Vernon & S.McKillop (Eds.), *The police and the pommunity* (pp. 89–106). Canberra, Australia: Australian Institute of Criminology.

Bingham, M. (1996). *Report on the review of the Queensland Police Service.* Brisbane, Australia: Kingswood Press.

Chan, J. (1997). *Changing police culture: Policing in a multicultural society.* Cambridge: Cambridge University Press.

Criminal Justice Commission (CJC). (1994). *Implementation of reform within the Queensland Police Service: the response of the Queensland Police Service to the Fitzgerald Inquiry recommendations.* Brisbane: Goprint.

Criminal Justice Commission (CJC). (1996). *Submission to the Queensland Police Service Review Committee.* Retrieved July 23, 2009, from http://www.cmc.qld.gov.au/data/portal/00000005/content/79048001200975124533.pdf

Crime and Misconduct Commission (CMC). (2009). *Public perceptions of the QPS Public Attitudes Survey.* Retrieved July 23, 2009, from http://www.cmc.qld.gov.au/data/portal/00000005/content/58351001241484546942.pdf

Coaldrake, P. (1990). Overview. In S. Prasser, R. Wear & J. Nethercote (Eds.), *Corruption and reform: The Fitzgerald vision* (pp. 157–159). Brisbane, Australia: UQP..

Dann, S., & Wilson, P. (1992). The Criminal Justice System Commission, Police and Prisons. In B. Stevens & J. Wanna (Eds.), *The Goss Government: Promise and performance of labor in Queensland* (pp. 202–214). Brisbane, Australia: Centre for Public Sector Management.

Davis, G. (1995). *A government of routines: Executive coordination in an Australian state.* Melbourne, Australia: MacMillan.

Dickie, P. (2004, June 6). Probing shady places. *The Age.* Available at http://www.theage.com.au/articles/2004/06/05/1086377185492.html

Dixon, D., & Chan, J. (2007). The politics of police reform: Ten years after the Royal Commission into the New South Wales Police Service. *Criminology and Criminal Justice, 7*(4), 443–468.

Finn, P. (1994). The significance of the Fitzgerald and the WA Inc. Commissions. In P. Weller (Ed.), *Royal Commissions and the making of public policy* (pp. 32–39). Brisbane, Australia: Centre for Public Sector Management.

Fitzgerald, G.E. (1989). *Report of the Commission of Inquiry into Possible Illegal Activities and Associated Police Misconduct.* Brisbane, Australia: Government Printer.

Fleming, J., & Lafferty, G. (2000). New management techniques and restructuring in police organisations. *Policing: An International Journal of Police Strategy and Management 23*(2), 154–168.

Fleming, J., & O'Reilly, J. (2008). In search of a process: Community Policing in Australia. In T. Williamson (Ed.), *The handbook of knowledge based policing: Current conceptions and future directions* (pp. 139–156). Chichester, United Kingdom: John Wiley.

Jarratt, J. (1990). Community policing — Gently does. It In S. Prasser, R. Wear & J. Nethercote (Eds.), *Corruption and reform, The Fitzgerald vision* (pp. 143–153). Brisbane, Australia: University of Queensland Press.

Lewis, C. (1999). *Complaints against police: The politics of reform.* Sydney, Australia: Hawkins.

Lloyd, C. (1989). Honest graft? Aspects of Queensland's Fitzgerald Report. *Politics,* 24(2), 125–133.

Nethercote, J. (1990). Reform of the bureaucracy — An overview. In S. Prasser, R. Wear & J. Nethercote (Eds.), *Corruption and reform, the Fitzgerald vision* (pp. 212–219). Brisbane, Australia: University of Queensland Press.

Prasser, S. (1990). The Fate of Inquiries: Will Fitzgerald be Different?. In S. Prasser, R. Wear & J. Nethercote (Eds.), *Corruption and reform, the Fitzgerald vision* (pp. 98–122). Brisbane, Australia: University of Queensland Press.

Prenzler, T. (1997). The Decay of Reform, Police and Politics in Post-Fitzgerald Queensland. *Queensland Review, 4*(2), 13–26.

PSMC. (1993). *Review of the Public Sector Management Commission.* Brisbane, Australia: Queensland Government.

PSMC. (1994). *Review of the Public Sector Management Commission.* Brisbane: Queensland Government.

QPS. (2009). *Queensland Police Service Annual Report, 2007–2008.* Retrieved July 23, 2009, from http://www.police.qld.gov.au/services/reportsPublications/

Savage, E. (1987). *Report: Public Sector Review.* Brisbane, Australia: Public Sector Review Committee, Government Printer.

Selth, P. (1991). The Queensland Public Sector Management Commission: An agent of change. *Australian Journal of Public Administration, 50*(4).

Stevens, B., & Wanna, J. (1992). The Goss Government: An agenda for reform. In B. Stevens & J. Wanna (Eds.), *The Goss Government: Promise and performance of Labor in Queensland.* Brisbane, Australia: Centre for Australian Public Sector Management.

Toohey, B. (1990). Fitzgerald — How the process came unstuck. In S. Prasser, R. Wear & J. Nethercote (Eds.), *Corruption and reform, the Fitzgerald vision* (pp. 81–88). Brisbane, Australia: University of Queensland Press.

Vickery, G. (1990). Did Fitzgerald go too far?' A response from the Queensland law Society. In S. Prasser, R. Wear & J. Nethercote (Eds.), *Corruption and reform, the Fitzgerald vision* (pp. 89–97). Brisbane, Australia: University of Queensland Press.

The Evolution of Human Resource Management in Policing

Jacqueline M. Drew and Tim Prenzler

The last two decades have seen significant changes in the way in which police around the world have sought to attract, recruit, retain, train and develop police personnel. In Australia, the findings of the Commission of Inquiry into Possible Illegal Activities and Associated Police Misconduct (hereafter referred to as the Fitzgerald Inquiry) represented a turning point for police in Queensland. The Fitzgerald Inquiry resulted in the Queensland Police Service (QPS) being thrust to the forefront of progressive human resource policies and practices in policing and it set an agenda for a more scientific approach to the management of personnel. This chapter outlines Fitzgerald's recommendations in the area of human resource management and charts the shifting interpretations and commitment that followed over 20 years. The QPS has made significant progress in a number of areas, including the police-to-population ratio; reform of the promotional system to embrace merit; civilianisation; the systems for recruitment and promotion; and in training and tertiary education. Significant progress has also been made in regard to Fitzgerald's recommendation about removing sex discrimination in recruitment, and substantial efforts have been made in recruiting indigenous people. However, the lack of external evaluation and of public record information make it extremely difficult to come to reliable conclusions about the extent of improvements.

Background and Context

While police personnel management was not part of the original terms of the Fitzgerald Inquiry, the operation of the police organisation was clearly a contributory factor to the corruption and inefficiency which was identified.

Methods of recruitment, training and the management of staff were evidently in need of major reform. Fitzgerald's analysis of deficiencies in the Queensland Police Force (QPF) was made against a backdrop of reform in other police organisations in Australia and across the world. Police administrators and scholars had long been discussing the issue of police professionalism with reference to increasing educational, recruitment and training standards. There was a growing recognition of the need to shape both police organisations and police personnel to promote professionalism, operational effectiveness, leadership excellence and accountability (Gillespie, Sicard, & Gardner, 2007, Lanyon, 2007; McCabe, 2000; Pierce, 2007, Price, 1976; Thurman, 2004). Many of these emerging principles were incorporated into Fitzgerald's diagnosis and recommendations for comprehensive reform.

This chapter focuses on police-to-population ratios, civilianisation, recruitment, education and training, equity and diversity in relation to women and indigenous people, and promotion by merit. The analysis draws on official data from the QPS and a number of major external reports to assess the implementation of the Fitzgerald recommendations on police personnel management. Insights into implementation are provided by the detailed studies generated by the Queensland Public Sector Management Commission (PSMC) in 1993, the reviews of the QPS by the Service Delivery and Performance Commission in 2008, a review led by Sir Max Bingham (the 'Bingham Review') in 1996, the Criminal Justice Commission (CJC) review in 1994, and the 1998 review of recruitment by the Police Education Advisory Committee (PEAC).

Police-to-Population Ratio

A fundamental issue when examining human resource management in policing is whether there are sufficient officers to fulfil the police function. The implicit assumption in examining police numbers is that more police will result in decreased crime rates (Walker, 1999). While the impact of police strength on crime rates continues to be debated; some studies have been supportive, finding increased police numbers and decreased crime rates in specific circumstances and for certain crime types (Kovandzic & Sloan, 2002; Levitt, 1997; Marvell & Moody, 1996). Adequate police numbers are essential not just for crime reduction but for the investigation and prosecution of crimes, support for victims of crime, and emergency services. In that regard, the Fitzgerald Report concluded that Queensland had the lowest police-to-population ratio in Australia and that this partly underlay its lacklustre record in crime control. While the ratio in Queensland had demonstrated slight improvements between 1972 and 1988, it had not kept pace with its organisational counterparts in New South Wales and Victoria (Fitzgerald, 1989).

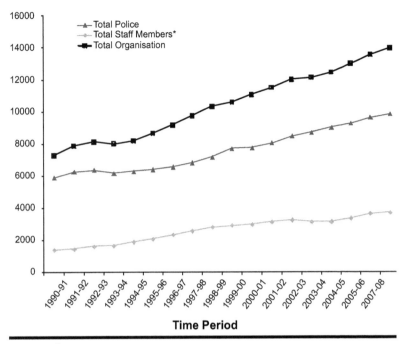

Figure 8.1[1]
Numbers of police and staff members, QPS, 1990–91 to 2007–08.
Note: *Staff members = Civilian staff
Source: *QPS Annual Reports, 1990–1991 to 2007–2008.*

The question of police strength was a major concern of subsequent reviews of the QPS. The Public Sector Management Commission Report (PSMC, 1993) noted that considerable efforts had been directed towards addressing the problem. The budget allocation to policing had increased by 53% in the period 1989–1990 to 1992–1993 (PSMC, 1993). However, despite these efforts, Queensland still had the lowest ratio (PSMC, 19931). It was concluded that budgeting for growth was too ad hoc and short-term (CJC, 1994; PSMC, 1993).

Submissions to the Bingham Review (1996) indicated there were still insufficient operational police and this was adversely affecting crime rates. The 2005 QPS Ten Year Staffing Plan indicated a projected strength of 9,106, involving an increase in police numbers from that time of 2,780 (Queensland Government, 2005; QPS Annual Reports 2000; 2002). Since then the number of Queensland police personnel has grown, as shown in Figure 8.1. The current strength, as reported in the 2007–2008 *Statistical Review* is 9,833 police officers and 4,115 staff members (QPS, 2008). Table 8.1 shows the police-to-population ratio of the QPS over the preceding 18 years. These data show the

Table 8.1
Police/Staff Member/Total Personnel-to-Population Ratio, QPS, 1990–1991 to 2007–2008

Time period	Police-to-population ratio	Total personnel-to-population ratio
1990–91	1:502	1:406
1991–92	1:478	1:404
1992–93	1:487*	1:400
1993–94	1:516	1:399
1994–95	1:527	1:396
1995–96	1:525	1:388
1996–97	1:523	1:375
1997–98	1:507	1:355
1998–99	1:490	1:340
1999–00	1:464	1:337
2000–01	1:467	1:328
2001–02	1:459	1:321
2002–03	1:446	1:315
2003–04	1:446	1:320
2004–05	1:440	1:318
2005–06	1:436	1:311
2006–07	1:429	1:305
2007–08	1:435*	1:306

Note: * Unexplained difference in ratio reported in QPS Statistical Review and/or Annual Report and actual calculation of Population divided by Number of Police Personnel. Figure represents authors' calculation of population and police personnel numbers as reported in the 'Summary Table' in QPS Statistical Review documents.

Source: QPS Statistical Review, 1990–1991 to 2007–2008.

QPS struggled with police numbers during the mid-1990s, but the overall trend since that time has been one of an increasing number of police per population. This trend is clearly illustrated in Figure 8.2.

Conjecture will remain in respect to the utility of using relative police strength to determine the adequacy of staffing. In addition, there are issues associated with how police are assigned to different regions. Nonetheless, the QPS has managed to achieve relative performance on this criterion in relation to interstate counterparts. Based on 2006 police numbers, Queensland had a police-to-population ratio of 1:436, compared to New South Wales of 1:468 and Victoria of 1:462 (Dean & Thorne, 20091). Most recently, the QPS police-to-population has been touted as equal to that of the national average (QPS, 2008).

Civilianisation

Since the 1980s there has been a commonly held view that police should employ a strategy for 'the use of suitably qualified civilian staff in positions not requiring police powers, skills or experience' (CJC, 1994, p. 98; also

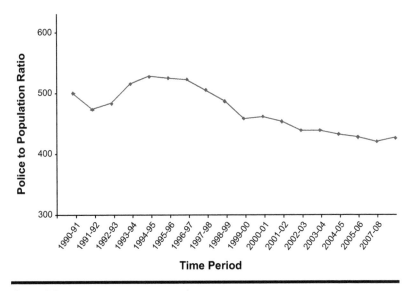

Figure 8.2

Police-to-population ratio, QPS, 1990–1991 to 2007–2008.

Source: *QPS Statistical Review, 1990–1991 to 2007–2008.*

Crank, 1989; Dick & Metcalfe, 2001). In theory, civilianisation allows police to more actively engage in operational, as opposed to administrative tasks; it provides a method of disjoining a closed culture, and facilitates a 'multi-disciplinary approach' to policing (Bingham, 1996, p. 79; also Dick & Metcalfe, 2001; PSMC, 1993). These elements of civilianisation were identified in the Fitzgerald Report (1989), along with the finding that police were often assigned to administrative positions as punishment or because of poor performance.

The Fitzgerald Report (1989) found that in the preceding 15 years the percentage of non-sworn employees in the Police had remained around 16% of personnel. It was recommended that a policy be adopted of replacing police officers with civilians in those positions of a primarily administrative and specialist nature. The PSMC Report (1993) concluded, however, that while some progress had been achieved, civilianisation had stalled and, in some cases, been reversed. The Police Commissioner attributed this to resource constraints, and conceded that while 90 police positions were civilianised in the 1989–1990 period, none had been civilianised in 1990–1991 (QPS, 1991).

Recommendations 26 and 31 of the Bingham Review (1996) called for greater efforts in civilianisation. It was concluded that between 700 and 1,000

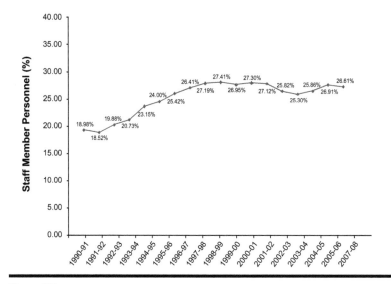

Figure 8.3

Percentage of staff members to total personnel, QPS, 1990–1991 to 2007–2008.

Note: A number of staff member positions were transferred from the QPS to a shared service provider, human resource management function during 2003–04 and 2005–06.

Source: *QPS Statistical Review, 1990–1991 to 2007–2008.*

positions within the QPS could be filled by civilians (Bingham, 1996), which would constitute a civilian target of 20.07% of total personnel. As evidenced in Figure 8.3, by the middle of 2005 the QPS exceeded this target, with a civilian percentage of 25.3%. Figure 8.3 shows solid gains in the 1990s, but since the late-1990s civilian numbers appear to have plateaued around 26–27%. The most recent analysis of the QPS civilianisation efforts concluded that the growth of civilianisation has not kept pace with the growth of police numbers (Service Delivery and Performance Commission, 2008). To provide an international comparison, Loveday (2005) reports that civilians comprise around one third of personnel employed in police organisations in England and Wales.

Following the Bingham Review (1996), the QPS Annual Reports for 1996–1997 and 1997–1998 stated that priority was being given to civilianisation, particularly in communication centres, computer training and roster and property offices. During 2004–2005 a civilian illicit laboratory investigation team was established to assist police investigators (QPS, 2005). In respect to the status of civilians, terminology was changed from 'civilians' to 'staff members', and a Staff Member Training Development Program was introduced as an essential element of human resource development (CJC,

1996). In response to a Bingham recommendation the QPS also established a Career Planning Unit and a Career Planning Officer Network (QPS, 2002). Interestingly, the 2008 report released by the Service Delivery and Performance Commission (2008) indicated that despite these efforts, developmental opportunities for staff members, such as training, continue to be limited in comparison to those provided to police.

The Service Delivery and Performance Commission's (2008) analysis of the QPS civilianisation program indicates that while progress has been made, a formal evaluation of the QPS civilianisation program is needed. Further, it recommended that the QPS develop a civilianisation plan which is regularly monitored and evaluated by the QPS Senior Executive Team.

Recruitment

One aspect of human resource management that has undergone significant change in the QPS is the recruitment of sworn officers. In 1989, at the time of the Fitzgerald Report, there were two entry programs into Queensland Police — the cadet and probationary programs. Cadets were Grade 12 graduates, and probationary recruits were between 18 and 40 years old who had completed Grade 10 (Fitzgerald, 1989, p. 245). Selection criteria covered height, education, intelligence, character, and health and fitness. The selection process involved written applications and tests and a panel assessment. There was a quota on the number of women. Fitzgerald (1989) criticised the selection process as being overly concerned with physical criteria and he argued that lack of maturity underlay high cadet drop-out rates. He observed that:

> Suitability for police work is assessed subjectively by a panel. Only limited formally validated instruments or tests directly applicable to police work are available to assist them. (Fitzgerald, 1989, p. 245)

Integrity screening was deemed to be overly reliant on referee reports. In addition, Fitzgerald (1989) noted that lack of lateral recruitment further cemented the insularity that buttressed corruption and incompetence. He recommended that more mature, tertiary qualified applicants should be sought who would support the community policing and social service orientation of the reform program.

The reforms to recruitment during and after the inquiry, while apparently sincere in their application, were less than optimal. On the positive side, height, weight, age and sex restrictions were removed. Selection criteria placed greater value on maturity, tertiary education and work experience. More thorough inquiries were made about the integrity of recruits, and community representatives were introduced onto interview panels. The cadet and probationary systems were replaced with one entry system. Many of these changes were endorsed by the PSMC (1993) review, although it found that changes to lateral entry had been implemented in an ad hoc manner and consideration needed to be given to more training credits for lateral entrants (CJC, 1993). However, a later CJC report found that screening of officers from other jurisdictions needed to be tightened to ensure behaviour problems were not being imported into Queensland (CJC, 1997).

The 1996 Bingham review also endorsed many of the changes, but questioned the validity of some of the entry tests being used and recommended a subcommittee of the Police Education and Advisory Council (PEAC) review all aspects of recruitment. The result was a substantial report, *Police for the Future: Review of Recruitment and Selection for the Queensland Police Service* (PEAC, 1998), which matched QPS practices against the best practice methods available in the scientific literature and a model system of general duties policing.

Police for the Future found that work experience was given too much weight vis-à-vis education, and that three psychometric tests — the gruelling 'mechanical reasoning', 'space relations' and 'numerical ability' tests — had poor predictive ability and should be abandoned. It also asserted that the 16PF psychological assessment instrument should be integrated into the selection process. A recommendation was made for making the interview procedure more structured and task-relevant. Interviewers needed to be trained, to be consistent in the questions they asked, but also to probe more deeply where appropriate. The report supported the fairly rigorous integrity checks in place, including exclusion for most criminal offences. However, it also suggested a greater degree of forgiveness for minor offences; and the addition of drug tests, financial checks, direct follow-up with all referees to verify their status and assertions, and creation of an 'integrity committee' to review candidates where ambiguity was flagged. The selection committee itself was deemed to operate with inconsistent information on candidates and no minimum cut-off. A recommendation was made that committee members be trained, that information standards and cut-offs be applied, and that the committee operate more democratically and provide reasons for its decisions.

The PEAC Report (1998) was the launchpad for a more sophisticated recruitment system that was occupationally valid and consistent with the Fitzgerald vision for police professionalism. The report also argued there should be a system for ongoing evaluation of recruitment processes. This does not appear to have eventuated — certainly not in terms of any public reporting of detailed findings (see CJC, 2001, pp. 20–21). The recent Service Delivery and Performance Commission Report (2008) also did not evaluate the implementation of the PEAC Report (1998), nor the relationship between education and police integrity. In fact it endorsed a move back to reduced tertiary qualifications for recruits — citing problems attracting sufficient applicants willing to serve outside south-east Queensland — and identified a need for more efficient processing of applicants.

Education and Training

The changes that occurred in police education are the subject of chapter 10 in this book, and a limited assessment is undertaken here. Fitzgerald identified a close association between the police culture of corruption and mismanagement and the absence of tertiary education in the police profile. He sought to apply research indicating that better educated police were more efficient and had more of a service orientation (Fitzgerald, 1989; see also Trofymowych, 2008). The report noted that:

> Police need more education to cope with their increasingly complex role. Officers should be encouraged to undertake higher education in colleges of advanced education and other tertiary institutions, along with students from other disciplines. There should be a long-term move to recruit more graduates. (Fitzgerald, 1989, p. 365)

Despite this, the summary recommendations did not prescribe a place for tertiary education in recruitment and training, nor in in-service training. Presumably this was part of the brief of 'a professional unit to be established within the Criminal Justice Commission', charged with reviewing 'all aspects of police education and training' (Fitzgerald, 1989, p. 365) — a recommendation that was not implemented.

Fitzgerald's recommendations regarding tertiary education were initially addressed through a dual system, operating from 1991 to 1993, whereby recruits attended one of two universities for one semester before academy training. At the end of the program they received an Advanced Certificate in Policing. At the universities, recruits studied ethics, law, social issues and communication; followed by a second semester of applied training at the academy (PSMC, 1993). The university component was intended to address Fitzgerald's idea that courses in criminal justice and social sciences should be 'attended by police along with people from other disciplines, to ensure the breadth of experience essential to the study and understanding of human behaviour' (Fitzgerald, 1989, p. 250).

The PSMC (1993) review found the dual system was costing the Police Service too much in payments to the universities, and evaluations by the CJC found the Advanced Certificate was not imparting sufficient practical skills (CJC, 1993). In any case, contrary to Fitzgerald, the university component did not involve study with non-police students nor did it include studies in broader criminal justice areas. A new system was introduced in 1994 that put recruits back entirely in the police academy, while maintaining the weight given to tertiary education in recruit selection.

Table 8.2
Stage 1: Minimum Application Requirements, QPS, 2009

Full-time employment experience	Required study
Less than 3 years employment	The successful completion of 3 or more full-time semesters of accredited study (or equivalent) within a Bachelor degree course
	or
	a completed accredited Diploma.
Between 3 and 5 years employment	Minimum of 400 hours of Diploma-level study (comprising at least 200 hours of level IV subjects or higher)
	or
	8 subjects of a Bachelor degree.
More than 5 years employment	Minimum of 200 hours of Diploma-level study (level IV subjects or higher)
	or
	4 subjects of a Bachelor degree.

Source: QPS, 2009b, p. 2.

The PEAC Report *Police for the future* cited QPS and CJC research showing that higher education levels of recruits correlated with higher academy performance, and endorsed the general association made by Fitzgerald between education and positive police attributes (PEAC, 1998; also Burke, 1993). However, the issue of graduate recruitment was not directly addressed. The recommendations, instead, focused on giving more weight to tertiary education and downgrading the weight given to work experience. The current educational and work experience criteria, based on the PEAC Report, are summarised in Table 8.2. The Service also introduced a Competency Acquisition Program linked to pay point progression, a tertiary level Executive Development Program, and a Management Development Program by distance education.

The educational profile of police has changed significantly since Fitzgerald. The PSMC (1993)review found the percentage of recruits with a tertiary degree increased from 5% in 1991 to 40% in early-1993. From 1993 to 2000 the percentage of recruits who had a completed degree at the time of commencement at the Academy was around 25%. On average, a further 25% had at least half a degree and a further 30% had a completed diploma (2–3 years study). Consequently, from 1993 to 2000, a consistent average of 80% of recruits had either a completed diploma or degree or a considerable portion of one (Jones, Jones, & Prenzler, 2003).

The present system has a number of advantages and disadvantages. On the one hand, a majority of recruits have some tertiary education while police retain flexibility and a wider pool of applicants than graduate recruitment might allow. The provisions also tend to keep out younger, more violence prone, males; with the average recruit age above 25 (CJC, 1997). The vague Fitzgerald recommendation regarding a 'long-term move to recruit more graduates' has been fulfilled. At the same time, the different entry requirements mean recruits lack a common foundational knowledge in those disciplines singled out by Fitzgerald, including 'sociology, psychology, communication, values and ethics' (1989, p. 249). Furthermore, as noted above, PEAC (1998) did not produce any follow-up reports on the state of police education and recruitment, including any analyses of the content of academy training.

The diverse profile of Queensland police recruits in terms of background knowledge is reflective of a wider problem in police recruitment and education in Australia. Fitzgerald's vision for a large role for tertiary education in police professional development has been taken up in quite different ways around the nation, including by full integration of police training into universities in some cases (Trofymowych, 2008; Wimshurst & Ransley, 2007). There are, however, no common standards in contextual knowledge; and each jurisdiction operates independently of the others, with quite different models of tertiary involvement.

Equity and Diversity: Women

Most jurisdictions in Australia introduced female police during World War I (1914–1918). Queensland avoided the trend until State Cabinet forced the Police to accept female officers in 1931 (Prenzler, Jones, & Ronken, 2001). Numbers were, however, kept to a handful until the reforming Commissioner Ray Whitrod increased the female intake in the early-1970s. The number of women peaked at around 10% across officers and recruits. In response to Police Union alarm over women taking men's jobs, in 1978 Commissioner Terry Lewis (later jailed for corruption as a result of the Fitzgerald investigations) introduced a quota on female recruits and reinstated a marriage bar.

The Fitzgerald Report (1989) criticised sex discrimination in recruitment, and associated the lack of women in the Force with the culture of isolation and cynicism that fostered corruption. Fitzgerald (1989) reported that women made up only 5.4% of police officers. Women were only permitted entry as probationaries, and the number selected for each intake was between 5% and 12%. This contrasted with an average applicant pool that was 25% female. The quota system was attributed to a misconception that training women was a waste of time because they were more likely to resign than men — whereas over the preceding five years women who resigned

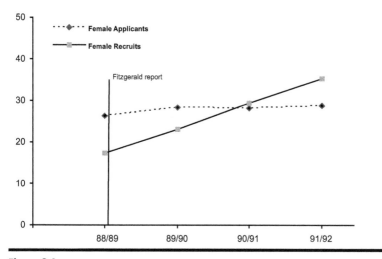

Figure 8.4
Percentage of female applicants and female recruits, QPS, 1988–1989 to 1991–1992.
Source: Prenzler, Jones, & Ronkin, 2001, p. 55.

from the Force had comparatively longer tenure than men who resigned. On the question of promotion of women, Fitzgerald could not identify a clear case of discrimination.

Fitzgerald's (1989) recommendations introduced an open system of non-discriminatory appointment by merit. An enlarged role for women was also envisaged as part of positive cultural change towards greater integrity. Figure 8.4 shows how in 1988–1989 women made up 26% of applicants but only 17% of recruits. Within four years a dramatic turnaround had occurred, with women making up 29% of applicants and 35% of recruits. A message of support for equity was given by Commissioner Noel Newnham with the promotion of five women to Inspector in 1990 and one woman to Superintendent in 1992. The Fitzgerald reforms were then overtaken by anti-discrimination legislation in 1992. With the introduction of the Queensland *Equal Opportunity in Public Employment Act* in 1993 more active measures were required to encourage equality. By 1993 Queensland had caught up to the national average of 12% of women police, and recruitment of women was well above the national average of 22% (Prenzler, 1994). Apart from increased opportunities to move up the ranks, women were also winning more places in specialist squads, and moving further out from Brisbane into regional areas.

The increases in the number of female recruits provoked renewed Union alarm, including uncorroborated claims of assaults against policewomen and threats to the safety of male police. When Frank O'Gorman, Assistant Commissioner Personnel and Training, retired in 1993 he was replaced in an acting capacity by Assistant Commissioner Greg Early. The stage was set for a backlash against women. Police Union President John O'Gorman argued that small female officers were jeopardising safety and called for the reintroduction of height and weight restrictions. At the academy, the officer in charge of physical skills devised a new 'physical competency test' (PCT), introduced into recruitment in 1994. Applicants were required to complete a military-style obstacle course test within a set time. The main effect was to exclude hundreds of female applicants and scores of less agile males in the six years it operated in different forms (Prenzler, 1996; see Figure 8.5).

The validity of the PCT was questioned in the Bingham Review (1996), which referred the issue of physical requirements to the PEAC subcommittee reviewing recruit selection. The PEAC Report concluded that the test had no job-related validity and was hypocritical given there were no requirements for police to maintain fitness (PEAC, 1998, chapter 10). Following the committee's recommendations the test was abandoned in 1999 and replaced with a medical screening test — despite a rearguard effort by police to save the test through a $100,000 consultancy to a university exercise science department (QPS, 1998). The whole fiasco demonstrated how lacking senior police

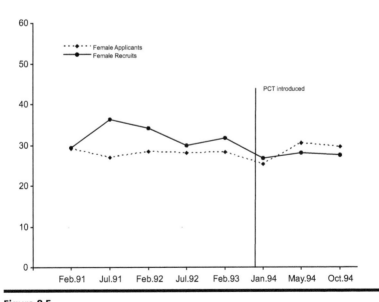

Figure 8.5
Percentages of female applicants and female recruits per Intake, QPS, February 1991 to October 1994.
Source: Prenzler, 1996, p. 318.

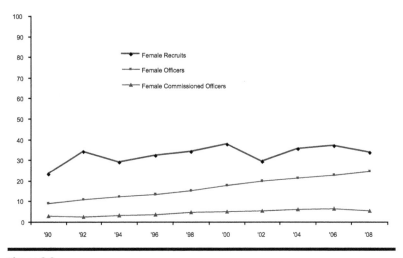

Figure 8.6

Percentages of female recruits, female sworn officers and female commissioned officers, QPS, 1989–1990 to 2007–2008.

Source: QPS Statistical Reviews.
Note: For 1990, Female commissioned officers include 'commissioned officers and managers'.

managers were in the kind of scientific approach to recruitment envisaged by Fitzgerald (1989) and the necessity of external controls to force police to comply with evidence-based policy.

Overall, QPS equity reports have been very mixed. An evaluation of the 1996 report found some positive data on progress for women (Prenzler, 1998). For example, figures showed that 18.1% of promotions went to women in the preceding 18 months — above the percentage of female sworn officers of 13.4%. Sexual harassment was identified as a problem but there was insufficient detail on harassment and discrimination complaints. Data were also missing in areas such as female application and progression rates in recruitment, and male/female deployment figures. A model set of strategies would have given more emphasis to targeted promotion campaigns and flexible employment opportunities, with more attention to the problem of female attrition due to family reasons (Bingham, 1996). Figure 8.6 covers the period since Fitzgerald and shows the proportion of female officers increasing at a snail's pace, with recruitment stuck around one-third and the very small proportion of commissioned officers increasing very slowly. For 2007–2008 the figures are 33.6% recruits, 24.7% all officers 5.6% commissioned officers. These proportions have been consistent with national averages for many years (e.g., AIC, 2006).

Equity and Diversity: Indigenous People

The Fitzgerald Report (1989) did not mention Indigenous staffing but the employment of Indigenous officers was consistent with the recommendations regarding equity and community policing, and became a significant goal after the introduction of the 1993 *Equal Opportunity in Public Employment Act*. The 1993 CJC review of recruitment and selection estimated that less than 0.5% of police personnel were of Indigenous heritage. However, the PSMC (1993) expressed support for the introduction in 1992 of a special entry program whereby potential Indigenous recruits completed a bridging program at certificate level at technical colleges in Brisbane and north Queensland.

A revised Aboriginal and Torres Strait Justice Entry Program (JEP) commenced in 2003 with a stipend paid to trainees and the training conducted at the two academies (Brisbane and Townsville). Up to mid-2008, out of 74 persons who began the program, 43 have been sworn in as constables (QPS, 2008a). What is lacking, however, are comprehensive statistics and reports on all aspects of the employment of Indigenous persons in the QPS. The most recent census in 2006 reported a figure of 2.3% Indigenous 'policemen' in Queensland, which can be compared to an estimated Indigenous population of 2.7% in the state in the same year (Productivity Commission, 2008, Table 6A.19). The figures, however, do not distinguish between regular sworn officers and 'Indigenous liaison officers' (QPS, 2009a) or 'Queensland ATSI Police' (QPS, 2008b, p. 140).

Promotion by Merit

The Fitzgerald Report (1989) initiated a review of the police promotion system. For promotion, officers were required to have specified experience, undertake appropriate training courses, pass mandated examinations, make an application for vacancies and then be assessed by a panel (Fitzgerald, 1989). Fitzgerald concluded, however, that performance of the officer was not given substantial weighting in the decision for promotion and that seniority appeared to be the predominant criterion. The Fitzgerald recommendations therefore emphasised the need to institute promotion by merit — a principle subsequently enshrined in the *Police Service Administration Act 1990*. The Fitzgerald Report also recommended that all vacancies be advertised and more senior police positions be advertised externally; that selection panels be regionally based, and that external education and performance appraisals serve as important indicators of merit. The report also recommended well-developed position descriptions be used as a method of assessing the suitability of applicants.

The implementation of this new system of promotion was somewhat difficult for the QPS. It was noted by Commissioner Newnham in the QPS

Annual Report 1990–91 that a promotion-by-merit system had been introduced throughout the police organisation; however, difficulties in implementation had been faced due to lack of understanding of the process and its conflict with the pre-existing system that was based on seniority. It was concluded that the new process required changes by both candidates and interviewers. However, despite these difficulties Commissioner Newnham (QPS Annual Report, 1990–91) stated that the changes were increasingly gaining credibility and would in the longer term ensure a better functioning human resource management system.

Submissions to the Bingham Review (1996) indicated that progress had occurred in regard to merit, but that officers lacked confidence in the new system. Particular concerns included a perception that applicants from within a region received preferential treatment, inconsistency in selection panel decisions, hostility to 'rank jumping', and an absence of common competencies at each rank. The recommendations that followed involved the introduction of a pre-qualifying program for promotions to sergeant and above, and the development of in-service education that focused on management, supervisory skills, law and procedures (Bingham, 1996). These latter points were implemented, in part, through the Management Development Program.

There was also a reform of selection panels and the appeals process. Based on recommendations, an accreditation process was introduced for panel convenors, and convenors were required to be external to the region where the vacancy occurred (Bingham, 1996). Independent community members and gender representation were also introduced into panels (Bingham, 1996). The CJC took over the appeals process, with an independent Review Commissioner who convenes the review process (CJC, 2005). In addition, in 1998 the QPS adopted an assessment development centre model for promotion to inspector (QPS, 1999).

A survey of QPS officers was conducted in 1998 in order to provide a measure of officer attitudes towards the promotional system. This baseline research (CJC, 1998) found that officers believed that cronyism, corruption and nepotism were major problems; that selection panels were inconsistent and there were too many delays; that education was overvalued and seniority undervalued; and that there was still a problem with bias towards applicants from the home region. A second review by the CJC in 2000 found officers still held negative perceptions towards the promotion process. However, in respect to consistency, bias and fairness, the responses from officers were comparatively more positive than those surveyed earlier (CJC, 2000). Generally, attitudes towards the assessment development centres were positive (CJC, 2000).

Reflecting on criticisms of the QPS promotion system in pre-Fitzgerald times, specifically the need for the promotion system to be fair and accountable, it is interesting to note the conclusions drawn by the Service Delivery and Performance Commission (2008). It was concluded that the current promotion system actually allows police to lodge an appeal against a promotion decision without substantial justification. While this ensures that process is conducted in a transparent and accountable manner, it has created substantial work for promotion panel convenors and hence has moved the promotion panel function to one characterised by over-complicated bureaucracy. The current focus on accountability and fairness has significantly altered, since Fitzgerald's recommendations, the procedural foundation on which the QPS promotion system is based.

The recommendations and reviews that have been undertaken by the QPS reflect the difficulties in developing and implementing a system of promotion, particularly within policing. This is reflected by Findlay (2004), who concludes that it is often difficult for those outside of the conventional police culture to understand that promotion-by-merit is a relatively new concept in policing and is significantly hampered by 'old school' police. Therefore, it is perhaps not surprising that while significant reforms have been instituted in the pursuit of a fairer and more equitable promotional system, QPS officers remain largely negative about the process. The CJC (2000) noted that despite the implementation of reforms the persistency of negativity of officers towards the system highlights the seemingly impenetrable attitudinal barriers to acceptance of the system. Undoubtedly, the QPS has significantly changed its approach to promotion since the Fitzgerald Inquiry. While negative attitudes among officers remain, continual improvements to the system and/or its acceptance must continue. However, it may be concluded that the system that is currently used, albeit not perfect, represents a giant leap in progress from the system of seniority that existed 20 years ago.

Conclusions

The QPS appears to have made considerable progress in implementing and maintaining the Fitzgerald reforms in human resource management. After a slow start it now has a police-to-population ratio that is equal to the national average, and the proportion of civilians has been increased. Many of the old biases have also been swept away from the recruitment process, which, to the extent that the 1998 PEAC recommendations have been implemented, appears to employ a more valid set of criteria than in the past. Higher education also has a much more prominent place in the profile of recruits and serving officers. Over the long term, there has been a steady improvement in the representation of women, although attrition and lower female recruit numbers limit the growth of sworn female officers and the pool available for promotion to higher ranks. Considerable efforts appear to have been put into recruiting Indigenous people.

Since the Fitzgerald Inquiry the QPS has also moved to institute merit in promotion. Establishing a system that is widely acceptable as fair and that selects the best people for the job is difficult in any occupation. The external reviews that have prompted further improvements of the promotion system reflect the need for regular evaluation. Unfortunately, the lessons from the evolution of the promotion system in the QPS appear not to have held across issues of recruitment and equity. The QPS has not been good at evaluating and improving its own systems, nor has it been good at providing information on the public record about what it does including performance outcomes. External agencies with significant capacity for research are needed to maintain a constant watch on police processes and drive a philosophy of continuous improvement.

Endnote

1 This is an original figure that was created by the authors of the chapter. The source indicates that the data used to construct the figure was sourced from data available in the QPS Annual Reports. Also, original figures and tables that have been created by the authors from QPS Annual Reports and Statistical Reviews include Figure 8.1, Figure 8.2, Figure 8.3, Figure 8.6, Table 8.1, and Table 8.2

References

Australian Institute of Criminology. (2009). *Composition of Australian Police services as at 30 June 2006.* Retrieved March 30, 2009, from aic.gov.au/stats/cjs/police/pol2006/html.

Bingham, M. (1996). *Review of the Queensland Police Service.* Brisbane, Australia: QPS Review Committee.

Burke, D. (1993). *Police recruit selection: Decision-making for success.* Unpublished master's thesis, University of Central Queensland, Australia.

Criminal Justice Commission. (CJC). (1993). *Recruitment and education in the Queensland Police Service: A Review.* Brisbane, Australia: Author.

Criminal Justice Commission. (CJC). (1994). *Implementation of reform within the Queensland Police Service: The Response of the Queensland Police Service to the Fitzgerald Inquiry recommendations.* Brisbane, Australia: GoPrint.

Criminal Justice Commission. (CJC). (1996). *Police recruit selection – Predictors of academy performance.* Brisbane, Australia: Author.

Criminal Justice Commission. (CJC). (1997). *Integrity in the Queensland Police Service: Implementation and impact of the Fitzgerald Inquiry reforms.* Brisbane, Australia: Author.

Criminal Justice Commission. (CJC). (1998). *Queensland police officers' perceptions of the promotion and transfer system: Results of 1998 baseline survey.* Brisbane, Australia: Author.

Criminal Justice Commission. (CJC). (2000). *Queensland Police Service promotion and transfer system.* Brisbane, Australia: Author.

Criminal Justice Commission. (CJC). (2001). *Integrity in the Queensland Police Service: QPS reform update.* Brisbane, Australia: Author.

Criminal Justice Commission. (CJC). (2005). *The review process: An Outline for QPS officers.* Retrieved March 30, 2009 from http://www.cmc.qld.gov.au/data/portal/00000005/content/51234001132635969543.pdf

Dean, G., & Thorne, C. (2009). Organisation and management of police. In R. Broadhurst & S. Davies (Eds.), *Policing in context: An introduction to police work in Australia* (pp: 49–68). Melbourne, Australia: Oxford University Press.

Dick, G., & Metcalfe, B. (2001). Managerial factors and organisational commitment: A comparative study of police officers and civilian staff. *The International Journal of Public Sector Management, 14(2),* 111–128.

Findlay, M. (2004). *Introducing policing: Challenges for police and Australian communities.* Melbourne, Australia: Oxford University Press.

Fitzgerald, G. (1989). *Report of a commission pursuant to orders in council.* Brisbane, Australia: Goprint.

Jones, D., Jones, L., & Prenzler, T. (2005). Tertiary education, commitment and turnover in police work. *Police Practice and Research: An International Journal, 6*(1), 49–63.

Kovandzic, T., & Sloan, J (2002). Police levels and crime rates revisited: A county-level analysis from Florida (1980–1998). *Journal of Criminal Justice, 30,* 65–76.

Lanyon, I.J. (2007). Professionalisation of policing in Australia: The implications for police managers. In M. Mitchell & J. Casey (Eds.), *Police leadership and management.* Sydney, Australia: The Federation Press.

Loveday, B. (2005). *The police modernization program in England and Wales: A reform too far?* Paper presented at the Annual Meeting of the American Society of Criminology, Royal York, Toronto. Retrieved March 29, 2009, from http://www.allacademic.com/meta/p32843_index.html

McCabe, K.A. (2000). Accreditation: Agency professionalization. In W.G. Doerner & M.L. Dantzker (Eds.), *Contemporary police organization and management: Issues and Trends.* Boston: Butterworth Heinemann.

Police Education and Advisory Council. (1998). *Police for the future: Review of recruitment and selection for the Queensland Police Service.* Brisbane: Criminal Justice Commission.

Prenzler, T (1994) Women in Australian policing: An historical overview. *Journal of Australian Studies.* 42, 78–88.

Prenzler, T. (1996). Rebuilding the walls? The impact of police pre-entry physical ability tests on female applicants. *Current Issues in Criminal Justice, 7*(3), 314–324.

Prenzler, T. (1998). Gender integration in Australian policing. *International Journal of Police Science and Management, 1*(3), 241–259.

Prenzler, T, Jones, L., & Ronken, C. (2001). *Journey to equality: An illustrated history of Women in the Queensland Police, 1931–2001.* Brisbane, Australia: Queensland Police Service.

Price, B.R. (1976). Police administrators' ambivalence towards professionalism. *Criminal Justice Review, 1*(13), 13–20.

Productivity Commission. (2008). *Review of government services.* Canberra, Australia: Productivity Commission.

Public Sector Management Commission. (1993). *Review of the Queensland Police Service.* Brisbane, Australia: GoPrint.

Queensland Government. (2005). *Budget, 2004–05.* Brisbane, Australia: GoPrint.

Queensland Police Service. (QPS). (1991). *Annual report, 1990–91.* Brisbane, Australia: Author.

Queensland Police Service. (QPS). (1993). *Equal employment opportunity plan 1993/94 and evaluation report 1992/3*. Brisbane, Australia: Author.

Queensland Police Service. (QPS). (1998). *Annual report, 1997–98*. Brisbane, Australia: Author.

Queensland Police Service. (QPS). (1999). *Annual report, 1998–99*. Brisbane, Australia: Author.

Queensland Police Service. (QPS). (2000). *Annual report, 1999–00*. Brisbane, Australia: Author.

Queensland Police Service. (QPS). (2002). *Annual report, 2001–02*. Brisbane, Australia: Author.

Queensland Police Service. (QPS). (2005). *Annual report, 2004–05*. Brisbane, Australia: Author.

Queensland Police Service. (QPS). (2008a). *Annual report, 2007–08*. Brisbane, Australia: Author.

Queensland Police Service. (QPS). (2008b). *Statistical review, 2007–08*. Brisbane, Australia: Author.

Queensland Police Service. (QPS). (2009a). *Police liaison officers*. Retrieved on 29 March 2009 from http://www.police.qld.gov.au/join/plo/default.htm

Queensland Police Service. (QPS). (2009b). Stage 1: Minimum application requirements. Retrieved March 24, 2009, from http://www.police.qld.gov.au/join/recruitment/selectionProcess/stageOne.htm#education

Service Delivery and Performance Commission. (2008). *Report on the Service Delivery and Performance Management Review of the Queensland Police Service*. Brisbane, Australia: Queensland Government.

Thurman, Q.C. (2004). Preparing police officers for success in the twenty-first century. In Q.C. Thurman & J. Zhao (Eds.), *Contemporary policing: Controversies, challenges and solutions* (165–177). Los Angeles, CA: Roxbury.

Trofymowych, D. (2008). Police education past and present. *Flinders Journal of Law Reform, 10*, 419–433.

Walker, S. (1999). *The police in America: An introduction*. Boston: McGraw-Hill.

Wimshurst, K., & Ransley, J. (2007). Police education and the university sector. *Journal of Criminal Justice Education, 18*(1), 106–122.

9

'Unusual Industrial Organisations': Police Unions, Fitzgerald and Reform

Richard Evans

In February 2009, the combined executive of the Police Federation of Australia (PFA), representing between them every Australian police union, held meetings with the Prime Minister, Kevin Rudd, and the leader of the Federal Opposition, Malcolm Turnbull. As the chief executive officer of the PFA, Mark Burgess, said:

> I don't think there'd be many groups in Australia that could confidently say that they've met with the Prime Minister and the leader of the Opposition in the one day ... you could probably count on one hand the number of groups that have that particular influence. (PFA, 2009a)

The PFA represents a combined membership of some 52,000 police officers across Australia. As a relatively new organisation — the PFA was formed in 1998 — such a level of access to high levels of government is indeed impressive. It is a clear demonstration, if any was needed, that police unions are powerful.

The work of the PFA also shows that police unionism has changed.

In 1970, Ray Whitrod was appointed commissioner of the Queensland Police Force. He attempted to make promotion in the force dependent on merit, which was already departmental policy, and introduce training in literacy and numeracy. The Queensland Police Union of Employees (QPU) responded with fury. It leaked stories to the media about Whitrod 'destroying the morale of the force', and continually campaigned against him. The union position was supported by Premier Joh Bjelke-Petersen, who memorably declared that police did not need to be Rhodes scholars (Whitrod, 2001).

In 2009, the PFA's submission to the National Police Audit argued in support of a national police registration scheme and 'further professionalization of policing'. It suggested that:

> ... there is a need for a police workforce planning study to be undertaken in a national, coordinated, and sector-wide manner. The study would examine both current and longer-term issues ... and would leverage previous research. (PFA, 2009a)

A police union advocating further training and research is something about which Ray Whitrod could only have dreamed. It is impossible to quantify the degree to which this change is attributable to the impact of the *Commission of Inquiry into Possible Illegal Activities and Associated Police Misconduct* (hereafter referred to the Fitzgerald Inquiry), but that the Fitzgerald Inquiry was important is, I would argue, beyond dispute. The depth and reach of this change is, however, still in question.

This chapter argues that the Fitzgerald Inquiry, by effectively exposing the ills of the police culture, presented a profound challenge to the QPU, and to other police unions in Australia. The response to this challenge has been mixed. Police unions remain effective industrial organisations, able to protect and improve the material wellbeing of their members. Some commitment to reform and responsible engagement with police management and outside stakeholders has also been displayed. However, crude and excessively militant campaigns, especially in response to court proceedings affecting police, continue to damage the standing of police and their unions. The public statements of some senior union officials continue to frustrate the Fitzgerald vision of accountable policing, founded on integrity and the rule of law.

Police Unions in Australia

Police unions have a long history in Australia. The first police union was formed in 1911 in South Australia; every other state had followed by 1923, with the two Commonwealth Territory Police Services unionised by 1945 (Fleming & Lafferty, 2001). Conservative commentators did worry that police unions would lead to a radical and hence unreliable force, but these fears proved groundless. The general experience of Australian police unions was that they fitted without much fuss into the system of industrial arbitration, that peculiarly Australian institution of quasi-courts which controlled wages and conditions until the 1990s. Through arbitration, police unions were able to pursue and win badly needed improvements in pay and conditions (Finnane, 2008).

Unable to strike, police unions used alternative strategies, from quiet lobbying to overt political campaigns, to place pressure on state governments (Fleming & Lafferty, 2001). There were periods of turbulence during the

1930s and 1940s, especially in New South Wales, but by the 1950s police unions had become an established part of policing in Australia. From the 1960s they were increasingly able to offer their members a valuable service: access to a legal defence fund for advice and representation should members be charged with a disciplinary or criminal offence (Finnane, 2002). In this period, too, police unions began to be more militant and more politically active in their pursuit of industrial objectives (Lewis, 1999).

With the consolidation of their position, however, police unions did face tensions in their role. Mark Finnane (2002) identifies one of the dilemmas of police unionism: protecting police from harsh and arbitrary discipline also tends to frustrate justified and necessary discipline. The success of unions in challenging the autocratic power of police management thus had the effect of reducing police accountability.

When, from the 1970s, pressure grew for police reform, unions were consistent in their opposition. In Queensland and elsewhere, police unions steadfastly and often vehemently defended the status quo (Smith, 1994).

The tendency for police unions to become part of the policing power structure, rather than a force for change, has been attributed to the 'iron law of oligarchy', the almost universal tendency for organisations to become bureaucratic and self-serving (Marks & Fleming, 2006). It is contended here that a more useful approach is Sherman's model of institutional capture (Sherman, 1978). By this view, if an organisation has control of important resources, outside interests will attempt to 'capture' it, and misuse those resources for other ends. For example, in the city-based police and government structure common in the United States, organised crime interests attempted to and often succeeded in gaining control over key city institutions, including the police and the district attorney's office (Carte & Carte, 1975).

Because police unions enjoy access to senior government officials and politicians are able to openly campaign on political and 'law and order' issues, and have control of significant financial resources including legal defence funds, police unions were obvious targets for organisational capture. And this is what occurred, in Queensland and elsewhere.

The Union Before Fitzgerald

Ray Whitrod's appointment as Queensland's police commissioner stands as one of the more unusual decisions made the Bjelke-Petersen government. Bjelke-Petersen had known, at least since 1964 and almost certainly much longer, that there was endemic and systematic corruption in the Queensland Police Force (QPF; Whitrod, 2001). Whitrod was well-known as a strict disciplinarian of high personal integrity, so conflict was inevitable.

As discussed above, Whitrod almost immediately clashed with the QPU over promotion by merit and education programs. He also tried to introduce a system to record details of paid informers; to allow regular transfer of police between regions; improve the level of supervision at regional and district level; and, introduce a course in 'Police Arts and Science'. The union resisted every one of these initiatives and derided Whitrod as 'an academic' who lacked practical police experience (Fitzgerald, 1989).

The union executive — all of whom were sergeants with Irish Catholic backgrounds, known as the 'Green Mafia' — used their direct access to the Premier and other senior ministers to denigrate Whitrod (Whitrod, 2001). By 1976, Bjelke-Petersen was openly intervening in operational police affairs, particularly in relation to internal investigations and discipline. When Terence Lewis was appointed Assistant Commissioner, Whitrod's position became untenable and he resigned (Lewis, 1999).

The union was also an important supporter of Terence Lewis. When, in 1976, Lewis wrote to Bjelke-Petersen putting forward his credentials as a potential commissioner, he stressed: 'I am very acceptable to the Queensland Police Union Executive and to over 95% of the members of the Police Force' (Fitzgerald, 1989, p. 43).

The further development of systemic corruption during the commissionership of Terence Lewis, and Lewis' close personal connections with Bjelke-Petersen and other senior ministers is discussed elsewhere (Lewis, 1999). Relevant here is that the QPU was an integral part of the police culture and system which allowed corruption to flourish.

The Fitzgerald Inquiry identified the union as a node of power within the corruption system. The union did not provide a challenge to corrupt management, nor did it support its own members who attempted to expose corruption. To the contrary, union officials were identified as among the powerful people who would bring retribution of those who attempted to reveal corrupt practices (Fitzgerald, 1989). The union was a significant cultural and organisational force opposed to reform and improved accountability.

One of the notable achievements of the Fitzgerald Inquiry was to emphatically refute the 'rotten apple' theory of corruption as a product of individual deviancy, and to identify the key sustaining role of the police culture and its 'code' in police corruption. By this code:

> … it is impermissible to criticize other police. Such criticism is viewed as particularly reprehensible if it is made to outsiders. Any criticism which does occur is kept under the control of those who have authority and influence within the Force. (Fitzgerald, 1989, p. 202)

The code tended to 'reduce, if not almost to eliminate, concern at possible apprehension and punishment as a deterrent to police misconduct'. It exaggerated 'the need for, and the benefits derived from, mutual loyalty and support', and this appeal to solidarity was exploited by corrupt officers to their advantage (Fitzgerald, 1989, p. 202).

The Fitzgerald Report also concluded that:

> Particular responsibility and enthusiasm for the police culture is to be found amongst some members of an elite within the Force, including senior officers, union officials and those with special appointments and functions, particularly detectives and other non-uniformed police. Members of the elite have been the major beneficiaries of the culture which they promote and exploit. (Fitzgerald, 1989, p. 200)

The nexus between the union and management was strong, as 'influential persons in the Police Union regularly become commissioned officers in the Police Force'. These connections were often exploited for negative purposes. Union officials used their greater freedom to speak publicly to support and promote the police culture, and to oppose 'any significant reform' (Fitzgerald, 1989, p. 212).

The report's strongest condemnation was reserved for the practice of informal discussions between union officials and senior politicians. In words which we shall have occasion to return to, the report argued:

> ... it is singularly inappropriate for the Union to demand the right to influence the selection of the Police Commissioner or Minister. In addition, any contact between the Unions and Government Ministers, (including the Premier) should only occur with the Police Commissioner and his Minister being present. (Fitzgerald, 1989, p. 280)

The Fitzgerald Report described the QPU and the (much smaller) Queensland Police Officers' Union as 'unusual industrial organisations', but accepted that they had 'a legitimate role to play in industrial matters affecting their members'. The Fitzgerald Report also acknowledged their 'interest in and support for many of the reform initiatives suggested in this report' (1989, p. 280).

It is poignant that in the wake of the exposure of corruption and misconduct by the Fitzgerald Inquiry, one of the architects of Whitrod's downfall, former QPU president Ron Edington, publicly expressed remorse:

> All that Ray Whitrod was trying to do was to lift the image of the Queensland Police Force ... We opposed him because we were old and we weren't prepared to accept change. I realise my mistake now ... (Fitzgerald, 1989, p. 36)

Reform and Regression

The Fitzgerald Report accepted that the police culture was too engrained among the existing 'elite' for those officers to abandon it. However, it was argued that:

> ... the attitudes of other officers can be changed over time by fresh leadership, better training and education and better recruitment practices ... The culture must be combatted if misconduct is to be controlled and the Police Force is to develop a mutually supportive relationship with the rest of the community. (Fitzgerald, 1989, p. 363)

The elements of this new culture included: respect for the criminal justice system; respect for the rule of law; a commitment to personal honesty and integrity; openness to new methods of management and policing; and, a willingness to censure, report and expose misconduct by colleagues.

In the immediate wake of Fitzgerald, the union leadership did accept the need for reform. The president of the union, John O'Gorman, was newly-elected in 1989 and had been heavily involved with the inquiry. In an interview with Colleen Lewis (1999), O'Gorman said:

> The Fitzgerald Inquiry was a watershed, not only in police history but in Queensland history. Therefore, it [the union] had to stand back and have a good hard look at all that Fitzgerald had uncovered and recommended ... because what we had before hadn't worked. (p. 128)

This extended even to issues on which the QPU, like most police unions, had been intransigent, such as civilian oversight of complaints against police. O'Gorman accepted that the Fitzgerald Inquiry had left the QPU in a weak bargaining position, and that there was little chance of blocking the creation of the Criminal Justice Commission. However, he also acknowledged that there was virtue in independent oversight body, and that Fitzgerald had created an historic window of opportunity to bring about reform. He did not want to be remembered as someone who had obstructed reform just so that some union members would see him as a 'tough bugger' (Lewis, 1999, p. 129).

The post-Fitzgerald environment was a challenging one for the QPU. Fleming and Peetz (2005) argue that, prior to 1990, the union employed to good effect the informal personal networks which characterised the Bjelke-Petersen government. The QPU initially struggled to adjust, and resisted the restructuring and organisational changes necessary to reform. Particularly resented were changes to systems of recruitment, training and promotions.

Fleming and Peetz (2005) describe the process by which both the QPU and the police service adopted a new professionalism in industrial relations. With the election of Labor governments in 1989, 1992 and 1998, the QPU had to accept the political reality of dealing with a Labor government, and adopt a lower public profile. The government and union learned to be polite and professional:

> Requests and queries are dealt with promptly, and issues are not allowed to get out of proportion … every effort is made to arrive at an outcome that is agreeable for all. (Fleming and Peetz, 2005, p. 291)

This happy state of affairs may well have existed in workplace negotiations, but the public face of the QPU too often remained provocative and reactionary.

The most spectacular example was the 1996 'Memorandum of Understanding' (MOU), a secret agreement between the QPU and the National Party, then in opposition. In the MOU, the Union asked for the powers of the Criminal Justice Commission to be reduced, for a weakening of police disciplinary processes, and for the removal of senior police, including the police commissioner, Jim O'Sullivan. The union also asked to be consulted about O'Sullivan's replacement. In return, the Union agreed to support the National Party in a crucial by-election, which could (and did) cause a change of government (CJC, 1996).

Whether the National Party leader, Rob Borbidge, intended to honour the MOU fully is moot. However, the scandal that resulted when the MOU was made public was damaging for the new government and the union. The MOU was an attempt by the police union to secretly negotiate changes of great public importance to policing. Some elements were clearly intended to roll back Fitzgerald reforms; for example, by demanding the right for the union to be consulted on the appointment of the commissioner (Fitzgerald, 1989).

However, if the Union was embarrassed by the MOU, it did not show it. In 2002, retiring Secretary Merv Bainbridge nominated the MOU agreement as the highlight of his 23-year union career (Franklin, Jones, & Stolz, 2002).

Other incidents have continued to tarnish the QPU, and raise questions over its commitment to a 'new culture'. In 2003, the union's monthly journal published a series of cartoons and photomontages intended to satirise the result of Islamic fundamentalists conquering the West. The images, which included a mock *Playboy* magazine cover with women wearing bikinis and veils, outraged Queensland's Muslim community. As the Islamic Council of Queensland pointed out, the cartoons were not just in poor taste: 'These are the people that are supposed to make sure that racial and religious vilification laws are being adhered to' (Macfarlane, 2003, p. 13). Respect for the rule of law, as well as respect for part of the policed community, was at issue.

In the same year, the Union reacted with outrage, and threatened industrial action and an anti-government advertising campaign, when the government proposed a new drug and alcohol policy for the police force (Parnell, 2003). Union president Gary Wilkinson threatened: 'Whenever you pick a fight with the coppers, you can't win it. Doesn't matter who you are'

(Wilson, 2003, p. 6). The union had a legitimate interest in such a policy, but such rhetoric was excessive and irresponsible.

This arrogant attitude, which implied police were above the law, was at its most damaging in the QPU's response to what became known as the Palm Island case. An Aboriginal man living on Palm Island, a troubled Indigenous community, was arrested on November 19, 2004, and later found dead in his cell. A riot followed, in which the island's police station was burned down (AAP, 2004).

The sequence of inquiries and court cases which followed is complex and the justice or otherwise of any part of the sequence is beyond the scope of this chapter. What are relevant are the public pronouncements made by senior QPU officials. The union vice-president, Denis Fitzpatrick, said a decision to grant bail to 19 men charged over the riot amounted to a 'betrayal' of the police (Gerard, 2004). A coronial investigation criticised the actions of the police, and found that one officer was directly responsible for the death (State Coroner Queensland, 2006). Immediately following the release of this finding, union president Gary Wilkinson held a press conference and accused the coroner of conducting a witch-hunt, 'cherry-picking' evidence and twisting the facts (Meade, 2007).[1] When a judicial review recommended that the officer be charged with manslaughter, industrial meetings were held across Queensland. Fitzpatrick said: 'We are not ruling out a march, protests, rallies or any form of industrial action. Police are incensed at this political interference' (Koch & McKenna, 2007). During the trial of the charged officer, the QPU issued blue wristbands as a fundraiser, and recommended that police officers wear the wristbands to signify support for their colleague. Many Aboriginal groups were furious that the police wore the bands, especially in court (Koch, 2007b). The officer was eventually acquitted: the union then ran a series of radio advertisements attacking the government, describing the officer as 'the first Queenslander ever to be prosecuted by a politician' (Koch, Murphy, & Parnell, 2007).

While the Palm Island affair did not involve police corruption, and no police have yet been convicted of misconduct,[2] the behaviour of the union raises serious questions about the organisation's commitment to key tenets of the Fitzgerald reforms. That a police union supports an officer during legal proceedings is entirely appropriate. However, respect for the rule of law and for the criminal justice system is incompatible with public expressions of outrage and threats of industrial action because an officer has been charged with an offence. It is also incompatible with public attacks on the independence and impartiality of holders of judicial office.

A change of leadership of the union in 2008 gave hope for a change of direction, but the reign of the new President, Cameron Pope, was short-lived

(Ironside, 2009). Pope resigned because of allegations of an improper sexual relationship, but more significant for the union as a whole were the bitter power struggles, frequently surfacing in public, which portrayed an organisation with serious governance problems: 'mired in internal troubles', as the acting President, Ian Leavers (2009), put it.

Impacts Outside Queensland

Similar patterns of resistance, reform and regression can be observed in other Australian jurisdictions.

When allegations of serious and systemic corruption in the New South Wales Police were raised in the mid-1990s, the state's Police Association responded initially in accord with the police code: denial and outrage. Association secretary, Lloyd Taylor, said the proposed royal commission was 'a devastating smack at the integrity of the force ... an expensive exercise into allegations we've all heard before' (Jones, 1994, p. 2). The deputy president advised an Association meeting that it could not support the royal commission, as it would be 'useless' (Harvey, 1994, p. 6).

The Wood Royal Commission, however, revealed endemic and systemic corruption and other misconduct. In its report, the Wood Royal Commission described the Police Association in a similar light to its Queensland counterpart a decade earlier: another player in the ruthless game of power. The corrupt 'elite' had a different name, the 'Barbeque Set', but the story of institutional capture was the same (Wood, 1997).

However, once the Wood Commission was established and demonstrated that it was a far-reaching and determined inquiry, the NSW Police Association responded well: providing administrative support and contributing to developing models for reform (Fleming & Lewis, 2002). The Association continues to work constructively with external oversight bodies such as the NSW Police Integrity Commission, for example, in developing an early intervention model for corruption prevention (Police Integrity Commission NSW, 2008).

The situation in Victoria is less positive. Mark Burgess argues that police unions have responded positively to the managerial and administrative reform of Australian police forces 'to varying degrees' (Burgess, Fleming, & Marks, 2006, p. 394). Those familiar with Victorian policing would agree that 'varying' is generous. Perhaps because Victorian policing has not been subjected to the searching scrutiny of a well-resourced public inquiry (with the partial exception of the Beach Inquiry in the mid-1970s), the Victorian Police Association has played a role which has been obstructionist, and often worse.

An historical overview of corruption in the Victoria Police prepared by the Office of Police Integrity (OPI) puts it bluntly:

[Among] influences that have impeded the effective operation of anti-corruption and anti-misconduct measures ... is a widespread 'culture' in the Force which, at the slightest criticism of police officers, closes protectively around the members under question. The Police Association as the industrial voice of rank and file members has at times played an important part in perpetuating this culture. (Office of Police Integrity Victoria, 2007a, p. 134)

In 2007, the OPI was itself at the centre of just such an episode. An OPI hearing revealed that several members of the Armed Offenders Squad had perjured themselves to obstruct an investigation into the physical abuse of suspected offenders, and that such abuse had, in fact, taken place. Association officials reacted with fury, criticising the investigation, encouraging industrial action by police, and organising a protest rally (Office of Police Integrity Victoria, 2008). Association Secretary Paul Mullett, condemned the OPI's public hearings as 'nothing short of a show trial and a Spanish inquisition' (Four Corners, 2007). No hint was given that the Police Association disapproved of lying to pervert the course of justice, or of beating suspects.

There were forces for reform in the union — but their experience was horrific. In October 2004, Janet Mitchell was elected President of the Association. She was the first female to be appointed to such a position in Australia, and her election was a signal that the 'old culture' was being challenged in the police union, as in Victoria Police generally. However, the 'old culture' fought back, with vicious personal attacks and intimidation. This campaign was intended to make Mitchell's position impossible, and was ultimately successful (Office of Police Integrity Victoria, 2007b). An external consultant's report on the Police Association's workplace culture gave a highly critical assessment, describing a climate of bullying, intimidation and poisonous factionalism (Brecht, 2006).

The impact of Fitzgerald is clearly limited in the Victorian union. The 'old culture' survives, based around denial and intimidation, rejection of the validity of external oversight, and implied and sometimes open, contempt for the rule of law.

Despite the many controversies which surrounded the Police Association, its political power seemed undiminished. In an episode eerily reminiscent of Bjelke-Petersen Queensland, the Victorian Premier, Steve Bracks, met personally with Paul Mullett without the knowledge of the Chief Commissioner, shortly before the 2006 state election. A secret five-page 'Record of Commitments' was agreed to: Bracks committed a Labour government to reimbursing the Police Association for the cost of legal representation before the OPI, and made commitments about upcoming wages negotiations. In return, the union publicly supported the government in the election (Austin, 2007; Hannan, 2007).

It was only after the election that Bracks reluctantly allowed the Record of Commitments to be made public. The disclosure was a humiliation for Chief Commissioner Christine Nixon and an embarrassment for the government. Many respected commentators condemned the deal, recalling the Fitzgerald Inquiry's view that 'any contact between the Unions and Government Ministers, (including the Premier) should only occur with the Police Commissioner and his Minister being present' (Fitzgerald, 1989, p. 280). Frank Costigan, QC, well-known in Australia for exposing corruption as a royal commissioner in the 1980s, said: 'Governments do secret deals with the police union at their peril, and ultimately at the peril of the community' (Rood and Oakes, 2007, p. 1).

In Western Australia, too, there has been a strong tradition of 'old culture' resistance to reform by the police union. In the late 1990s, the West Australian Police Union of Workers (WAPU) president Mike Dean attacked the Anti-Corruption Commission, which had been established following well-documented revelations of government and police corruption, calling the body 'a Spanish inquisition because it answers to no one and can do whatever it likes' (Laurie, 1998).

This attitude of defiance continues. In the first half of 2009, the WAPU website prominently displayed images from a union rally. One is of a woman holding a placard: 'Hang the lawyers with the criminals they defend!' (West Australian Police Union of Workers, 2009). This rally was in response to the acquittal of three people charged with assaulting and badly injuring a police constable (Stanley, 2009). The response of Mike Dean:

> ... it was the last straw and the last insult from a judicial system which over decades ... has dispensed verdicts all too frequently bereft of justice ... The ignorance and arrogance of a small group of very vocal defence counsel only aggravated the situation ... the vast majority of West Australians made it very clear that they were incensed ... For the first time, the do-gooders of our academic and legal system – which constantly pressure our parliamentarians — are being questioned as to their agenda and recommendations. (Dean, 2009)

As in the Palm Island affair, it is not in dispute that this court case raised legitimate issues for a police union. But twenty years after Fitzgerald, it is hard to excuse a senior police union official launching an invective, and demeaning whole sections of the policed community, undermining respect for the law and due process, and implying that police officers are above the law. The Fitzgerald Report made clear connections between the many failings of the Queensland Police in the 1980s and a culture which 'includes contempt for the criminal justice system [and] disdain for the law' (Fitzgerald, 1989, p. 200).

Troubling also is the overly-frequent use by police unions of motions of no confidence in police commissioners. In recent years, these have occurred or have been threatened in Western Australia against Commissioner Barry Matthews (Kelly, 2002), in Victoria against Christine Nixon (AAP, 2005), in Queensland against Bob Atkinson (Lund, 2007), and in Tasmania against Richard McCreadie (Stedman, 2008).

The picture is, however, not all negative.

Forces for Reform

A significant development in police unionism in Australia came in 1998, with the creation of the Police Federation of Australia, an umbrella body which represents state and territory police unions nationally. The importance of the PFA lies in it being a well-resourced body which has influence with both governments and police services, but is also removed from the hard-nosed industrial haggling which preoccupies unions and employers at state level (Lyons & Fleming, 2004).

Traditionally, Australian police services and their unions have been inward-looking, concerned with affairs in their own jurisdictions. The development of a genuinely federal employee association at a time when policing clearly requires a more national approach is welcome, especially as the PFA has made concrete steps towards improving training and working towards cultural change in policing (Burgess et al., 2006, p. 397).

An emerging body of scholarship suggests that police unions have the potential, perhaps beginning to be realised, to be forces for reform and democratic policing in Australia (Marks and Fleming, 2008). A study of the Queensland Police Union reported perceptions by police officers that their union was democratic and responsive to their interests (Fleming & Peetz, 2005). The experience of democracy within their own workplaces, it is argued, strengthens the appreciation police will have for democratic ideals more generally — in established liberal democracies and emerging democracies alike (Marks and Fleming, 2006).

There is some evidence that this is occurring in Australia. The New South Wales Police Association has reformed its organisational structure, allowing for greater member involvement and accountability (Burgess et al., 2006). The Northern Territory Police Association has been engaged with efforts to improve policing in remote Aboriginal communities (Marks & Fleming, 2006; Northern Territory Police Association, 2007). A 2005 PFA submission on mental health and policing has been deservedly praised as an excellent contribution to resolving a major social problem (PFA, 2005).

A PFA submission to the National Human Rights Consultation is similarly reassuring (PFA, 2009b). Concerns about 'un-elected judges' having the task of interpreting human rights law are a little ironic, given frequent protests by state police unions about 'political interference' in the justice system (Koch, 2007a, p. 5). Nonetheless, the submission is a measured and worthwhile contribution to the debate over the need for a specific human rights instrument.

Conclusion

In developments such as those outlined above, it is possible to see the beginning of the realisation of the Fitzgerald vision of a reformed police culture: one which combines effective policing with a 'mutually supportive relationship' with other stakeholders and the policed community, and of which police unions are an active part (Fitzgerald, 1989, p. 363).

Police unions have a legitimate role protecting the interests of their members, and it is accepted that this role requires robustness and independence. As a QPU official put it: 'we're not a Union that will lie down and have our tummies tickled' (Sycz, 2009). It is not suggested that they should be. However, an effective union can still be a responsible actor in the criminal justice system, contributing to the reform process. Progress towards this goal in the twenty years since the Fitzgerald Report has been mixed.

Endnotes

1   Wilkinson was later convicted of contempt of court for his comments.
2   A CMC review of the initial investigation of the death is still to be finalised.

References

Austin, P. (2007, February 20). Premier tarnished, Nixon humiliated, Mullett wins. *The Age*, p. 1.

Brecht, G. (2006). *Health and Well-being Review: A risk management initiative.* Melbourne, Australia: Grant Brencht and Associates.

Burgess, M., Fleming, J., & Marks, M. (2006). Thinking critically about police unions in Australia: Internal democracy and external responsiveness. *Police Practice and Research, 7*(5), 391–409.

Carte, G.E., & Carte, E.H. (1975). *Police reform in the United States: The era of August Vollmer, 1905–1932.* Berkley, CA: UC Press.

Criminal Justice Commission. (CJC). (1996). *Report on an investigation into a memorandum of understanding between the Coalition and the QPUE and an investigation into an alleged deal between the ALP and the SSAA.* Brisbane, Australia: Author.

Dean, M. (2009). Police officers' loud call for justice. *WA Police News, 4.*

Finnane, M. (2002). *When police unionise: The politics of law and order in Australia.* Sydney, Australia: Sydney Institute of Criminology.

Finnane, M. (2008). No longer a 'workingman's paradise'? Australian police unions and politcal action in a changing industrial environment. *Police Practice and Research, 9*(2), 131–143.

Fitzgerald, G.E. (1989). *Report of a Commission of Inquiry Pursuant to Orders in Council.* Brisbane, Australia: Queensland Government.

Fleming, J., & Lafferty, G. (2001). Police unions, industrial strategies and political influence: Some recent history. *International Journal of Employment Studies, 9*(2), 131–140.

Fleming, J., & Lewis, C. (2002). The politics of police reform. In T. Prenzler & J. Ransley (Eds.), *Police reform: Building integrity* (pp. 83–96). Sydney, Australia: Federation Press.

Fleming, J., & Peetz, D. (2005). Essential service unionism and the new police industrial relations. *Journal of Collective Negotiations, 30*(4), 283–305.

Four Corners. (2007, February 12). *The culture.* Sydney, Australia: ABC.

Franklin, M., Jones, C., & Stolz., G. (2002, August 16). Labor MPs blast police union. *The Courier-Mail,* p. 7.

Gerard, I. (2004, December 7). Bail 'betrayal' angers police. *The Australian,* p. 7.

Hannan, E. (2007, February 21). Bracks's dirty deal. *The Australian,* p. 3.

Harvey, S. (1994, May 14). Inquiry no use: Union. *Sydney Morning Herald,* p. 6.

Hooper, C. (2009). *The tall man: Death and life on Palm Island.* Melbourne, Australia: Penguin.

Ironside, R. (2009, March 17). Upheaval for the force. *The Courier Mail,* p. 7.

Jones, M. (1994, May 12). Fahey anger over inquiry. *Daily Telegraph,* p. 2,

Kelly, J. (2002, March 17). Police chief loses vote of confidence. *Sunday Times* [WA], p. 5.

Koch, T. (2007a, January 29). No strike on Palm charge, top cop tells force. *The Australian,* p. 1.

Koch, T. (2007b, June 22). Police ads slam Beattie over Palm case. *The Australian,* p. 6.

Koch, T. (2007c, June 22). Pussycats in jackboots totally bereft of class. *The Australian,* p. 6.

Koch, T. (2007d, June 9). Symbol clash at Palm cop's trial. *The Australian,* p. 9.

Laurie, V. (1998, June 30). Crisis of confidence. *Bulletin with Newsweek,* p. 22.

Leavers, I. (2009, April). Acting General President's Message. *Queensland Police Union Journal,* p. 2.

Lewis, C. (1999). *Complaints against police: The politics of reform.* Sydney, Australia: Hawkins Press.

Lund, M. (2007, September 22). Misconduct in the ranks. *The Courier-Mail,* p. 6.

Lyons, M., & Fleming, J. (2004). A study of union mergers: The strange case of the Police Federation of Australia. *New Zealand Journal of Employment Relations, 29*(2), 1–16.

Macfarlane, D. (2003, March 26). Police journal insults Muslims. *The Australian,* p. 13.

Marks, M., & Fleming, J. (2006). The right to unionize, the right to bargain, and the right to democratic policing. *The ANNALS of the American Academy of Political and Social Science, 605,* 178–199.

Marks, M., & Fleming, J. (2008). Having a voice: The quest for democratic policing in Southern Africa. *Journal of Organizational Change Management, 21*(4), 451–459.

Meade, K. (2007, March 20). Contempt for Palm comment. *The Australian,* p. 5.

Nine in police custody after island riot. (2004, November 27). *Sydney Morning Herald,* p. 3.

Northern Territory Police Association. (2007). *Indigenous policing proposal unrealistic.* Darwin, Australia: Author.

Office of Police Integrity. (2007a). *Past patterns — Future directions: Victoria Police and the problem of corruption and serious misconduct.* Melbourne, Australia: Author.

Office of Police Integrity. (2007b). *Report on the 'Kit Walker' investigations* . Melbourne, Australia: Author.

Office of Police Integrity. (2008). *The Victorian Armed Offenders Squad: A case study.* Melbourne, Australia: Author.

Parnell, S. (2003, April 16). Police union lodges drug policy protest. *The Courier-Mail,* p. 16.

Police Association confidence in Nixon 'on the table'. (2005, August 23). *Australian Associated Press* (AAP) news release.

Police Federation of Australia (PFA). (2005). *Submission to Senate Select Committee on Mental Health.* Canberra, Australia: Author.

Police Federation of Australia (PFA). (2009a). *National Police Audit: Submission from the Police Federation of Australia.* Canberra, Australia: Author.

Police Federation of Australia (PFA). (2009b). PFA in the halls of power. *Police Journal,* April, 20–23.

Police Federation of Australia (PFA). (2009c). *Submission from the Police Federation of Australia to the National Human Rights Consultation.* Canberra, Australia: Author.

Police Integrity Commission. (2008). *Annual Report 2007–2008.* Sydney, Australia: Author.

Rood, D., & Oakes, D. (2007, February 23). Costigan hits out at Bracks deal. *The Age,* p. 1.

Sherman, L.W. (1978). *Scandal and reform: Controlling police corruption.* Berkley, CA: UC Press.

Smith, D. (1994). The political and social constraints to reform Brisbane. In K. Bryett & C. Lewis (Eds.), *Un-Peeling tradition: Contemporary policing.* Brisbane, Australia: Centre for Australian Public Sector Management.

Stanley, W. (2009, October 21). Thousands turn out at parliament to support police. *Australian Associated Press,* new release.

State Coroner (Qld). (2006). *Findings of inquest into the death of Mulrunji.* Brisbane, Australia: Queensland Coroner's Court.

Stedman, M. (2008, October 21). McCreadie canned, reasons unclear. *Mercury,* p. 3.

Sycz, D. (2009). Assistant General Secretary's Message. *Queensland Police Union Journal,* May, p. 4.

West Australian Police Union of Workers. (2009). *Strength in unity.* Retrieved May 5, 2009, from https://www.wapolun.org.au/.

Whitrod, R. (2001). *Before I Sleep: Memoirs of a modern police commissioner.* Brisbane, Australia: University of Queensland Press.

Wilson, A. (2003, September 12). Union warns Beattie not to blue with cops. *The Australian,* p. 6.

Wood, J.J. (The Hon). (1997). *Royal Commission into the New South Wales Police Service, Corruption (Vol. 1).* Sydney, Australia: Royal Commission into the New South Wales Police Service.

The Reformative Powers of Higher Education for Policing?

Kerry Wimshurst

A major recommendation of the *Commission of Inquiry into Possible Illegal Activities and Associated Police Misconduct* (hereafter referred to as the Fitzgerald Inquiry) was the urgent need for reform of police education and training in Queensland. A key strategy for reform saw the introduction of university programs designed for police officers and other criminal justice personnel. The Fitzgerald Inquiry's prescription for police higher education, and particularly the reform of recruit education, has since been invoked in support of similar attempts at reform in other states. The Inquiry concluded that police were not adequately educated to meet the demands of an increasingly complex society. The Fitzgerald Report stated that:

> Police need a deeper appreciation of social, psychological and legal issues which are intrinsic to their work — an understanding which can only be acquired by higher education. United States research confirms that authoritarian tendencies are lower and tolerance higher among better educated police. Better educated police also perform more effectively. Education programs in tertiary institutions which provide basic knowledge of criminal justice processes and foundations of social science are needed. The courses would be ideally attended by police along with people from other disciplines, to ensure the breadth of experience essential to the study and understanding of human behaviour. (Fitzgerald, 1989, p. 250)

This chapter builds on Buerger's (1998) thesis for the United States where he argued that educational reforms almost always follow from periods of crisis in police organisations. That is, following some sort of public crisis of confidence, changes in education and training are embraced in an attempt to reform the organisation. Such educational restructuring may be internal only to the organisation and does not necessarily involve the higher education sector. However, in Australia, attempts to bring about attitudinal change among personnel, and to rehabilitate police organisations, have almost invariably looked to developing partnerships with universities. The Fitzgerald Inquiry and its educational aftermath is a clear example of the crisis control function of education reform, and since then similar recommendations have been made by commissions of inquiry in other states. For a time, a partnership was forged between a police service in considerable disarray and tertiary education providers. This arrangement was short-lived and the chapter argues that police organisations commonly assert their seniority and power in educational partnerships.

The source of the Fitzgerald Inquiry's certainty about the liberalising influence of higher education on policing is not clear. References to reduced levels of authoritarianism and increased tolerance echo the conclusions reached in American studies reviewed by Carter, Sapp and Stevens (1989). These studies, many of them dating from the late 1970s and early 1980s, generally portrayed considerable benefits for police departments employing tertiary educated personnel. They were published at a time when authorities in the United States were still justifying the millions of dollars invested in new college programs for law enforcement officers. The unprecedented injection of federal funds and consequent growth of college programs for police during the 1970s arose from concerns about social unrest, and especially concerns about the quality of officers who might have to respond to such unrest (President's Crime Commission, 1967).

The focus of educational reform in the United States was on providing tertiary education for serving officers. While the quality of this first generation of higher education for police was often criticised as little more than revamped academy training, and hence intellectually compromised, evaluations also questioned the organisational level at which this funding was pitched (Carlan, 2007; Roberg & Bonn, 2004). Evaluations recommended that funding should be directed toward providing quality pre-service education and attracting better educated recruits in the first place. Thus, an important question which continues to run through overseas and Australian debates about higher education for policing emerged early, and this question asked whether society and police organisations derived greatest benefits from 'recruiting the educated' or 'educating the recruited'.

In fact, studies since the early 1990s have been less optimistic about the supposed benefits of higher education in the quest for quality policing. Advocates of mandatory higher education for police claim that the benefits have been clearly established. However, reviewing several decades of research, Courtright and Mackey (2004, p. 312) concluded that the 'jury was still out' in terms of mandating university studies for police officers:

> There has been an abundance of research investigating the utility and benefits of a college degree for law enforcement practitioners although … little evidence exists demonstrating that educated police officers are more effective crime fighters or that education has a significant influence on police officer behaviour.

There is little doubt that individual officers may derive considerable personal and professional benefits. Graduate officers, for example, often readily acknowledge the personal benefits from their degree studies such as enhanced confidence and self-esteem, broadened outlooks and greater tolerance for divergent points of view. On the other hand, they have difficulty articulating how such personal accomplishments contribute to doing better police work, or even how higher education has contributed to their careers.

The chapter begins with an analysis of the educational reform and reactions to reform which followed the Fitzgerald Inquiry's recommendations. While the research literature overseas continues to look for empirical confirmation that higher education produces better on-the-job policing, attention has moved to related questions. Two of these are addressed later in the chapter because Australian research has provided important insights. First, there is the question of whether level of education is related to job satisfaction and commitment. Second, there is growing interest in what *kind* of higher education is most beneficial, a question which explores tensions between contrasting models of police education. The chapter concentrates on pre-service/recruit education because this was the primary concern of the Fitzgerald Report (1989), and has also been an important concern of subsequent interstate inquiries.

Educational Reform

The findings of the Fitzgerald Inquiry shattered the image and morale of the Queensland Police Service (hereafter referred to as QPS). The president of the police union characterised the period 1987–1992 as the years of 'shame, despair and degradation for decent police officers' (Queensland Police Union of Employees, December, 1992, p. 4). Police executives from interstate were appointed and given a mandate to reform the QPS. In this climate police management was prepared to experiment with radical changes to education and training. The Criminal Justice Commission (hereafter referred to as CJC), a standing justice commission established as a result of the Fitzgerald Inquiry to oversee police reform, advocated the possibility of 'shifting some of the (recruit) training away from the academy to other tertiary institutions' (*Sunday Sun*, July 29, 1990).

The state's political upheaval saw a Labor government come to power (the first non-conservative government in Queensland for over 30 years), which promised to substantially boost operational police numbers. The government placed considerable pressure on the police service and two participating universities to quickly deliver a new program for recruits (Public

Sector Management Commission, 1993). The new Advanced Certificate in Policing featured content in social and behavioural sciences, communications, accountability and ethics, criminology and law, and police competencies (Bryett, 1992; CJC, 1993; Lewis & Prenzler, 1993). Recruits spent the first semester at the university and a longer second semester at the police academy. The QPS then required first-year constables to undertake a further probationary year of intensive field training under the supervision of experienced officers.

The Advanced Certificate in Policing was short lived (1991–1993) but it was important in the history of police higher education in Australia. Civilian academics not employed by the police academy had significant input into curriculum design and delivery. It provided a broad liberal studies (policing and society) education and training package for the 1040 recruits who passed through the program. It also made some university study mandatory for all police recruits and provided credit for the first year of the new baccalaureate criminal justice degrees developed at the same time by the participating universities, also as an aftermath of the Fitzgerald Inquiry.

The Advanced Certificate received national coverage and was widely portrayed as a 'world first' in police education. Reports anticipated 'Policing on a Higher Plane' and noted the improved educational backgrounds of recruits (*Courier-Mail*, 8 March, 1993). Criminal Justice Commission surveys showed a significant improvement in public respect for the police (CJC, 1995), and the enhanced image was attributed in part to the police-university link. The universities were keen to participate in the recruit program because the partnership established a link with a new industry group and new source of funding in the increasingly marketised environment of higher education. That a synergy of diverse interests was accommodated post-Fitzgerald should not detract from the achievements of the police-university partnership. The police union of employees (QPUE), at times very critical of what it saw as the over-emphasis on tertiary qualifications, nevertheless acknowledged that given the crisis of confidence in the state's police, academics and police had 'delivered their best efforts to produce something new in police education and training' (QPUE, November, 1992, p. 5).

Educational Reaction

Yet within three years the university-academy program ceased and a number of pressures for dissolution can be identified. First, as public and media scrutiny declined, along with recollection of the corruption scandal, the 'reformist' police executives became increasingly isolated within the QPS. In 1992, the contract of the post-Fitzgerald Police Commissioner (Newnham) was not renewed. The reformers had broadcast widely that in future promotion to commissioned ranks would require a degree. The incoming regime appeared to place less emphasis on the possession of tertiary qualifications although, in fact, tertiary qualifications remained important for promotion to senior positions. The focus of the new Commissioner (O'Sullivan) was on street policing. Under the headline 'Back on the Beat', he stressed in his first press interview his commitment to operational policing: 'Every available police officer should be out on the streets, being seen, doing what is expected of them — ensuring the lives and property of citizens are protected' (*Courier-Mail*, 16 October, 1992).

Second, an 'operational imperative' came to dominate police views of the new program. The CJC (1993) noted the lack of integration between the university and academy components. Recommendations of the Fitzgerald Inquiry for educational reform indicated broad directions only, which then translated to a lack of clear goals for the new program, and difficulty trying to evaluate it with precision. Thus, operational criteria emerged as the 'de facto standard' to fill the vacuum left by the absence of clearly stated professional and educational goals (CJC, 1993, p. 74). Supervising police officers complained that the first year constables lacked 'street wise' practical knowledge and skills, that the new program was 'bookish' and 'theoretical'. The CJC pointed out that 'first year constables undertaking their field training cannot be expected to have the experience to be deployed as fully operational police officers' (CJC, 1993, p. 81). Nevertheless, the fixation on operational concerns neutralised much of what was potentially positive in the Advanced Certificate. Although recruits were generally positive about their university-based experiences, it was not surprising that over 90% of them claimed they much preferred the academy semester.

Third, educators from within policing remained suspicious of university influences and intentions. Police educators acknowledged that the university partnership had 'revitalised' education and training at a time of crisis, but claimed that universities were intent on controlling police education: 'The takeover bids (by universities) constantly interfere with fostering mutual ideas and developing excellence and integration of education and training content for police (because) many academics involved in police education at universities lack an understanding of what policing is all about' (Barrow & Pitman, 1995, p. 18). Police educators were not anti-higher education, many had degrees themselves, but they were adamant that universities should never become senior partners. Their comments about 'developing excellence and integration of education and training content for police' reflected aspects of the 'professional policing' model of higher education then emerging and which is discussed below.

Fourth, the review of post-Fitzgerald reform conducted by the Public Sector Management Commission (hereafter PSMC) concluded that the education and training focus had swung too much toward recruits to the detriment of serving officers. It was as if experienced officers were being denied the career-enhancing benefits that (supposedly) would flow to post-Fitzgerald recruits from mandatory university study, as if longer-serving police were still being punished for the corruption scandal. Thus, the PSMC recommended that the QPS invest in developing its own in-service education and training packages. The review was really saying that by 1993 the crisis of confidence had apparently passed. The review considered that the university component of the program was too expensive ($11 million over 3 years, 60% of which went on recruit salaries). With the enhanced image of policing, it was suggested that the QPS could directly recruit any number of applicants with at least some tertiary education (PSMC, 1993). Fitzgerald's aims, concluded the PSMC, had been realised and there was no pressing need to continue the university-academy partnership. Full delivery of recruit education and training in Queensland returned to the police academy from 1994 onwards.

Catching a Rising Educational Tide?

It is worth considering the educational condition of recruits prior to the Fitzgerald Inquiry, since the official view of the Inquiry tended to portray the earlier situation as pretty dismal. The CJC (1992, pp. 4–6), for example, noted there were numerous calls in the 1980s to make fundamental changes to 'basic' training, but added that 'change was slow' until after Fitzgerald's recommendations. At least one of these earlier reports was glowingly endorsed by then Commissioner Lewis (later gaoled for corruption). Lewis agreed that there was a need for better educated recruits. Higher education levels would help to improve police interpersonal skills, enhance the way they related to minority ethnic groups, and would help officers understand wider social issues (Commissioner's Report, 1984). In fact, a comparison of recruits prior to the Fitzgerald Inquiry with those entering the university-academy program 1991–93 suggests continuity in recruit quality rather than a radical break with the past.

The cadet system, discontinued after the Inquiry, provided the majority of young males (17–19 years) recruited in the 1980s. However, the main mode of recruitment and training was through the adult probationary system. Most probationers were older males (20–29 years), while small numbers of women were recruited only through the probationary system. A study by Lidgard (1988) of 650 recruits indicated that by the late 1980s their educational backgrounds were relatively high. Seventy-nine per cent of men and 74% of women had completed the final year of secondary school and, while possession of a degree was rare, 21% of men and 41% of women had some further/higher education. By comparison, Hyde & Wimshurst (1993) noted that 20% of post-Fitzgerald recruits at one of the participating universities had degrees, and that twice the proportion of female recruits had degrees compared with males. Thus, while there were many more female recruits post-Fitzgerald, and more recruits had degrees, women still had higher educational levels than males, as they had in the pre-Fitzgerald years.

Hyde & Wimshurst (1993) found that a high proportion of recruits entered policing for 'employment security', and that the opportunity for university study was given by 24 percent of them for joining. Thus, a sizeable proportion of these recruits saw the university-academy program as the way to enhance career and personal prospects. Overall, an average 30% of recruits entered with degrees during the period 1991–1993 (Bragg, 1998) and this remained consistent through the 1990s after the demise of the Advanced Certificate. Nevertheless, given the relatively high educational levels of recruits prior to the Fitzgerald Inquiry, it may be that the university-academy partnership caught a rising tide of recruit quality already in train.

Higher Education, Satisfaction, and Commitment to Policing

When the QPS shifted focus to in-service education, two programs were developed and mandated for promotion to the level of Inspector. The programs were initially received in very different ways by serving officers. The Constable Development Program (CDP), consisting of modules in police competencies, personal and professional development, was launched in 1995 under the banner of 'Developing Quality People for a Quality Service'. The union supported the CDP, claiming that it combined the best aspects of apprenticeship along with reflectivity. Orderly progression through the modules also promised to prevent 'rank jumping' and premature deployment to specialist positions.

The Management Development Program (MDP) encountered considerable opposition. Completion of the program was necessary for promotion above Senior Constable. The QPS began flagging the introduction of the MDP from 1996, and the program became mandatory for promotion from 1999. The QPS and the union were at loggerheads throughout 1998. Critics of the MDP were often officers who had been exposed over the previous decade to conflicting messages about the value (or otherwise) of different visions of education and training. Some had undertaken degree studies post-Fitzgerald, but these earlier efforts now did not seem to count for much in terms of career progression. The union criticised the 'shifting goalposts' of educational criteria for promotion. The MDP (initially dubbed 'Managing

Disillusioned Police') was arguably based on a limited conception of professional development (police law and management), but of considerable concern was that the program had no tertiary recognition and might carry little recognition outside a police career. Tensions began to ease when the QPS reached agreement with an interstate university that the MDP receive substantial credit toward specified degrees (*The Australian*, December 9, 1998).

The union remained critical of 'tertiary educated careerists', a position that at first glance appeared to be anti-higher education:

> In the past 15 years there has been a push within the QPS to recruit staff who hold tertiary qualifications. It is our position that there has been little or no managerial or operational benefit to the QPS from this policy. This is due in part to the fact that these tertiary qualified officers quite often have an unreasonable expectation as to their career and promotional prospects. (Mitchell & Musgrove, 2006)

On closer view, it seems that the union's position has been consistent over time; that priority go to supporting educational opportunities for serving officers (including university studies), but that tertiary qualifications should not be a prerequisite for 'employment, promotion or advancement'.

A study of officers who graduated in the 1990s (Wimshurst & Allard, 2007) found an intriguing divide between those who were undecided (even hostile) about the benefits of tertiary study, compared with another group who were satisfied with educational and employment-related outcomes. It seems that as the reform impulse waned in the mid-1990s, and the QPS mandated its own programs, some serving police became increasingly doubtful about the usefulness of their degree. On the other hand, those who became police after commencing their degrees clearly felt that tertiary education opened the door to recruitment. In addition, some of the more experienced police (who were comfortable with their careers) reported that they undertook their degree for educational and self-improvement reasons, with no great expectations for instrumental career benefits.

Recruit education did not disappear from public scrutiny after the demise of the university-academy program. Recruit education had, after all, been a major concern of the Fitzgerald Inquiry and for much of the 1990s a series of CJC reports monitored pre-service education. There was a sense that the CJC was reassuring stakeholders, including the QPS, that the attitudes of recruits to higher education remained positive, that there had not been some educational backlash among them. In fact, while findings were said to be 'mixed', there was continuing support for tertiary education (CJC, 1996). Most recruits (79%) believed that academic qualifications improved the prospects for officers should they leave policing. The majority (63%) believed that 'tertiary education develops a better police officer' (although recruits with university qualifications were more likely to believe this). On the other hand, 43% of recruits felt there should be less emphasis on academic education, and more on practical training.

These mixed, but mainly positive, results were confirmed a year later (CJC, 1997) when the educational views of recruits at the larger Oxley academy in the capital city were compared with recruits at the recently established academy in regional Townsville. There were significant differences between the two academy campuses. Sixty-seven per cent of recruits overall agreed that a tertiary education developed a better police officer, however 74% of the metropolitan recruits agreed compared with only 52% of provincial recruits.

Nevertheless, the CJC (1994, p. 140) warned that 'the transition to a more qualified workforce may present difficulties in later years for the QPS'. A study from the United Kingdom (Smithers, Hill, & Silvester, 1990) had found that graduate officers may have 'higher career aspirations and greater expectations of the work' than non-graduates, and that graduates were inclined to resign earlier because of limited career prospects. Two Queensland studies have since investigated whether there are relationships between levels of education and job-related attitudes.

Bragg (1998) found no relationship between level/type of education, job satisfaction and job commitment. By way of explanation, he suggested that younger officers were also likely to be better educated, but as yet had not had the time to become dissatisfied. It was also suggested that police culture (and the close knit bond between officers) might offer surrogate satisfaction in place of rapid promotion and increased pay. However, elsewhere the study suggested that the QPS had successfully introduced processes, such as secondments across areas of specialisation, from which educated officers might derive job satisfaction. Similarly, Jones, Jones and Prenzler (2005) found no significant relationship overall between level of education, job satisfaction and commitment. Nor were degree holders more likely to resign from the QPS than those who did not have degrees. Again, the explanation offered was that post-Fitzgerald reforms produced a police service flexible enough to offer compensatory challenges in place of accelerated promotion and pay.

What is interesting about both these studies was that the authors felt the need to explain why they had not found significant relationships between educational levels and job satisfaction. The assumption in each case was that well-educated officers would be less satisfied with their lot, that degree holders would expect accelerated opportunities. An equally valid counter-explanation may be that in a police organisation where many officers have tertiary qualifications, there would be no particular reason why individuals would expect special consideration based on higher education.

Contemporary Models of Police Education

The literature from the United States often implies that questions about the professional benefits of higher education for police have already been settled, largely in the affirmative (e.g., Carter, Sapp, & Stephens, 1989; Roberg & Bonn, 2004), and that the one big question remaining is when to make tertiary qualifications mandatory for all police. This is despite the lack of empirical 'certainty' about benefits, or the fact that still only about 15% of police departments require some level of college education as a minimum standard for recruitment, although some estimates suggest that up to 25 percent of officers in the field have degrees (Roberg & Bonn, 2004). Higher education is seen as an essential requisite for professional standing in the community, and for police officers to be able to comprehend and cope effectively with the complex demands of contemporary law enforcement. Tertiary-educated officers, it is claimed, are more likely to monitor and modify their own styles of policing within diverse communities, and to utilise problem-oriented and community policing strategies. On the other hand, the kind of higher education they should receive remains very much open to debate (Polk & Armstrong, 2001; Wimshurst & Ransley, 2007).

Liberal Education

The characteristics of a 'good' police officer and the opportunities for self-development outlined above are strongly indicative of the outcomes of liberal education. Flanagan (2000, p. 3) notes that while there is 'no uniform conceptualisation of liberal education', the idea generally describes an education which focuses on encouraging informed analysis of current social issues, constructive critical thinking, flexible approaches to problem-solving, and a capacity to understand values and beliefs beyond one's immediate life experiences. These are presumably desirable attributes for those entering rapidly changing and complex work environments such as the criminal justice system. Queensland moved to a model of recruiting liberally educated officers after the Fitzgerald Inquiry from the mid-1990s. While it might be argued that this was largely by default (the academy-university partnership having dissolved), the QPS recruits graduates from across a range of disciplines, including those from broad criminology/criminal justice programs.

In fact, a trend in Australia over the past two decades is that the liberal ideal for police education has been endorsed by two further commissions of inquiry (Kennedy, 2004; Wood, 1997). For example, the *Royal Commission into the New South Wales Police* (1994–1997) made recommendations very similar in spirit to Fitzgerald's prescriptions for Queensland reform. Royal Commissioner Wood championed the apparently restorative powers of a liberal education when he insisted that 'recruits (must) have an exposure to the external influence of an open campus in which they can interact with students studying in other disciplines, thereby limiting potential for entrenchment of the negative culture, which might be encouraged if their entire training was conducted in a closed and isolated residential college' such as the police academy (Wood, 1997, p. 276).

Wood clearly had the liberalising potential of higher education in mind when he recommended that recruits complete an 'external tertiary qualification provided through a civilian education in all but the core policing skills which were better delivered by experienced police trainers' (Wood, 1997, p. 276). However, he qualified some of his own recommendations, commenting that while such 'external' programs should derive from 'the Arts, Social Sciences or similar disciplines', they should also be courses which were 'relevant to policing studies'. Thus, considerable interpretive latitude, and potential for implementation 'drift', opened between the Royal Commission's pronouncements on the need for liberal education and, on the other hand, the 'professional policing' model which was subsequently implemented.

There remains an overwhelming faith in the reformative powers of university-based education to fix problems of corruption, misconduct and mal-administration. It was thus not surprising when the Royal Commission into whether there had been corrupt or criminal conduct by any Western Australia police officer (2002–2004) also endorsed the reformative powers of higher education in its attempt to heal a police service confronted by allegations of 'corrupt or criminal conduct' (Kennedy, 2004). It recommended that recruiting preference go to those with 'advanced qualifications' beyond high school level. The Inquiry recommended that the police build 'partnership relationships (with the university) in the development and delivery of education and training at tertiary level' and, reminiscent of the earlier Fitzgerald and Wood inquiries, that 'where appropriate, academy students should participate in joint study with (other university students) to gain additional perspectives and experience a diversity of views' (Kennedy, 2004, p. 332).

It is apparent, however, that while commissions of inquiry have identified serious organisational problems and indicated directions for educational reform, they have been less precise about ways to achieve that reform. Gilligan (2002) noted that the roles and outcomes of Royal Commissions vary considerably. While often very effective at gathering evidence, and indicating directions for reform, they may be less prescriptive about solutions, and perhaps this is even more so when justice commissions pronounce on educational matters. Thus, the model that has emerged after commissions in some other states resembles more the 'professional policing' model of recruit education.

Professional Policing

In the early 1990s, prominent police educators developed a model called the 'full professional' paradigm of police education (Bradley, 1996; Bradley & Cioccarelli, 1994). These educators were adamant that police organisations could never be reformed through 'gentrification', that is simply by recruiting generalist graduates (Bradley, 1996, p. 93). They advocated a partnership between universities and the police in order to develop a 'discipline of policing' (Bradley & Cioccarelli, 1994), but argued that police must take prime responsibility for initiating and carrying through these developments. Policing must utilise university expertise, particularly research expertise, however the police would remain firmly in control of their own professional destinies, setting the agendas for such partnerships. This vision for the future of Australian policing presumed 'the existence of highly educated and skilled officers operating on a foundation of rigorous applied research' (Bradley, 1996, p. 86). While the 'full professional' model was hailed as a new paradigm for police/university research collaborations, it has also informed education partnerships with some universities, including pre-service education.

These partnerships tend to intersperse blocs of academy training with academic education on a university campus. The resulting credential may be a 'named' degree in policing. Ultimately, these programs reflect the 'professional policing' model of higher education where the police organisation remains essentially the dominant partner by way of its gatekeeping role into the profession. According to this model, policing students may be effectively quarantined from their mainstream peers, thus minimising the potential 'liberalising' effect of attendance at university. In short, liberal education gets displaced by a model developed and owned by police organisations.

There is some evidence of the potential negative effects of sequestering police-oriented students from other tertiary students. Research on the Advanced Certificate experience in Queensland (Christie, Petrie, & Timmins, 1996) indicated that university education had some positive impact on attitudes and values of recruits, but deterioration set in as recruits encountered the 'substantial and deliberalising' impact of academy training and in particular the early years of socialisation on the job (Christie et al., 1996, p. 299). The CJC (1993) also found that recruits surveyed at the end of their university-academy year, and again after their field training, revealed a 22% decline among those who rated as important learning about 'the role of police in society' and 'social issues'. More recently, research comparing different educational pathways into policing (associate degree and full degree) in one university–police partnership found that 'social reasons' provided by students for wanting to become a police officer ('making a difference in the community', 'helping others') declined considerably after the academy practicum experience for both groups (Jennett et al., 2008).

Concluding Comments

Following the recommendations of the Fitzgerald Inquiry the Queensland Police Service experimented with university-based education for recruits and serving officers and, for a short time, a broadly liberal concept of police education was attempted. Elsewhere in Australia, following similar crises of public confidence in policing, other police organisations have developed partnerships with universities. Several commissions of inquiry in the period 1987–2004 advocated the need for a significant component of liberal education for police recruits. Currently two models have emerged for police higher education. One is a liberal model whereby police organisations recruit the best people available, preferably with a tertiary education. The other is a 'professional policing' model which specifies a vocationally oriented higher education for (intending) recruits. The latter model may raise standards of operational policing, but it is not clear how it will contribute to making police organisations more diverse, representative, and accountable. Neither model at this time provides sufficient graduates entering policing and so organisations maintain multiple pathways into the job.

There is no obvious reason, of course, why police organisations should not form educational partnerships with universities. In Queensland, for instance, a police–university partnership could conceivably build on in-service programs to provide a baccalaureate qualification which articulates with the Diploma of Public Safety, which is awarded to sworn constables after their initial training, combined with the CDP and the MDP discussed earlier. However, this would be an in-service program for serving officers, awarded after several years of policing experience, higher education, and reflection. It would not constitute a mode of pre-service selection into the job. The rationale even for in-service partnerships needs to be carefully delineated and progress monitored, especially by the university provider. Carlan (2007), for example, noted that criminal justice degrees utilised by serving police (and valued by them for a number of positive reasons), may slide toward police operational and management needs, and away from big questions about policing a liberal-democratic society.

In any case, the research literature is ambivalent about the relation between university education and police professionalism. Doubtless, individual officers benefit from degree studies, but how this translates into doing a better job of policing remains largely unexplored in Australia. A decade ago, Baro and Burlingame (1999), surveying the American scene, claimed that we should not expect to identify positive connections because much policing did not require those skills apparently gained from a degree. They concluded that if universities wanted to contribute to police professionalism and accountability, then they were better advised to establish research and other working partnerships with police organisations, rather than seeking to secure student numbers through involvement in police education.

References

Baro, A., & Burlingame, D. (1999). Law enforcement and higher education: Is there an impasse? *Journal of Criminal Justice Education, 10*(1), 57–73.

Barrow, P., & Pitman, G. (1995). Queensland police education policy development (1989–1993): The untold story. *Criminology Australia, 6*(3), 15–20.

Bradley, D. (1996). Contemporary police education in Australia. In D. Chappell & P. Wilson (Eds.), *Australian policing: Contemporary issues* (pp. 85–110). Sydney, Australia: Butterworths.

Bradley, D., & Cioccarelli, P. (1994). A new accountability: Education and the liberation of policing. In K. Bryett & C. Lewis (Eds.), *Un-Peeling tradition: Contemporary policing* (pp. 72–83). Melbourne, Australia: Macmillan/CAPSM.

Bragg, D. (1998). *An analysis of the influence of higher education on the job satisfaction and organisational commitment of Queensland police officers.* Unpublished PhD thesis, Queensland University of Technology, Australia.

Bryett, K. (1992). The preparation of police recruits, Queensland style. *The Police Journal, 65*(1), 49–55.

Buerger, M. (1998). Police training as a Pentecost: Using tools singularly ill-suited to the purpose of reform. *Police Quarterly, 1*(1), 27–63.

Carlan, P. (2007). The criminal justice degree and policing: Conceptual development or occupational primer? *Policing: An International Journal of Police Strategies & Management, 30*(4), 608–619.

Carter, D., Sapp, A., & Stephens, D. (1989). *The state of police education: Policy direction for the 21st century.* Washington, DC: Police Executive Research Forum.

Christie, G., Petrie, S., & Timmins, P. (1996). The effect of police education, training and socialisation on conservative attitudes. *Australian and New Zealand Journal of Criminology, 29*(3), 299–314.

Courtright, K., & Mackey, D. (2004). Job desirability among criminal justice majors: Exploring relationships between personal characteristics and occupational attractiveness. *Journal of Criminal Justice Education, 15*(2), 311–326.

Criminal Justice Commission (CJC). (1992) *Pre-evaluation Assessment of the Police Recruit Certificate Course.* Brisbane, Australia: Author.

Criminal Justice Commission (CJC). (1993). *Recruitment and education in the Queensland Police Service: A review.* Brisbane, Australia: Author.

Criminal Justice Commission (CJC). (1994) *Implementation of Reform within the Queensland Police Service.* Brisbane, Australia: Author.

Criminal Justice Commission (CJC). (1995). *Public attitudes towards the Queensland Police Service.* Brisbane, Australia: Author.

Criminal Justice Commission (CJC). (1996). *Briefing Note: Key Findings of Pre-Training Survey (May 1996 Recruit Intake).* Brisbane, Australia: Author.

Criminal Justice Commission (CJC). (1997). *Queensland Police Service Academy Training: The Views of Recruits.* Brisbane, Australia: Author.

Fitzgerald, G., Commissioner. (1989). *Commission of inquiry into possible illegal activities and associated police misconduct.* Brisbane, Australia: Government Printer.

Flanagan, T. (2000). Liberal education and the criminal justice major. *Journal of Criminal Justice Education, 11*(1), 1–13.

Gilligan, G. (2002). Royal Commissions of Inquiry. *Australian and New Zealand Journal of Criminology, 35*(3), 289–307.

Hyde, M., & Wimshurst, K. (1993, April). *Police recruits in 1991 and 1992: Past and future contexts.* Paper presented at the Police Education in Australia: The Way Ahead conference, Brisbane, Australia.

Jennett, C., Islam, M., Bull, D. & Woolston, R. (2008, November). *Occupational identity of police recruits.* Paper presented at the Australian and New Zealand Society of Criminology conference, Canberra, Australia.

Jones, D., Jones, L., & Prenzler, T. (2005). Tertiary education, commitment, and turnover in police work. *Police Practice and Research, 6*(1), 49–63.

Kennedy, G.A., Commissioner. (2004). *Royal commission into whether there has been corrupt or criminal conduct by any Western Australian police officer, Vol. 2.* Perth, Australia: Government Printer.

Lee, M., & Punch, M. (2004). Policing by degrees: Police officers' experience of university education. *Policing & Society, 14*(3), 233–249.

Lewis, C., & Prenzler, T. (1993). Teaching police ethics. *Queensland Researcher, 9*(1), 1–14.

Lidgard, C. (1988, August). *How expectations change? The changing expectations of Queensland police recruits after fifteen months education.* Paper presented at the XXIV International Congress of Psychology, Sydney, Australia.

Mitchell, G., & Musgrove, R. (2006). Policing by degree? *Queensland Police Union Journal, March,* 14–15.

Queensland Police Union of Employees. (1992). *Queensland Police Union Journal.* November, p. 4; December, p. 5.

Police Commissioner's Report. (1984–85). *Queensland Parliamentary Papers, Vol. 3,* Report No. 90, pp. 6–11.

Polk, O., & Armstrong, D. (2001). Higher education and law enforcement career paths: Is the road to success paved by degree? *Journal of Criminal Justice Education, 12*(1), 77–99.

President's Commission on Law Enforcement and Administration of Justice. (1967). *The challenge of crime in a free society.* Washington, DC: US Government Printer.

Public Sector Management Commission. (1993). *Review of the Queensland Police Service.* Brisbane, Australia: Government Printer.

Roberg, R., & Bonn, S (2004). Higher education and policing: Where are we now? *Policing: An International Journal of Police Strategies & Management, 27*(4), 469–486.

Smithers, A., Hill, S., & Silvester, G. (1990). *Graduates in the police service.* School of Education, University of Manchester, UK.

Wimshurst, K., & Allard, T. (2007). Criminal justice education, employment destinations, and graduate satisfaction. *Australian and New Zealand Journal of Criminology, 40*(2), 218–235.

Wimshurst, K., & Ransley, J. (2007). Police education and the university sector: Contrasting models from the Australian experience. *Journal of Criminal Justice Education, 18* (1), 106–122.

Wood, J. (Commissioner). (1997). *Royal Commission into the New South Wales Police Service, Vol. 2: Reform.* Sydney, Australia: Government Printer.

The Renewal of Parliament: A Fitzgerald Legacy?

Noel Preston

During the closing decades of the 20th century an international focus on the need to 're-invent' government and, along with this, to re-examine and reform ethical conduct developed in public institutions. Legislators and their parliaments around the world were not immune from this trend. The doctrine of ministerial accountability in Westminster-derived parliaments was a key element of this focus. Furthermore, some argued that the regeneration of the institution of parliament itself and a restatement of the obligations issuing from the protection of parliamentary privilege were essential components for such a revitalisation of governance in public life.

In the United States, the legacy of the Watergate scandal of the 1970s was still being played out through the establishment of the Office of Government Ethics in Washington. In a parallel development, many legislatures across the United States were establishing Codes of Ethics and House Ethics committees. North of the border in Canada, in a quiet but thorough way, government in Ottawa, along with provincial legislatures, instituted various manifestations of Ethics Commissions or Ethics Counsellors. European parliaments were also undergoing transformation. Symptomatic of this process was the implementation in the United Kingdom of a 1995 report by Lord Nolan into ethical standards in public life, resulting in the establishment of a Parliamentary Commission for Standards. Generally it was not some high-minded vision of reform that aided these developments but the exposure of scandals involving legislators as were the 'Sleaze' and 'Cash for Questions' affairs in Britain.

In Australia a range of inquiries following allegations of misconduct and corruption by elected and non-elected officials had similar consequences.

New South Wales led the way in 1988 with the establishment of the Independent Commission against Corruption, a standing commission with a brief which included investigating and reporting on the conduct of politicians. At the same time in Queensland Tony Fitzgerald QC was leading a *Commission of Inquiry into Possible Illegal Activities and Associated Police Misconduct* (hereafter referred to as the Fitzgerald Inquiry). As the terms of this inquiry widened it became apparent that the 238 days of public inquiry would lead to a report with widespread ramifications for the State of Queensland. The Fitzgerald Inquiry quickly developed from an examination of salacious allegations about prostitution and police corruption to what was effectively scrutiny of misconduct in government administration including that of politicians, along with some far-reaching analysis of what had contributed to this misconduct. Moreover, its impact extended beyond Queensland especially via what may be loosely termed the 'Fitzgerald phenomenon'. The inquiry's report was a catalyst issuing in the agencies formed as a result of the inquiry, which led to numerous research reports and recommendations. The Fitzgerald Inquiry generated an ongoing influence characterised by a public discourse about administrative and institutional reform including, but not confined to, criminal justice systems. In particular the *Report of a Commission of Inquiry Pursuant to Orders in Council* (hereafter referred to as the Fitzgerald Report) contributed directly to attempts at parliamentary reform in Queensland and thereby was linked, to some degree, with the international movement of legislative reform alluded to in this introduction.

This chapter is essentially a Queensland case study of how effective the Fitzgerald-inspired initiatives proved to be in the renewal of Parliament and how widespread beyond Queensland was its influence. Such an assessment first requires a quick overview of the state of Queensland's Parliament pre-Fitzgerald.

Australian state legislatures were spawned in the Westminster tradition, a system of government which assumes that the executive (or the cabinet) is accountable to the legislature whose members represent the will of the people. Not uniquely, but patently, there has been a long history of dominance by the executive over the legislature in the Queensland Parliament. Fifty years before the Fitzgerald Inquiry, echoing words of a former Chief Justice in Australia, a Queensland government backbencher, Jack Duggan (later leader of the ALP Opposition from 1957), told the Legislative Assembly: 'If Parliament becomes a mere sounding board for Cabinet, the danger is that parliamentary government will fall into contempt'.[1]

It is popularly argued that this inability of members of the Legislative Assembly in Queensland to challenge Cabinet and the premier, or even scrutinise legislation, derives from the abolition of the Legislative Council in

1922. This is too simplistic an explanation, as it assumes that the restoration of an upper house would restore the capacity for legislative review which was absent in pre-Fitzgerald days. There were, and are, many other long-standing structural defects in the procedures and practices of the Queensland Parliament contributing to the abuse of parliament by a succession of governments (Ransley, 2008).

The government led by Johannes Bjelke-Petersen (1968–87) contributed significantly to the weakening of Parliament. As premier he mercilessly denied the Opposition the resources that might have enabled them to be more effective participants in the parliamentary process. Electorally he dominated, in part by manipulating a famous gerrymander inherited from earlier ALP governments. In 1974, the ALP Opposition was reduced to a record low of 11 members only in a Legislative Assembly of 82 members. As head of a coalition government Bjelke-Petersen was often ruthless with Members of Parliament (MPs) from the coalition's junior partner, the Liberal Party.[2] The procedures of Parliament offered little scope for scrutiny of government: routinely, ministers were not subject to questions without notice, parliamentary sitting days were abysmally few, citizens were frequently vilified under privilege with no citizens' right of reply and, in particular, there was virtually no committee structure through which backbenchers could influence the public policy agenda while, for all practical purposes, a succession of pro-government Speakers provided no balance to the overbearing dominance of the government in the unicameral parliament. The result was that the Queensland Parliament was an impotent forum. Notwithstanding this record, when Premier Joh Bjelke-Petersen was honoured with a knighthood by Her Majesty in 1984, the citation for the award referred to his belief in parliamentary democracy and improvements to the parliamentary process (Murphy, Joyce, Cribb, & Wear, 2003).

When Mike Ahern succeeded Sir Joh, he became the first premier since the early 20th century to espouse parliamentary reform as a high priority. He immediately took steps to establish a Public Accounts Committee and Public Works Committee, while in April 1989 he introduced a Register of Members Interests which passed into law in the hiatus between termination of the Fitzgerald Inquiry and the release of the Commission's Report. Of course, he also famously made a promise, which his own party denied him the opportunity to keep, that he would institute the Fitzgerald Report 'lock, stock and barrel'.

Parliamentary Reform According to Fitzgerald

In the plain speaking and accessible style of the report, Commissioner Fitzgerald laid out the 'role of Parliament':

> Parliament is meant to be the forum in which the necessity and worth of proposed laws ... can be debated. It should also serve as an inquest in which all or any aspects of public administration can be raised. (Fitzgerald, 1989, p. 123)

He went on to link Parliament's role to the eradication of the corrupt activities his inquiry had revealed:

> It is much less likely that a pattern of misconduct will occur in the Government's public administration if the political process of public debate and opposition are allowed to operate, and the objectives of the parliamentary system are honestly pursued. (Fitzgerald, 1989, pp. 123–124)

As a means to that end, the report notes the importance of an 'impartial speaker' and an 'effective opposition' in the operation of Queensland's unicameral legislature. Fitzgerald wrote of the need for an informed parliament. In particular, he argued for a considerably improved parliamentary committee system which would lead to more informed membership enhancing the capacity of parliament to scrutinise the actions of government:

> Elsewhere the effective and efficient operation of Parliament has been enhanced by the setting up of all-party policy and investigatory committees. (They) have become a vital and energetic part of giving effect to the democratic process ... They serve as Parliament's research arm and as an independent source of information to aid proper Parliamentary debate. (Fitzgerald, 1989, p. 124)

In the structures proposed for implementation of the report, Fitzgerald underlined the supremacy of parliament in a Westminster democracy. Parliament, via two new all-party parliamentary committees — the Parliamentary Criminal Justice Committee (PCJC) and the Parliamentary Committee for Electoral and Administrative Review PCEAR) — not the Executive, was entrusted with the power of supervision and review of the two standing commissions charged with examining the report's recommendations (the Criminal Justice Commission (CJC) and the Electoral and Administrative Review Commission (EARC)). The possibility of executive interference in the preparation of final recommendations was thereby significantly minimised while public input into the process was potentially maximised.

The report's call for a review of electoral laws directly links the establishment of fair and free elections with the capacity of Parliament to reflect the public will through legislation, as well as to be a check and balance on the misuse of executive power.

> ... the institutional culture of public administration risks degeneration if, for any reason, a Government's activities ceased to be moderated by concern at the possibility of losing power. (Fitzgerald, 1989, p. 127)

Secrecy in government was raised as a major impediment to executive government's accountability, and as a matter directly linked to the abuse and misuse of parliament:

> Secrecy and propaganda are major impediments to accountability, which is a prerequisite for the proper functioning of the political process. Worse, they are the hallmarks of a diversion of power from the Parliament. (Fitzgerald, 1989, p. 126)

The recommendations for consideration by the proposed EARC, issuing from the section of the Fitzgerald Report captioned 'The Political Context', went beyond the matters canvassed above. They included better resourcing of non-government MPs, review of the guidelines for registration and disclosure of members' and ministers' financial interests, establishment of a register of donations to political parties, and review of the Code of Conduct for Public Officials. Taken together they represented a brief for comprehensive parliamentary reform. Moreover, they assumed this reform was not merely desirable but necessary, and, by implication, not a matter to be left simply to the Members of Parliament themselves.[3]

Parliamentary Reform in Queensland

Less than six months after the publication of the Fitzgerald Report, the Goss Labor Government was elected with a strong mandate to institute the report's recommendations. The new Premier, Wayne Goss, brought a clear understanding of accountability and the proprieties of public office to the leadership of government. Reform of the police service and the public sector proceeded at a furious rate. At the same time, the new government was reluctant to implement fully the numerous reports tabled in Parliament by PCEAR and the PCJC. The new Government resourced its Opposition more generously than had been previous practice, while a revamped electoral system reduced the malapportionment of voter distribution by electorates (although a zonal system was retained, giving weight to certain remote electorates). However, when it came to the reform of Parliament itself there was a greater reluctance to advance the agenda. Several factors conspired to slow the reform of parliamentary practice, while other reforms such as an independent speaker and an increase of sitting days were never really considered.

Executive government continued to dominate the legislature, partly because the Goss Government was inclined to view Parliament (to borrow the words of one Goss biographer) as 'an unwelcome interruption to the smooth running of government business from the executive building in George Street' (Murphy et al., 2003, p. xvi). This attitude complemented the long-standing tendency among elected members to differentiate themselves from unelected public officials and to be protective of their own interests under the cover of parliamentary privilege. In turn they embraced a rationale that no body external to Parliament should create impositions on MPs. This view was consolidated in the reaction of many parliamentarians to the CJC's adverse *Report on Parliamentary Travel Entitlements* in 1991. The investigation leading to the report fostered an acrimonious relationship between the CJC and many parliamentarians who believed the commission had 'exceeded its authority by launching the investigation' (Fleming and Holland, 2001, pp. 130–132). However, the government was forced to take action against some of its own members accused of travel entitlement irregularities, arguably because public opinion was sensitively attuned to political misconduct, influenced as it was by recent memories of the Fitzgerald Inquiry itself. In the Goss Government's first term, fuelled by other episodes such as the partial legalisation of prostitution, tension also emerged between Cabinet and the parliamentary committee overseeing the CJC, headed as it was by the high profile and independently minded Peter Beattie. Altogether, the Parliament strengthened in its resolve to protect itself from external, reforming pressures.

Nonetheless, across subsequent years, many Fitzgerald-inspired reforms were adopted. Most notable of these is a significantly augmented parliamentary committee system. However, almost 20 years after Fitzgerald's work was completed, one researcher (Ransley, 2008), who has studied developments in Queensland's Parliament, concluded: 'Fitzgerald's vision of Parliament as an inquest of government administration has proved largely illusory'.

EARC tabled its report on parliamentary committees in November 1992. As was the process, the PCEAR reviewed EARC's report and proposed an amended committee model. That model moved from EARC's approach, which would have based committees on policy areas, to that preferred by the PCEAR: committees divided on a functional basis. In September 1995 the Goss Government introduced the Parliamentary Committees Bill.[4] The subsequent Act provided for seven substantial committees. Although the Goss Government had reformed the budget process as early as 1992, Estimates Committees (for budget accountability in each portfolio) were added later by resolution of the Assembly, although in Janet Ransley's judgment (2008, p. 249) 'perusal of the transcripts of these hearings shows this examination is brief, fragmented, and hardly probing'.

Very recently in May 2009, the *Parliament of Queensland Act 2001* (Qld) was amended. It made significant changes to the parliamentary committee system, effectively moving it much closer to EARC's original model. Three new policy committees have been established on economic development, environment and resources, and social development, and the functions of the former Legal, Constitutional and Administrative Review Committee have been absorbed in the new Law, Justice and Safety Committee. It is too early to assess the work of these new committees.

Apart from the PCJC (now the Parliamentary Crime and Misconduct Committee [PCMC]) the new committees in the 1995 Act reflecting the reform agenda that encouraged bipartisan scrutiny were the Members' Ethics and Parliamentary Privileges Committee (MEPPC), the Scrutiny of Legislation Committee (SLC) and the Legal, Constitutional and Administrative Review Committee (LCARC). Over time each committee has been prolific in preparing reports for Parliament. LCARC has released more than 60 reports, ranging from freedom of information to a major review of the Queensland Constitution. A vital innovation in the 1995 Act, which was consistent with Fitzgerald's emphasis in his discussion of Parliament, was a requirement that ministers respond to recommendations from committee reports within 3 months, at least in an interim way, with final responses made within 6 months. Over time, full compliance with this provision has, regrettably, been rare.

In its review of the Office of Parliamentary Counsel (Report, May 1991) EARC emphasised the need for a system to check on legislation ensuring that legislation conforms to defined, but not enforceable, legislative principles (Laurie and Timperley, 2001). The SLC is the committee charged with that task. Since its inception, across several parliaments, the SLC has diligently issued reports on legislation. However, responses to the committee's suggestions by ministers and sponsors of Bills have been spasmodic and inconsistent. In recent years (as Ransley reports), around 40% of the reports have lapsed without a proper response. Ransley (2008) offers the conclusion that while this committee does perform scrutiny functions they often have 'little effect in terms of government response'.

Potentially, the MEPPC is a major vehicle for enhancing accountability, transparency and improved parliamentary conduct. However, it has rarely examined the behaviour of individual parliamentarians or government ministers in particular. Recently, for instance, in examining allegations that Minister Nuttall lied to an Estimates' Committee in 2006, the Beattie government bypassed the MEPPC, instead dealing with the issue in the Legislative Assembly where its will could be imposed unquestioningly. One major task of the Ethics and Privileges Committee is to review the Act governing declarations by all MPs in the Pecuniary Interests' Register. Again, the committee was bypassed in the early years of the Beattie Government, when a motion to reduce the requirements for declaration of hospitality received by members was introduced to the Parliament as a whole by Minister Terry Mackenroth. This government-led action was effectively a defiance of the earlier *Report on Pecuniary Interests* by the MEPPC.

The MEPPC also oversees the administration and interpretation of the Members' Code of Ethical Standards. All new members are offered induction training on the Code document. In practice, the occasions when the code is invoked are few. Drafting a Code of Ethical Standards for Members was a key task given MEPPC at its inception. In addition, the parliamentary reference to the committee was to develop a process for complaints about breaches of the code. The 1992 *Report on the Review of Codes of Conduct for Public Officials* EARC declared:

> To the Commission it seems inescapable that if the elected government is to work effectively, the ethical standards of elected officials need to be declared publicly, and a continuing effective process for disciplining breaches of those standards needs to be developed and implemented ... recourse to the ballot box every two or three years has been shown to be largely ineffective as a process for achieving such discipline. (Electoral and Administrative Review Commission, 1992, p. 146)

When the *Public Sector Ethics Act 1994* (Qld) was passed enshrining a code for unelected officials, the legislation was silent about requirements for elected officials.[5] Indeed it was another seven years before the Parliament endorsed a code for MPs. In 1998, an excellent and thorough report on the MEPP Committee's research into the development and use of a code was published. Three years later a code was adopted by Parliament that restates the obligations of parliamentarians such as the use of allowances, disclosure of interests, conduct in the Legislative Assembly, requirements of electoral laws and appropriate use of information. These provisions are set in their ethical context by an aspirational preamble, which includes a Statement of (6) Fundamental Principles.

While advice in interpreting the code resides with MEPPC and the Clerk of Parliament, the appointment of an integrity commissioner in 2001 provided some further capacity for ethical advice, but not to the Parliament as a whole. The Integrity Commissioner is a part-time official with limited powers accessed voluntarily by certain designated persons including ministers and government members of parliamentary committees. In 2009 Premier Bligh announced an expansion of the role of the Integrity Commissioner. One reform is the inclusion of all Members of Parliament as 'designated persons'. In introducing the amendments to the *Public Sector Ethics Act*, which provide for the appointment of the Integrity Commissioner, Premier Beattie linked this initiative to the range of 'pioneering reforms' established by 'Queensland Labor governments since the Fitzgerald Inquiry' (Fleming & Holland, 2001, Ch. 10). This and other initiatives, despite their limitations, are welcome additions to the administrative edifice made possible since the Fitzgerald Inquiry. Similarly, periods of public proactivity and scrutiny since 1989 from various auditors-general and other statutory officers who report to Parliament have been facilitated in a climate of public opinion substantially changed since Commissioner Fitzgerald's report.

Limited reform of parliamentary procedures since the 1989 election is evident, but its links to the post-Fitzgerald reform reports are indirect. Question Time is potentially an occasion when opposition and backbench government MPs can scrutinise government performance. Generally, however, Question Time is a politically managed exercise. It took until March 21, 1995, for the Legislative Assembly to adopt new procedures making Question Time a forum for asking Questions without Notice, instead of the previously over-used practice of asking and answering Questions on Notice during Question Time. Significantly, many of the reforms liberating a greater proportion of sitting days for direct contributions by Opposition, Independent and government back-bench members emerged in the period of minority government under Premiers Borbidge and Beattie (in his first term). In the Borbidge years (1995–1998), the Leader of Government Business initiating procedural changes was another Tony FitzGerald who was responsible for expanding these opportunities through grievance debates and private members' bills. The change to minority government raised briefly the possibility of an independent speaker, but this was abandoned when the coalition government decided to return to the convention of appointing a government member, indeed, in this case, one from the former Bjelke-Petersen government, Neil Turner MP, who promptly and controversially sacked an appointee of previous Speaker Jim Fouras, the Deputy Clerk, whose major brief was to manage parliamentary changes in the post-Fitzgerald era.

In her detailed analysis of parliamentary procedural changes since the Fitzgerald Report, Ransley (2008) concludes that they have resulted in 'nominal' improvement only. The Parliament still meets relatively infrequently, while even though there are more ministerial statements and on sitting days a period of Questions without Notice, there is little indication that these trends lead to more scrutiny of government within the Parliament.

In summary, there is little evidence that 'the Fitzgerald phenomenon' has renewed the Queensland legislature; indeed, with the exception of the parliamentary scrutiny committees (PCMC, LCARC, SLC, MEPPC) such reforms as have occurred can barely be traced to the implementation of the Fitzgerald Report, and, as this discussion shows, the ongoing effectiveness even of these committees is questionable. Twenty years after the Commission of Inquiry finished its business there is a strong case for revitalisation of the Queensland Parliament in ways that have more prospect of enhancing government accountability. Structural reforms may be needed, such as reducing the proportion of members under the mantle of Cabinet (a consequence of the increasing raft of Parliamentary Secretaries), as well as revisiting EARC's original proposals for parliamentary committees that focus on particular portfolios and policy functions.[6] In the Beattie Government years (and now the Bligh Government years) the lopsided majorities commanded by ALP governments, which serve to disenfranchise the legislature's power to challenge and scrutinise government, have raised questions about the effective functioning of Queensland's unicameral legislature. The case for reform of the electoral process and consequent changes to the composition of the Parliament, which might eliminate the possibility of huge majorities for government, has once again assumed some urgency.

Fitzgerald's Impact in Other Jurisdictions

Undeniably, the Commission of Inquiry led by Tony Fitzgerald QC and its consequences impacted in jurisdictions beyond Queensland, and its story has been alluded to in many international forums concerned with accountability and ethics in government. However, it can hardly be claimed that there is a direct connection between the 'Fitzgerald phenomenon' — a term explained at the outset of this chapter — and parliamentary reforms elsewhere that aim at greater scrutiny of executive government. There is a plausible suggestion that the Fitzgerald Inquiry process and its aftermath was particularly noted by Lord Nolan in the United Kingdom, whose report in the early 1990s led to a range of reforms in Westminster.[7] That granted, international legislative ethics reforms, such as the institution of an ethics committee or the appointment of an ethics counsellor as in Canadian parliaments, generally preceded the Queensland changes outlined in this chapter and were motivated by factors within the experience of those particular jurisdictions. So, rather than being the catalyst for global parliamentary reform, the Queensland changes themselves (whether procedural or of the parliamentary committee system or the adoption of codes and ethics advice) were influenced and developed in light of the experience of other jurisdictions. Indeed, an account of the diverse influences and interactions leading to reforms of parliamentary practice in other Australian states and the Parliament in Canberra — or, on the other hand, the procrastination and avoidance delaying such reforms — reveals little that supports a case that they were the result of 'the Fitzgerald phenomenon', although that phenomenon (and especially the reports generated by it) was inevitably a contributor to the discussion, advocacy and research surrounding Australian parliamentary reforms of the 1990s. In what follows, the outline of developments in other jurisdictions shows that where parliamentary practice has been subject to moves aimed at enhancing capacity for scrutiny and monitoring of integrity standards, the genesis of such reforms was usually quite independent of 'the Fitzgerald phenomenon' in Queensland.

In New South Wales, spurred on by the actions of independent members of Parliament and after years of controversy about alleged corruption affecting senior politicians, the Independent Commission Against Corruption (ICAC) was formed in 1988, prior to the date Commissioner Fitzgerald completed his work in Queensland. The impact from ICAC on parliamentarians in NSW was acute during 'the Metherell Affair'. In April 1992 the NSW Legislative Council and Legislative Assembly asked ICAC to inquire into the circumstances surrounding Dr Terry Metherell's resignation from Parliament and subsequent appointment to a senior public service position (Fleming & Holland, 2001). The upshot of this was the resignation of Nick Greiner as Premier and his Minister for the Environment, although the Supreme Court later that year exonerated Greiner and his minister from the charge of corruption. This episode understandably heightened the wariness of politicians across Australian jurisdictions about interference by external watchdog bodies in the exercise of their political role. In part, although there were other factors at work, (such as the advocacy and leadership of the former NSW Assembly Speaker, Kevin Rozzolli), this experience gave impetus to the work of the Members' Ethic committees in both NSW Houses during the 1990s. This work resulted in an ethics code and the appointment for the first time in an Australian parliament of a part-time (and non-member) ethics adviser. In practice, these reforms were very disappointing and minimally reformist at best (Preston, Sampford, & Connors, 2002; Preston, 2001; Preston, Sampford, & Bois, 1998).

If a parliamentary code is a benchmark of accountability within a legislature then Victoria might have been well ahead of other states. As early as 1978 Victoria adopted a code focusing on conflicts of interest in the *Members of Parliament (Register of Interests) Act*. When in 1996, the Premier Jeff Kennett was accused of confusing private and public interests in his wife's acquisition of 50,000 shares in Guandong Corporation,[8] the code enshrined in the Act was shown to be ineffective, except as a reference in the political debate surrounding allegations of the Premier's misuse of office. Rather, it was other abuses of power by the Kennett government that led to its defeat by the ALP. Led by Premier Bracks, whose election platform promised parliamentary reform chiefly through electoral reform of the Upper House, structural changes are now in place that make it more difficult for future governments to dominate the bicameral legislature.

In Western Australia (WA) allegations of corruption led to a *Royal Commission into Whether There Has Been Corrupt or Criminal Conduct by Any Western Australian Police Officer* (what was popularly known as WA

Inc.). This investigation of illegal business dealings in WA in 1992 resulted in a former state premier and other high ranking party figures being jailed. One consequence of this commission was the establishment of the Public Sector Standards Commission, which framed a program developed independently of, but nonetheless influenced by, reforms in Queensland. Again, there was little impact on Parliament (although it was in the Western Australian Parliament that the Annual Conference of the Australian Study of Parliament Group met in 1998 on the theme of legislative ethics and codes). Only when a crisis — generated by findings of the WA Anti-Corruption Commission about misconduct by certain Members of Parliament in their dealings with lobbyists — engulfed the Carpenter Labor Government across 2006–2008, were there moves to clarify expectations for ethical conduct by members and institute a program of ethics training for members of parliament in 2009.

A postscript to this section might note that there has been no sustained attempt to develop a comprehensive ethics regime in the Parliament of Australia, although half-hearted, recurring attempts by various Prime Ministers of the Commonwealth to establish standards of accountability for their Ministers have characterised administrations in the recent past.

A Concluding Assessment

In summary, it is reasonable to conclude that, rather than subjecting themselves to new standards of accountability and improved strategies for scrutiny of executive government as Tony Fitzgerald QC had signalled in 1989, parliaments across Australian jurisdictions have practised resistance and delay, rather than reforming zeal, when it comes to such reforms (Preston, 2001). In no way does this conclusion diminish the rigour or importance of the reports, research and documentation generated in the wake of Commissioner Fitzgerald's work; in particular, that produced by EARC, which goes back to fundamental principles of the Westminster system and has implications for parliamentary practice. Overall, that work led to John Uhr's conclusion that Queensland's reforms are 'the boldest policy measures that have emerged in recent years in Australian public service ethics' (2005, p. 131). Of course, Uhr's judgment is about government in general, not of parliament in particular. In fact in that regard, although there have been clear improvements in the functioning of the Queensland legislature, in practice that parliament falls well short of the ideals espoused by Fitzgerald.

That said, Queensland's Parliament is not alone in falling short of the ideal. Self-evidently, there is no easy corrective to these ills in a two-party adversarial system. Properly functioning parliamentary committees independent of the executive remain essential, as Fitzgerald emphasised. However, too much can be expected of parliamentary committees (Lewis, 2000). A range of ongoing reforms are necessary to deal with this malaise. Structural changes, such as a reduction in the disproportionate numbers of elected members under the control of the executive are also required. In Queensland's case, as a unicameral legislature, there would be merit in a review of the electoral system to better reflect minority electoral opinion, as happens in the New Zealand Parliament since the introduction of a mixed member proportional system, where coincidentally the committee system has considerable influence on government. Arguably, improvement in the calibre of parliamentarians is another facet of the change required; to achieve this and to support other accountability reforms the culture of political parties must also be challenged continually.

As the Fitzgerald phenomenon demonstrates — unpalatable as it seems to those (usually MPs themselves) who champion parliamentary privilege as if it were an absolute principle — external bodies supported by a critical body of public opinion can have a positive impact on the capacity of parliament to review and challenge executive government. That is why, in Queensland's case, a standing body similar to the EARC, regrettably terminated a few short years after the Fitzgerald Report was published, may be necessary.

Endnotes

1   Jack Duggan was quoting Sir Isaac Isaacs, one-time Chief Justice of Australia (Preston, 1997).
2   This tension between the coalition parties culminated in the withdrawal from coalition of the Liberal leader, Terry White, following White's futile insistence on the introduction of a Parliamentary Accounts Committee. After the 1984 election the defection of two Liberal members of cabinet allowed Bjelke-Petersen to bypass coalition and form a stand alone National Party government.
3   The PCEAR is no longer a Committee of the Parliament. It ceased its operations after processing all the work of EARC which itself was terminated in the second term of the Goss Government.
4   The 1995 Act was later superseded by the *Parliament of Queensland Act 2001*.
5   The 1995 Act establishing MEPPC required the Committee to take account of the Public Sector Ethics Act. For a fuller discussion of the development of the Queensland Code for MPs see Preston (2001).
6   In recent times the Parliament has used select committees (the Review of Organ and Tissue Donation Procedures and Investigation into Altruistic Surrogacy Committees) to produce excellent research and policy recommendations.
7   In an interview with the then Research director of the Queensland MEPPC, I was told that when the Queensland Committee visited the UK and met Nolan Commission officials, the conversation with those officials implied that they had already been helped considerably by the Queensland EARC Reports.
8   *The Age*, May 15, 1996 and *The Weekend Australian*, May 18–19, 1996.

References

Electoral and Administrative Review Commission (EARC). (1992). *Report on the Review of Codes Conduct for Public Office*. Brisbane, Australia: Author.

Fitzgerald, G. (1989). *Report of a Commission of Inquiry pursuant to Orders in Council*. Brisbane, Australia: Queensland Government.

Fleming, J., & Holland, I. (2001). *Motivating ministers to morality*. Aldershot, UK: Ashgate, Dartmouth Publishers.

Laurie, N. (2008, July). *Size matters — The problem of proportionally shrinking Parliaments*. Paper presented at the Presiding Officers and Clerks' Conference, Adelaide, Australia.

Laurie, N., & Timperley, A. (2001). Enhancing scrutiny. *The Parliamentarian, 3*, 59–64.

Lewis, C. (2000). The politics of civilian oversight: Serious commitment or lip service. In A.J. Goldsmith & C. Lewis (Eds.), *Civilian oversight of policing: Governance, democracy and human rights*. Oxford: Hart Publishing.

Murphy, D., Joyce, R., Cribb, M., & Wear, R. (Eds.). (2003). *The premiers of Queensland*. Brisbane, Australia: UQP.

Preston, N. (2001). Codifying ethical conduct for Australian Parliamentarians 1990–1999. *Australian Journal of Political Science, 36*, 45–60.

Preston, N., Sampford, C., & Bois, C.-A. (1998). *Ethics and political practice*. Sydney, Australia: Federation Press.

Preston, N., Sampford, C., & Connors, C. (2002). *Encouraging ethics and challenging corruption*. Sydney, Australia: Federation Press.

Ransley, J. (2008). Illusions of reform: Queensland's Legislative Assembly since Fitzgerald. In N. Aroney, S. Prasser & J.R. Nethercote (Eds.), *Restraining elective dictatorship — the upper house solution?* (pp. 240–253). Perth, Australia: University of WA Press.

Uhr, J. (2005). *Terms of trust*. Sydney, Australia: UNSW Press.

Freedom of Information (FoI) in Queensland and its Fitzgerald Origins

David Solomon

The Fitzgerald Proposal

The first Order in Council establishing what became known as the Fitzgerald Inquiry focused on the activities of five named people in relation to prostitution, unlawful gambling and illegal drug dealing, and whether any police corruption was involved. There was also a question whether any of the five made a corrupt payment to a political party in Queensland of $50,000. The second Order in Council, almost a month later, expanded the terms of reference only slightly. The third, a year and two months later, transformed the inquiry by empowering it to inquire into:

> 4. Any other matter or thing appertaining to the aforesaid matter or any of them *or concerning possible criminal activity, neglect or violation of duty, or official misconduct or impropriety the inquiry into* which to you shall seem meet and proper in the public interest. (Fitzgerald, 1989, p. A29)

The italicised words were additional to those included in the second Order in Council. The unamended paragraph was not included in the first Order in Council.[1]

This chapter is concerned with just one aspect of what Commissioner G.E. Fitzgerald QC considered relevant, in the public interest, to consider. He raised the problem under the heading 'secrecy', and wrote in part:

> The ultimate check on public administration is public opinion, which can only be truly effective if there are structures and systems designed to ensure that it is properly informed. A government can use its control of Parliament and public administration to manipulate, exploit and misinform the community, or to hide matters from it. Structures and systems designed for the

purpose of keeping the public informed must therefore be allowed to operate as intended. Secrecy and propaganda are major impediments to accountability, which is a prerequisite for the proper functioning of the political process. Worse, they are the hallmarks of a diversion of power from the Parliament. Information is the lynch-pin of the political process. Knowledge is, quite literally, power. If the public is not informed, it cannot take part in the political process with any real effect. (Fitzgerald, 1989, p. 126)

He dealt next with Freedom of Information:

> Freedom of Information Acts along the lines of the United States model has been adopted to grant a general right of access to documents held by government and government agencies. The professed aim of such legislation is to give all citizens a general right of access to government information. Appeals are allowed to an external independent review body when a request for information is refused in whole or in part, or when a person objects to a decision to release information about their affairs, or when the accuracy or completeness of personal information held by government is disputed by the person it concerns.

> It is true that where such legislation has been enacted in Australia (the Commonwealth, Victoria and more recently New South Wales) there has been criticism. Government agencies say that answering requests has been costly and disruptive. Applicants claim that some agencies are obstructive, that the exemptions are too wide or are abused, and that increasing charges make the cost of requests prohibitive.

> The importance of the legislation lies in the principle it espouses, and in its ability to provide information to the public and to parliament. It has already been used effectively for this purpose in other Parliaments. Its potential to make administrators accountable and keep the voters and Parliament informed are well understood by its supporters and enemies. (Fitzgerald, 1989, p. 129)

Fitzgerald proposed the establishment of an Electoral and Administrative Review Commission (EARC; see chapter 5) and made it clear that one of its priorities should be 'an investigation into Freedom of Information legislation and its desirability' (Fitzgerald, 1989, p. 371). EARC began functioning in late 1989. It did in fact treat Freedom of Information (FOI) as a priority, publishing an issues paper (its third) in May 1990. It presented its final report on the matter, including draft legislation, in December 1990. The report was then considered by the Parliamentary Committee for Electoral and Administrative Review (PCEAR) which produced its own report and gave its response to EARC's recommendations. Both the EARC and PCEAR reports were then considered by the Queensland Government. Legislation enacting FOI was assented to in August 1992.

That there was a need for FOI legislation, following the Fitzgerald Report and its revelations, and the adoption of FOI by most other Australian jurisdictions, was scarcely questioned. EARC said in its report:

The Commission, in the light of the widespread support for FOI legislation in the submissions [to EARC], does not propose to labor [sic] the arguments in support of giving persons access to government information. Suffice it to say that the Commission considers that information is the grist of government processes. The fairness of decisions made by government, and their accuracy, merit and acceptability, ultimately depend on the effective participation by those who will be affected by them. Further, when access to information is denied to the public it is thereby denied its right to exercise control over government. FOI legislation is crucial if access to information is to be obtained, and thereby participation in the processes, and control of, government is to be achieved. (EARC, 1990, p. 16)

Of the 116 recommendations in the EARC report, 109 were accepted by PCEAR and the remaining seven accepted with some modification. The government accepted 100 of the proposals in the PCEAR report, modified another 13, rejected just two and took no action on one other. A rejected recommendation was a proposal to establish a register of cabinet decisions to be published on a continuing basis with details of all decisions made by cabinet, but the information would be entered on the register 'at the discretion of the Premier' (EARC, 1990, p. A15). Among the modifications adopted by the government were two decisions that potentially reduced the availability of documents that could be accessed under FOI: first, an increase in the availability of Ministerial certificates and second, a limitation on the way FOI might override secrecy provisions in other Acts.

EARC's proposals largely followed the scheme of the Commonwealth *Freedom of Information Act 1983*, and took account of the FOI laws that had been enacted in most other States and the Australian Capital Territory, as well as the New Zealand *Official Information Act 1982*. One important change was to provide for external review of decisions by an independent Information Commissioner (a function given initially by the Queensland Government to the ombudsman, who, when acting as the Information Commissioner, would have a determinative power). The Commonwealth Act provided for external review by the Administrative Appeals Tribunal whereas the New Zealand Act gave that function to the Ombudsmen, who were able only to make recommendations, not determinations.

The first FOI legislation was adopted in Sweden more than 200 years ago. But it was not until the United States adopted its FOI law in 1966 that most western democracies began seriously considering adopting similar measures. In Australia, FOI was put on to the political agenda in the policies advocated by E.G. (Gough) Whitlam in the 1972 federal election campaign. This followed the publication of a book, *Secrecy*, written by James Spigelman (1972), who was to become Whitlam's private secretary after Labor won the 1972 election. Despite the creation by Whitlam of an interdepartmental committee (on which Spigelman sat) to consider FOI, no public progress was made by the Whitlam Government. The Fraser Government took up the project after it took power at the end of 1975, and in 1978 the cabinet approved a Bill that was to be put to parliament. Progress, however, was slow as the Bill was referred to a Senate Committee for investigation and report. The FOI legislation was eventually passed in 1982 (Solomon, 2009). Canada and New Zealand adopted FOI laws at about the same time and these three countries became the first with Westminster-style governmental systems to do so.

The Queensland law, at least initially, was used as a model by many countries. The *Irish Freedom of Information Act 1997*, for example, was modelled on the Queensland, Commonwealth and New Zealand laws and on the laws of some Canadian provinces (O'Reilly, 2007). The Queensland Government had high aspirations for its legislation. In introducing the measure the Attorney-General, Dean Wells, said:

> [T]his Bill will effect a major philosophical and cultural shift in the institutions of government in this State. The assumption that information held by government is secret unless there are reasons to the contrary is to be replaced by the assumption that information held by government is available unless there are reasons to the contrary. The perception that government is something remote from the citizen and entitled to keep its processes secret will be replaced by the perception that government is merely the agent of its citizens, keeping no secrets other than those necessary to perform its functions as an agent. Information, which in a modern society is power, is being democratised. (1991, p. 3851)

Backward Steps

However, the Queensland Parliament was soon involved in watering down one of the most important provisions of the legislation, the exemption covering cabinet materials. In 1993, in response to a decision by the Information Commissioner[2] the first of two important amendments was passed. It removed the requirement that to qualify for exemption, a document must be brought into existence for the *purpose* of submission to cabinet. The amendment made it sufficient that the document had been submitted to cabinet for its consideration. The change also narrowed the definition of what constituted 'merely factual matter' that was not covered by the exemption. In 1995, in response to a further Information Commissioner decision[3] the exemption was further broadened by removing the requirement that a document be 'for its [cabinet's] consideration'. Any purposive element was thus removed and it became sufficient for a document to fall within the exemption that it had been submitted to cabinet. The exception concerning factual matter was completely removed. It thus became possible for a document to be covered by the cabinet exemption even if it had never been intended that it should be considered by cabinet and even if it was not considered. It was sufficient for a document to be exempt under FOI if the document was taken into the cabinet room and made available to members of cabinet. Any document could gain the 'protection' of the cabinet exemption simply by being taken into the cabinet meeting room.[4]

Thus within a few years the Goss Government had managed to undermine and diminish the effectiveness of one of the key provisions of its own legislation. As a consequence of these two sets of amendments, information would be made available under FOI only if it was not inconvenient to the government to do so. The government had no need to issue conclusive certificates to protect information; rather it had available a very simple means of protecting a document; a minister could simply take the document into the cabinet room so that, under the terms of the amended legislation, the document would be entitled to the protection that was originally intended be afforded only to a genuine cabinet document.

These legislative changes, and the way they impacted on FOI, had critics even within the senior ranks of the Labor Party. Labor lost office in 1996. At the beginning of 1998 its new leader, Peter Beattie, introduced a private member's bill, intended to ensure, inter alia:

> ... that the cabinet exemption from FOI applies only for proper cabinet purposes and not for the improper purpose of merely evading FOI access. (1998, pp. 118–119)

However, on regaining government later that year, Beattie did nothing to implement this reform. His government also did not implement most of the reforms proposed in a report by the Queensland Parliamentary Legal, Constitutional and Administrative Review Committee in 2001. That committee had taken up proposals made in the report of the Australian Law Reform Commission/Administrative Review Council in 1995 for an information commissioner to have a role as FOI monitor.

Forward Leaps

It was not until Beattie retired and was replaced as Premier by Anna Bligh, that any real action to improve the prospect of disclosure of government information under FOI was taken. In September 2007, Bligh took to her very first cabinet meeting as premier (four days after her appointment) a proposal to establish a review of FOI in Queensland by an independent panel of three people. The review was expected and intended to carry out 'a complete overhaul' and produce 'an entirely new freedom of information act' (Bligh, 2007).

The panel was chaired by the author of this chapter while its two part-time members were Simone Webbe, a former Deputy Director-General of the Department of Premier and Cabinet and Dominic McGann, a partner in a firm of solicitors, McCullough Robertson. All three members had legal qualifications. All three had at some period worked for EARC, Webbe and McGann in 1990 and 1991, and Solomon as its chair from 1992 till its end in late 1993. The panel produced a discussion paper in January 2008 and their final 400-page report in June 2008. Unusually, the panel was invited by the premier to present that report directly to the cabinet before the premier made it public and generally endorsed its approach.

Less than two months later, cabinet began to consider a line-by-line analysis of its recommendations prepared by the Premier's Department. Cabinet took three weeks to complete its task. The results were then released on 20 August 2008 by the premier in a document, *The right to information — A response to the review of Queensland's Freedom of Information Act*. She said: 'the Queensland Government supports in full 116 of the report's recommendations, and either partially or in principle supports another 23 recommendations. Only two recommendations are not supported' (Queensland Government, 2008). In early December 2008, the government released two consultation drafts, the Right to Information Bill 2009 and the Information Privacy Bill 2009, incorporating the proposals adopted by cabinet.

In its official response to the panel's report, the Queensland Government said the report:

> ... proposes a complete rethink of the framework for access to information in Queensland. At the core of the report is a clear recommendation that government implement real enhancements to openness and accountability through a comprehensively developed change statement on information policy. The Queensland Government agrees that there is a need for government to renew its commitment to freedom of information through a new policy and legislative approach to freedom of information ... (Queensland Government, 2008, p. 2)

The government said it would implement 'a new legislative framework for access to information, as recommended by the panel, and agrees that the recommended title, Right to Information Act, will make the primary purpose of the new legislation clear' (Queensland Government, 2008, p. 5). Among the recommendations adopted were:

- Access and amendment rights for personal information should be moved from right to information legislation to a new Privacy Act.
- A reduced number of 'true' exemptions.
- Reframing the 'public interest test' to provide in legislation a list of factors that might arise for consideration in the process of deciding whether the disclosure would, on balance, be contrary to the public interest.
- Introduction of a purposive element into the cabinet exemption.
- Giving the cabinet exemption a maximum life of 10 years.

- Reducing the 30-year rule for cabinet materials held in archives from 30 to 20 years.
- Application of the legislation to most government-owned corporations.
- Ensuring accountability, through government agencies, of non-government organisations that receive funding or support from the government.
- Reduction of time limits for processing requests.
- Enhancing and expanding the role of the Information Commissioner to be both a champion and monitor of the right to access information.
- Development of a central electronic right to information (e-RTI) facility.
- Proactive release of information, including cabinet material.

(Queensland Government, 2008, p. 9)

The government concluded:

> The Independent Panel's Report has set some significant challenges for government. Implementing the recommendations in *The Right to Information Report* will require fundamental changes to government administration and organisational culture. It will also require clear leadership and commitment, and significant investment of time and resources. The Queensland Government recognises that we are not going to achieve the administrative and cultural change that is required to do this overnight. Nonetheless, the government has expressed its commitment to a new information policy paradigm and new legislation through the Right to Information Bill and a new Privacy Bill. This response is the first step down that path, and the beginning of a new era of openness, transparency and accountability for the Queensland Government. (Queensland Government, 2008, p. 9).

The government's response to the panel's recommendations was hailed by an independent Sydney FOI consultant, Peter Timmins, who wrote:

> There are still steps to be taken to translate intent into law, and to change attitudes in government about the public right to access information, but this is rolled gold reform. A whole of government information policy to increase proactive release of information, with CEOs to be told to get cracking now to see what can be done straight away; a new simplified act to be called the Right to Information Act with a strong objects clause to ensure disclosure considerations don't get waylaid by 'exemption creep'; clear governance responsibilities for making all this work assigned to the Premier and the Director General of her department. This is seriously good stuff ... Not surprisingly there is room for a few quibbles but not today. For the moment at least, Queensland has set the standard for the rest of the country, where reform is still in the air. Some such as the Federal Minister John Faulkner, the ACT and Tasmanian governments have shown real interest in what's been happening in Queensland (Timmins, 2008a).

The Commonwealth's FOI legislation was subject to a detailed review in the mid-1990s by the Australian Law Reform Commission (ALRC), in conjunction with the Administrative Review Council. Their report included numerous recommendations for reform — though not for radical changes — but all its proposals were ignored throughout the whole of the term of the Howard Government. In 2007, the Liberal Attorney-General, Philip Ruddock, gave a new reference on FOI to the ALRC, but this review was halted early in 2008 by the incoming Rudd Government.

The Queensland panel's discussion paper in January 2008 had noted that the policy platform of the new Labor Party federal government, elected in November 2007, included the following proposals:

a. revision of the *FOI Act* to promote a culture of disclosure and transparency;

b. appointment of a statutory Freedom of Information Commissioner;

c. rationalisation of the exemption provisions, and publication of guidelines, so that information is only withheld where this is in the public interest;

d. review of FOI charges to ensure they are not incompatible with the objects of disclosure and transparency — a scale of charges should be determined by the Information Commissioner, and access to an applicant's personal information should be provided free of charge; and

e. abolition of conclusive certificates, to ensure the public interest test is applied more thoroughly and consistently and to establish a pro-disclosure culture throughout government. (Independent Review Panel, 2008a, p. 40)

Senator John Faulkner was appointed Cabinet Secretary in the Rudd Government and made responsible for implementing the FOI reforms. On 24 March 2009 Senator Faulkner announced the major reforms the government intended to make to FOI at the Commonwealth level, having previously introduced legislation to abolish conclusive certificates. His media release said the key proposals were:

- Establishing two new statutory positions — Information Commissioner and FOI Commissioner — and bringing them together with the Privacy Commissioner in a new Office of the Information Commissioner. In terms of FOI, the new office will promote a culture of pro-disclosure across the government.

- Giving the new Information Commissioner the power to conduct merits based reviews of FOI decisions by agencies, including the power to use alternative dispute resolution tools.

- Introducing a new information publication scheme requiring agencies to proactively disclose more information to the public — and giving the Information Commissioner a key role in assisting agencies and monitoring their compliance with the scheme.

- Reduction of the Archives Act's 30-year rule for access to all documents to 20 years, and bringing forward access to cabinet notebooks from 50 to 30 years.

- Important changes to the fee regime — including the abolition of all FOI application fees; the abolition of all charges for a person seeking access to their own information; a charge-free first hour of decision making time for all FOI requests; and for not-for-profit organisations and journalists, a first five hour charge-free decision making period.

- Introducing a single, clear pro-disclosure public interest test, and ensuring that factors such as *embarrassment to the government*, or *causing confusion and unnecessary debate*, can no longer be relied on to withhold access to documents.

- Extending the FOI Act to cover documents held by service providers contracted to the government.

- Introducing a strong new objects clause in the FOI Act, which emphasises that information held by government is a national resource, reinforcing that the aim of the FOI Act is to give the Australian community access to information held by government. (Faulkner, 2009)

In August 2008 the new Tasmanian Premier, David Bartlett, announced a plan to strengthen trust in democracy and political processes in Tasmania. The first item in the 10-point plan was 'A review of the Freedom of Information Act' (Tasmanian Government, 2009, p. 7). Mr Bartlett said in a press release, the government would undertake:

> [a]n immediate review of the *Freedom of Information Act*, with a view to improving, if necessary, access to information for all Tasmanians, as well as of the administration of the act. This will include a thorough look at the recommendations of the reviews already conducted of both the Commonwealth legislation and the recent Queensland act review. In fact, the Solomon Review of the Queensland FOI system will be the starting point for this review. Secondly, we will significantly strengthen the implementation of the act by providing additional resources in the training, salary and staff numbers of FOI officers and units, as well as the development of rigorous manuals and guidelines for use by people working in this area across government agencies. The Department of Justice will oversee this review, but it will be conducted with the use of independent FOI experts from outside of our government and outside of Tasmania ... This is something which we will commence now. (Bartlett, 2008)[5]

In April, 2009 the Department of Justice issued a directions paper indicating that many of the proposals adopted in Queensland were also likely to be adopted in Tasmania. The Tasmanian proposals include:

- increased publishing of core information to improve accountability and improve public debate;

- a new *Right to Information Act*;

- an enhanced role for the ombudsman in relation to both external review and the monitoring of release of information;

- an overarching public interest test detailed in legislation; and transfer of requests for personal information to the *Personal Information Protection Act.*

In New South Wales the ombudsman, Bruce Barbour, initiated his own review of the NSW FOI Act in April 2008 'after a continuing lack of interest by government' (NSW Ombudsman, 2009, p. 4). That State also had a change in leadership in 2008, with Nathan Rees taking over as Premier. Shortly after, he was reported as promising an overhaul of FOI to improve transparency and accountability, and to introduce world's best practice (Timmins, 2008b). The premier made it clear to the ombudsman's office he wanted reforms that would match those in Queensland (Private communication).

The final report by the ombudsman echoed many of those in Queensland. The recommendations included:

- emphasising the need for proactive disclosure and release of information;
- moving personal information matters to the Privacy and Personal Information Protection Act;
- providing for a right of access to information 'unless, on balance, it is contrary to the public interest to disclose that information (the Queensland public interest test)';
  — makes both Houses of Parliament liable to FOI;
- eliminates 'exemptions' and refers instead to reasons for refusal based on a recognised detriment or harm which could reasonably be expected to be caused if particular information is released;
  — narrows the cabinet document exemption and makes it purposive; and
- creates an Information Commissioner, established within the ombudsman's office.

It proposes the new FOI legislation should be called the *Open Government Information Act.*

On May 6, 2009, Premier Rees released three Bills for public comment, based, he explained, on the recommendations of the NSW Ombudsman and the Queensland and Commonwealth reforms (Rees, 2009). Timmins described them as close to gold star and said:

> The scheme itself follows what is emerging as an Australian standard — a clear statement of objects based on the concept of responsible and representative government that is' open, accountable, fair, and effective'; emphasis on proactive disclosure; a simplified set of refusal reasons, some e.g. cabinet documents absolute, most with a public interest test and the presumption in favour of disclosure unless an overriding public interest against; a codified list of other provisions in acts that override this act; an independent information

commissioner to provide leadership on achieving the objects, deal with complaints and review etc. (Timmins, 2009)

The Fitzgerald Legacy

As noted earlier, Fitzgerald said in his report of FOI:

> The importance of the legislation lies in the principle it espouses, and in its ability to provide information to the public and to parliament. It has already been used effectively for this purpose in other Parliaments. Its potential to make administrators accountable and keep the voters and Parliament informed are well understood by its supporters and enemies. (1989, p. 129)

There can be no argument about the importance of the principle espoused in FOI. The legislation adopted in Queensland gave expression to that principle of open and accountable government. But the supporters of FOI would have been disappointed that its potential 'to make administrators accountable and keep the voters and Parliament informed' was not fully realised. As soon as the government found itself having to disclose information it wanted kept secret it changed the law to limit disclosure. It kept doing so. And the direction of change was constant. FOI in Queensland became incapable of delivering open and accountable government to the extent that Fitzgerald had envisaged was necessary.

Elsewhere in Australia, FOI also fell short of its full potential. As in Queensland, one of the main problems was the 'culture' at a ministerial and (often) agency level. This was unsympathetic to the notion of FOI and even antagonistic towards it, although no-one was prepared to declare themselves publicly to be an enemy of it in the way that Sir Joh Bjelke-Petersen had when he told a Senate Committee inquiry into the first draft Commonwealth FOI legislation that the ideas and concepts involved were 'alien' to the Westminster system (Senate Standing Committee Legal & Constitutional Affairs, 1979).

While the media (and to a lesser extent, Opposition politicians) complained about the way FOI was administered, about the over-use of exemptions and of conclusive certificates and of excessive and prohibitive charging, FOI rarely became a political issue that engaged the public. FOI was not mentioned by either of the political leaders in the 2009 election campaign in Queensland, despite the fact that Premier Anna Bligh had initiated the process that resulted in her tabling, in December 2008, draft legislation that was intended to give Queensland open, transparent and accountable government.

New political leadership, rather than media, Opposition or public pressure, is delivering the massive changes in FOI currently occurring in Australia. Bligh, Barnett, Rees (who was able to capitalise on the initiative of the NSW Ombudsman) and Kevin Rudd, backed by John Faulkner (who pushed for Federal Labor's pre-election commitments and then expanded on them when he took office as Cabinet Secretary) all committed themselves at the very beginning of their terms to making government more open and accountable than it had been under their predecessors.

The younger political leaders who have embraced FOI reform have all emerged in the post-Fitzgerald era and advocate the need for reforms. FOI is but one initiative among a number of measures that generally enhance openness and accountability (to varying degrees, admittedly). For example, at the Federal level, Faulkner is promoting (or has introduced) changes to the 30-year (archival) rule, codes of conduct for ministerial staff, registration of political lobbyists, restrictions on post-departure employment of senior public servants and ministers and whistleblowing, transparency and merit based selection when appointing senior public servants, political donations and electoral reform and controls over government advertising (Faulkner, 2008, 2009; Keane, 2009). Tasmanian Premier Bartlett's plan to strengthen trust in democracy included reviews of whistleblower laws, registering lobbyists and codes of conduct for MPs, ministers and ministerial staff (Bartlett, 2008). The Queensland and NSW Premiers are involved in some of these areas (Rhiannon and Thompson, 2009).

None directly acknowledged their debt to Fitzgerald. However, their commitments to provide people with a '*right* of access to government information' (as Fitzgerald put it — emphasis added) is central to the reforms they have endorsed and are in the process of enacting. Their FOI reforms go beyond legislative tinkering and are aimed at ensuring the 'right' is not evaded by government.

Fitzgerald was not concerned with the detail of FOI. Indeed, as mentioned earlier, his final proposal was that EARC should investigate FOI legislation 'and its desirability' (Fitzgerald, 1989, p. 114). Fitzgerald's concern was, on the political level, with what is now characterised as openness and accountability. Under the heading 'The Political Context' he wrote:

> Good government is more likely to result if opposition, criticism and rational debate are allowed to take place, appropriate checks and balances are placed on the use of power and the administration is open to new ideas, opposing points of view and public scrutiny. (Fitzgerald, 1989, p. 358)

This message, this legacy, appears to be motivating those Australian politicians now advancing FOI and other reforms that will provide for more open and accountable government.

Endnotes

1   The three relevant Orders in Council are reproduced in Fitzgerald (1989, pp. A25–29).
2   Re Hudson/Fencray and the Department of the Premier, Economic and Trade Development (1993) 1 QAR 123.
3   Re Beanland and the Department of Justice and Attorney-General, Information Commissioner Qld. decision number 95026, 14 November 1995.

4   For a full discussion of the changes in the Act, see Gregorczuk (1999, pp. 26–27). For an analysis of the effect of the changes see also Independent Review Panel (2008b, pp. 106–121).

5   Most of the consultants who worked on the project were senior public servants or officials in Tasmania. The two external consultants were Rick Snell, lecturer in law at the University of Tasmania, and the author of this chapter.

References

Bartlett, D. (2008). *Premier Bartlett's 10 point plan: Ten Point Plan to Strengthen Trust.* Retrieved August 7, 2009, from http://www.tashealthydemocracy.com/?q=node/40

Beattie, P. (1998). Queensland Parliamentary Debates, March 4, 1998, 118–119. Retrieved August 5, 2009, from http://www.parliament.qld.gov.au/view/legislativeAssembly/hansard/documents/1998/980304ha.pdf

Bligh, A. (2007, September 21). *ABC Stateline Program.* Brisbane, Australia: ABC.

Electoral and Administrative Review Commission (EARC). (1990). *Freedom of information.* Brisbane, Australia: Queensland Government.

Faulkner, J. (2008, July 22). *Press conference: Freedom of information reform.* Retrieved August 7, 2009, from http://www.smos.gov.au/transcripts/2008/tr_20080722_freedom_of_info.html

Faulkner, J. (2009). *Media release:* FOI reform. Available at http://www.smos.gov.au/media/2009/mr_122009.html

Fitzgerald, G.E. (1989). *Report of a Commission of Inquiry pursuant to Orders in Council.* Brisbane, Australia: Goprint.

Gregorczuk, H. (1999). Freedom of information: Government owned corporations, contractors and cabinet exemptions, *Research Bulletin* (Vol. 5/99). Brisbane, Australia: Queensland Parliamentary Library.

Independent Review Panel. (2008a). Enhancing Open and Accountable Government [Electronic Version]. Retrieved August 4, 2009, from http://www.foireview.qld.gov.au/FOIDiscussionpaper240108.pdf

Independent Review Panel. (2008b). *The right to information: Review of Queensland's FOI Act.* Retrieved August 4, 2009, from http://www.foireview.qld.gov.au/documents_for_download/FOI-review-report-10062008.pdf

Keane, B. (2009). F*aulkner's Freedom of Information shake-up.* Retrieved August 7, 2009, from http://www.crikey.com.au/2009/03/24/faulkners-freedom-of-information-shake-up/

NSW Ombudsman. (2009). *Opening up government — Review of the Freedom of Information Act 1989.* Sydney, Australia: NSW Government.

O'Reilly, E. (2007, November). *Address.* Paper presented at the Fifth International Conference of Information Commissioners, Wellington, New Zealand.

Queensland Government. (2008). *The Right to Information — A response to the review of Queensland's Freedom of Information Act.* Retrieved August 4, 2009, from http://www.thepremier.qld.gov.au/library/pdf/initiatives/foi_review/Right_to_Information.pdf.

Rees, N. (2009, May 6). *Press release.*

Rhiannon, L., & Thompson, N. (2009). What? No More Fundraisers? Retrieved August 7, 2009, from http://newmatilda.com/2009/08/05/what-no-more-fundraisers#comments

Senate Standing Committee Legal & Constitutional Affairs. (1979). *Freedom of Information, Report on the Freedom of Information Bill 1978.* Canberra, Australia: Australian Government Publishing Service.

Solomon, D. (2009, January 1). Reviewing the Cabinet Archives 1978. *The Courier-Mail.*

Spigelman, J. (1972). *Secrecy, political censorship in Australia.* Sydney, Australia: Angus and Robertson.

Tasmanian Government. (2009). *Strengthening trust in government — Everyone's right to know. Review of the Freedom of Information Act 1991* (Directions Paper). Retrieved August 4, 2009, from http://www.justice.tas.gov.au/legislationreview/foi_act_1991/foireview

Timmins, P. (2008a). *Queensland takes gold on FOI reform.* Available at http://foi-privacy.blogspot.com/2008_08_01_archive.html

Timmins, P. (2008b). Transparency 101 briefing prompts more fundamental interest in best practice [Electronic Version]. *Open and Shut,* from http://foiprivacy.blogspot.com/2008_08_01_archive.html

Timmins, P. (2009). *NSW FOI reforms — close to gold star. Open and Shut.* Retrieved August 6, 2009, from http://foi-privacy.blogspot.com/

Wells, D.M. (1991). *Queensland Parliamentary Debates: 5 December, 3851.* Retrieved August 5, 2009, from http://parlinfo.parliament.qld.gov.au/

13

Global Lessons From Fitzgerald: From State and National to Global Integrity Systems

Charles Sampford

Tony Fitzgerald's visionary leap was to see beyond localised, individual wrongdoing. He suggested remedies that were systemic, institutionalised, and directed at underlying structural problems that led to corruption. His report said 'the problems with which this Inquiry is concerned are not merely associated with individuals, but are institutionalized and related to attitudes which have become entrenched' (Fitzgerald Report 1989, p. 13). His response was to suggest an enmeshed system of measures to not only respond reactively to future corruption, but also to prevent its recurrence through improved integrity systems. In the two decades since that report the primary focus of corruption studies and anti-corruption activism has remained on corruption at the local level or within sovereign states. International activism was largely directed at coordinating national campaigns and to use international instruments to make these campaigns more effective domestically. This reflects the broader fact that, since the rise of the nation state, states have comprised the majority of the largest institutional actors and have been the most significant institution in the lives of most individuals. This made states the 'main game in town' for the 'governance disciplines' of ethics, law, political science and economics.[2]

Over the last 20 years, however, the flow of money, goods, people and ideas across borders has threatened to overwhelm the system of sovereign states. Much activity has moved outside the control of nation states. Simultaneously, nation states have 'deregulated', effectively transferring power from those exercising governmental authority at the nominal behest of the majority of its citizens to those with greater wealth and/or greater knowledge in markets in which knowledge is typically asymmetric.

In an increasingly globalised world, the domestic and the foreign, the national and the international become more and more enmeshed. This is true of corporations, investments, markets, environmental problems. For these reasons, globalisation requires effective governance, but in the increasingly globalised world this cannot be driven by and through nation states alone, but will require interstate cooperation and transnational networks that go beyond states. Even if nation states retain many of their present functions, effective governance will require more extensive international institutions and avenues for cooperation (see Keohane, 2001, p. 364). It is now recognised that many governance problems have arisen because of globalisation and can only be addressed by global solutions. It must also be recognised that governance problems at the national level contribute to governance problems at the global level and vice versa. Weaknesses in one exacerbate weaknesses in others. This is true of current issues from the melting Greenland glaciers to the ethical and financial meltdown of Wall Street. It is also true of traditional issues involving the relationship between domestic and international conflict and the toxic symbiosis of foreigners paying bribes to officials which are deposited in off-shore secretive banks.

The 'integrity systems' approach taken to fighting corruption within sovereign states is the most promising way of tackling global governance problems. Such an approach has ethics and values at its heart. This chapter examines the various issues facing a rapidly globalising world. It suggests that much can be learned from the approach suggested by Fitzgerald in 1989, Queensland's attempts at implementation, the exemplar it produced, and the thinking it generated.

Learning Lessons From the Fight Against Corruption Within Sovereign States

Before addressing those global problems and potential global solutions, it is useful to quickly review some of the progress in thinking about the nature of corruption within sovereign states and the best means of combating it, as concentrations of power within states continues to provide ongoing temptations and opportunities for corruption.

Westphalian States, Absolute Power and the Enlightenment

The strong sovereign nation-states that emerged from the chaos of the Thirty Years' War (1618–1648) in 17th century Europe were generally highly authoritarian and justified as such.[3] Hobbes argued that rational people would mutually agree to subject themselves to an all-powerful sovereign to avoid a 'state of nature' in which the life of man would be 'poor, nasty, brutish and short' (Hobbes, 1991, p. 89). It was better to allow a sovereign to enforce his preferred religion and for those who did not agree to leave than to allow other sovereigns to intervene on behalf of their co-religionists.[4] Once internal order had been restored, this 'social contract' did not appear advantageous. While sovereigns were entrusted with absolute power to preserve social order, such power was a recipe for corruption for reasons set out clearly by Lord Acton's aphorism that 'power tends to corrupts and absolute power corrupts absolutely' (Dalberg-Acton, 1949, p. 364). The 18th century Enlightenment sought to civilise these authoritarian states by holding them to a set of more refined and ambitious values — notably liberty, equality, citizenship, human rights, democracy and the rule of law. Some of these were adaptations of classical city state ideals to the much larger polities of the time. Nineteenth century thinkers extended the range of rights championed and added concern for the environment and for practical and social equality. By the mid-20th century, disputes had moved on to the interpretation and ranking of those rights — especially between civil and political rights, and social and economic rights (Sampford, 1999).

However, governance is not merely a matter of articulating values. Values are rarely self-implementing: they require institutions to realise them. This was recognised from the beginning by 18th century *philosophes* — although the institutional mechanisms of their initial proposals were inadequate to the task. Some sought to implement the English constitution as they misunderstood it (e.g., Montesquieu).[5] Others sought to reform the institutions they knew and sought to persuade existing despots to become 'enlightened' ones.[6] It was not until the end of the 18th century that more promising institutional innovations emerged in the United States (federalism, tripartite separation of powers with constitutionally entrenched powers to review executive and legislative acts and, generally, a system of 'checks and balances'), and in England where the loss of the American colonies helped crystallise 'responsible' (or 'parliamentary') government.[7] In both countries, bicameral parliaments were retained and the press became more critical. Scotland and then Germany developed universal education; France experimented with universal suffrage; and, the Swedish developed the ombudsman to institutionalise and supplement the support British MPs provided their constituents. This development of governance values and the institutions to realise them can be seen as an 'enlightenment project'.

Modern Developments

While the adoption and institutionalisation of liberal democratic and social democratic values spread, and many of the relevant values were enshrined in international instruments, the concentration of power within states have continued to provide a temptation for corruption. Various scandals demonstrated that democratic polities could be highly corrupt — and not all states were democracies. More was required and two models emerged. The Hong Kong model (a strong law and a powerful agency), which was the general model for fighting corruption, was prevalent in the 1980s and early 1990s. Indeed, when the new Premier of New South Wales wanted to address corruption in that state the year before Fitzgerald reported, he explicitly adopted the Hong Kong model.

Instead of adopting the Hong Kong model, Fitzgerald (1989) suggested that there were a series of interrelated problems in Queensland that should be addressed by the Electoral and Administrative Reform Commission (EARC), as well as the direct response to corruption to be provided by the Criminal Justice Commission (CJC). This led to an approach to reform in which several institutions, agencies and laws sought to simultaneously promote integrity and limit corruption,[8] initially called an ethics regime (Sampford, 1994b). The OECD (1999) called it an 'ethics infrastructure'. But the term that endured was that used by Transparency International's (TI) Jeremy Pope following a visit to Queensland in the mid 1990s — a 'national integrity system' (NIS; Pope, 2000, 2008, pp. 48–49). This approach was widely followed and the approach Fitzgerald had inspired became the model for anti-corruption reform.

As Fitzgerald had clearly understood, reforms that focus systemically on corruption networks are likely to be more effective than interventions that rely on a single agency or focus solely on individual behaviours. Reform networks that build strong reform institutions and systems are more effective in focusing continuing attention on long-term corruption reform. Strong government institutions have effective checks and balances in place and keep elected officials accountable for their actions to ensure a fair degree of transparency in the political process. Strong institutions have legal systems that uphold the rule of law and property rights, administrative bureaucracies that deliver public goods and services in an efficient, impartial and timely manner, limited and predictable business regulation, and low levels of political and administrative corruption (Manzetti & Wilson, 2007, p. 955). The emerging challenge is how to design strong and effective institutions and mechanisms of governance for a polity of unprecedented size and diversity.

While there are many institutions commonly found in successful integrity systems, different integrity systems display much variety based upon history and circumstance; however, a values-driven approach strengthens the ethical culture of government.

Integrity and Corruption

Integrity is the unifying virtue of ethical public service and good governance. The choice of the term 'integrity system' rather than 'anti-corruption' system first coined by Transparency International was inspired. Defeating corruption (the abuse of entrusted power for personal gain) is a derivative concept and a derivative goal to promoting integrity[9] (Génaux, 2004; Philp, 1997, 2002, 2006; von Alemann, 2004).[10] As we have long argued, integrity and corruption are conceptually linked opposites (Sampford, 2000). One cannot know what an abuse is without knowing what the legitimate uses of those powers are (Sampford, 1990).

If the goal was to avoid government corruption, in theory that perhaps could be achieved by not having government and, in practice, instituting anti-corruption methods that encourage government inaction. The potential for corruption is built into all institutions because of the dynamics of collective action and agency (Heidenheimer, 2004; Montinola & Jackman, 2002) based on the fact that institutions collect power, people and resources for publicly justified purposes, but those powers can be used for other purposes (Sampford, 1990).

The reason why we create and support governments, joint stock companies and international NGOs is because it is believed that more can be achieved collectively than individually with the pooling of people power and resources for shared goals (Warren, 2004).[11] That decision, however, opens the possibility that institutional leaders may turn that entrusted power to their own benefit or use against their citizens/stockholders/bondholders (Keohane, 2006).[12] While it is not true that all power corrupts, it has to be recognised that it will not only attract those who wish to exercise it for its publicly justified purpose but also those who wish to use it for their own purposes.

A National Integrity System (NIS) evolves to increase the probability that entrusted powers will be used for its publicly justified and democratically endorsed ends and reduce the likelihood that such powers are abused. The NIS will vary from state to state with similar functions being performed by different institutions. A NIS can vary in completeness and effectiveness, but there is almost always some base on which it can be built (Sampford, Smith, & Brown, 2005). Coalitions of leaders are needed to create, reinforce and integrate the institutions of the NIS and to coordinate their activities (Sampford and Connors, 2006).[13] While a NIS may be seen as the best way to promote integrity, the corrupt are often far more organised and in some states national corruption systems (NCS) may be better organised, better resourced and more effective — with long established patterns of behaviour, strong institutions, clear norms and effective positive and negative sanctions. The NCS will seek to disrupt and corrupt the NIS. As a corollary, the NIS should positively react. It should not merely seek to deter, detect and prosecute bribe-givers and bribe-takers but should first set to map and understand the corruption system then plan how to disrupt and destroy it.

Lessons Learned

The first lesson is that corruption does matter. As Fitzgerald showed, corruption is not a minor issue, let alone a sustainable alternative route to development. There is little evidence 'that on net, corruption encourages much of anything except slower economic growth, under investment, capital flight, and a general malaise with respect to the legitimacy of political institutions' (Klochko & Ordeshook, 2003, p. 259).

New evidence of corruption by leading politicians and businesses surfaces in virtually every corner of the globe and few, if any, countries have escaped unscathed. Because of the close intersection between business and government at all levels, every regulation, law and public program can be manipulated to favour particular interests. Companies may try to influence these decisions though legitimate lobbying but some are also tempted by the huge sums involved to bribe and use other unlawful means to influence outcomes. Such rent-seeking has a long history in the literature on political economy (see for example, Faccio, 2006; Johnson, Kaufmann, McMillan, & Woodruff, 2000; Johnson & Mitton, 2003; Kaufmann & Wei, 1998; Klochko & Ordeshook, 2003; Theobold, 1999). But rent-seeking has grown dramatically because public spending and regulation are now so extensive. Politicians and bureaucrats may be no more mercenary than other groups, but they can face unusually strong temptations to sell their power for money and other gains.

Corruption, in any form, distorts the functioning of an economy because it leads government officials to take actions that are not in the general interest. It can choke economic development by discouraging honest entrepreneurs and by arbitrarily raising the cost of doing business. Corruption is a symptom indicating that state–society relations are dysfunctional. It undermines the legitimacy of the state and lead to wasteful public policies. The end result is that good policies are unlikely to be chosen or to be carried out effectively without honest institutions (Rose-Ackerman, 2008). Effective global institutions of cooperation delivering a sufficient proportion of their promises are needed.

While corruption is not necessarily related to the decline of the state or the decay of moral values, it is linked to the failure of states to achieve set goals for the very simple reason that the power, people and resources allocated to achieving those goals are used for other purposes. Corruption involves unjustified exclusion and is a violation of the norm of empowered inclusion of all affected (Warren, 2004).

Corruption flourishes in well-established networks where trust is present on both sides of the exchange relationship and is as old as human civilisation; its forms subject to continual change and redefinition (von Alemann,

2004). Too often, moral accusations are aimed at the failings of individuals, thus distracting from institutional and structural patterns of corruption. Systemic, pervasive subsystems of corruption can and have existed across historical periods, geographic areas and political economic systems. A key operating feature of corruption subsystems is that they are relatively stable networks rather than exceptional, independent, individual events (Neilsen, 2003).[14] Such networks support the common good of particular social groups rather than uphold the national public good. The failure of public trust leads to solidarity networks within a state. It is important is understand how corrupt and unethical subsystems operate in order to reform and change them.

The second lesson is the approach to be taken in combating corruption. For Fitzgerald, this involved a multi-pronged, systemic approach encompassing electoral, governmental and legal reforms and the creation of new institutions. If corruption involves the abuse of entrusted power for personal gain, the attempt to limit corruption in an emerging global order involves identifying:

- areas of significant power;
- the ostensible purpose used to publicly justify the existence of that power and the ends for which it may be legitimately used;
- potential abuses of that power by those who hold it and the benefits they and others will gain;
- potential corruption systems that may emerge to organise those abuses of power; and,
- potential integrity systems that disrupt corruption systems and increase the likelihood that powers are used for their ostensible purpose and not abused through illegitimate use.

Integrity System Degradation and Correction

There is, however, a natural tendency for integrity systems to degrade, and the simple reason for this is that a concentration and use of power may be to further the highest possible ideals, but it is not always the case. If a power holder is faced with a strategy that will be of significant individual benefit and will do limited damage to the office that the person holds, some will choose the avenue that furthers their personal benefit or gain. There are also those who seek to increase their power at the expense of independent organisations. This should not come as a surprise.[15] Rather, there needs to be awareness that such actions may lead to a downward spiral. The scandals that arise in relation to the abuse of power are the reason why societies do not end up in a permanent downward spiral despite the regular attacks against integrity institutions. The reason for this is that the corruption scandal results in it being in the interests of the political elite to introduce integrity mechanisms in response to the corrupt conduct. Knowledge that integrity mechanisms are implemented largely in response to corrupt practices, informs us that corruption systems are adaptive to their relatively static target. The adaptive nature of corruption means that the ability to develop an integrity regime is a result of the experience of corruption. The development of the system takes time in response to the history of corruption a country has experienced. However, just because an effective response is dependent on the experience of corruption does not mean that meaningful progress is unachievable at will. Integrity reforms will generate institutions with the purpose of furthering reform and providing mutual support to the constituencies seeking reform, and they may also increase the likelihood of uncovering scandals and pursuing them.

Power and Corruption in a Globalising World

The contemporary challenge is to apply the lessons learned, and contribution made by the Fitzgerald process, to a globalising world where corruption crosses national borders. The use of power concentrated in government institutions is justified by ascertaining and furthering values that are of importance to the citizenry. In this way, the institutions that hold the power are able to justify the use of that power in terms of the values that the institution is seeking to achieve and uphold, resulting in the risk of abuse being accepted. As a result of the concentration of power, governments have the potential to commit acts that further the common good as well as acts which abuse the power entrusted to them by the citizenry. This is not only an issue of fundamental importance to governmental concentrations of power but also in term of concentrations of power in any organisation or institution. In a globalising world, the impact of problems in one place on conditions in other places is more pronounced and faster in the current era than ever before. Conversely, the impact of both public sector and private sector solutions to these problems through institutional activities has the potential to be more rapid than in any previous age with international exchanges and organisations proliferating and with the potential to shape and influence institutional systems and environments.[16]

Identify and Develop Relevant Global Values

What are the values that will inform sustainable global governance, form the base of a potential global integrity system, and inform the ethical decisions of officials of multilateral, transnational and global institutions? Put simply: what values should sustainable globalisation seek to sustain? Asking the fundamental questions about values provides the core of ethical standard setting, as the answers to the values questions provide the principles upon which to base reform measures in relation to the interpretation of laws governing institutions. Identified values also provide a mechanism by which to assess the implemented institutional reforms as they constitute the fundamental ethical standard.

When discussing the use of questions about values to order public life and provide justification for actions, it is necessary to develop a concept of whose values we are talking about. When developing the concept of applicable values, it is imperative that ideological dead ends are avoided. This account of integrity does not intend to employ an orientalism-like construct to facilitate a reason why constructs and institutions from outside the context will improve the problem of corruption. Such an account implies that members of that environment are not capable of being objective in relation to corruption but mechanisms from outside are, by the mere fact that they are from outside the context. Similarly, simplistic universalism whereby all cultures are considered to be the same is not the approach to be adopted.

A cultural relativist approach is also inappropriate for this account as such an approach would use cultural explanations as justification for actions. This results in condemnation of practices in a given context being considered as culturally particularist judgements. Indeed, experiences of corruption and particular contextual factors do differ but not in terms of some supporting good governance and some being inimical to it. All longstanding cultures have different accounts of major social issues and a range of answers reflecting different interpretations of the ideals. Again, it is emphasised that this integration of integrity is not focused on exporting Western values (Brown & Cloke, 2004).[17] The answer to achieving an application of appropriate values is the use of dialogues (Castells, 2008).[18] The implementation of dialogues will tend to produce a convergence of values. The dialogue process assumes that most cultures will include values that are very similar to Western liberal–democratic values. These values will not be identical to western values but will be nuanced and influenced by the context in which they arose. Using ethics to ask value questions recognises that the contextual environment within which governance measures operate is not static and for that reason ethical standard setting can be responsive to the given situation.

This should not be a difficult lesson to apply. International norms are an intrinsic part of international society. While similar values can be found in all cultures and in the writings of Confucius, Buddha, Christ and Mohamad, such values can only be called universal at levels of abstraction that are not particularly helpful and deny the very real philosophical development that has taken place between and since those to whom the relevant writings have been attributed. Truly universal values may appear at the asymptote of infinite dialogue but not before. What can be found is 'congruent values': values with similar meaning and effect that are nonetheless subtly different because of the different histories and contexts in which they arose (Küng, 1993).[19] These form a much stronger base on which to form global values which can inform global governance (see Robinson, 2002).[20]

Good governance and bad governance are not the preserve of any particular culture. All long-standing cultures, religions and traditions have experienced good governance and bad governance. The West managed to produce both Nazism and Bolshevism in a single century as well as some of the finest expressions of human rights, democracy and the rule of law. Individuals, such as Gandhi and Dr King, were acutely aware that such values were 'good ideas' needed to be put into practice.

Global values may well emerge as versions of good governance values proposed for nation states or they may emerge as combinations of values.[21] What, then, are these values?

Transparency, Rule of Law, Liberty and Human Rights

These values underpinned most of Fitzgerald's recommendations, and may translate fairly directly from sovereign state to global community. Transparency is an essential part of the operation of integrity systems — both of the agencies and institutions monitored and the agencies and institutions undertaking the monitoring. This might appear to be an imperialistic statement about one governance value. However, similar stories can, and often are, told about other values; at times, 'liberty', 'human rights', 'the rule of law', and, nowadays, 'sustainability'. What the statement above actually sets out is the interconnectedness of governance values in theory as well as in the practice of national integrity systems.

Equality

This is a highly contested value within sovereign states with some emphasising formal equality and others advocating substantive equality along at least some dimensions. This consideration becomes all the more complicated when dealing with differences across states as well as within them (Horton & Patapan, 2006). Perhaps, the simplest way is to consider the democratic value of equality, is to view individuals as 'autonomous'[22] moral and political agents, particularly in societies which are in the midst of social and economic transition (Hellsten and Larbi, 2006).

Citizenship and Democracy

These ideas were developed in city states and changed significantly when they were applied to sovereign states. Their application to the institutions found in a globalising world are likely to involve further significant development – perhaps embracing claims to membership of, and a say in, the critical institutions that affect lives (Horton & Patapan, 2006). When sovereign states were the preeminent model, the claim to membership and influence was centred on sovereign states. Such claims may now legitimately extend to international agencies and corporations (see Dahan et al., 2006; Heidenheimer, 2004; Rodriguez, Siegel, Hillman, & Eden, 2006; Stubbs, 2008).

Accountability

Accountability might not change much as a concept — the key issue is who is to be accountable, to whom, and for what? Accountability is important as it helps to prevent the abuse of power. We need to think about how to design a pluralistic accountability system that relies on a variety of types of accountability, for example, fiscal, legal, market, reputational (Keohane, 2006).[23] Institutionalised accountability relationships controls power without imposing enormous costs that can be involved in the application of coercion.

Environment

These values were developed within sovereign states. In 19th century England, environmental values led to the formation of the National Trust and attempts to clean up the Thames. These values maybe global; however, 'conventional environmentalism has so far failed to win over hearts and minds either within the electorate at large or within today's political elites' (Porritt, 2005, p. 19). The prevailing version of capitalism is unsustainable and unjust:

> The case for sustainable development must be as much about new opportunities for wealth creation as about outlawing irresponsible wealth creation; it must draw on a core of ideas and values that speaks directly to the people's desire for a higher quality of life emphasising enlightened self-interest and personal well-being of a different kind. (Porritt, 2005, p. 20)

The quality of environmental governance at all levels is critical for realising the possible environmental gains from globalisation. Governments, however, have an important role to play in creating a framework that encourages and sustains environmental innovation and the dissemination of more environmentally-friendly technologies in global markets (OECD, 2008).

Institutionalising These Values

The next question at national and global levels is how we can institutionalise these values: that is, what institutions will best realise those values? Following the Fitzgerald inspired reforms we have the model of a set of interrelated institutions within a 'national integrity system'. But how can this model be translated to a global level? In order to properly understand the complex phenomenon of global governance, peoples' values and social orientations should be taken into account. Even if the main repository for such diverse values may be various international institutions, these organisations also exist in a broad cultural setting. It is argued, however, that this will not be through global government — 'the sovereign state writ large'. The answer lies in global governance through a global integrity system — a range of institutions to achieve these values. This approach requires clarity as to the values/public goods the institutions are expected to achieve, and the creation of a set of institutions that can realise global values. Some of the institutions will already be established, some will need major reform, and some new institutions will have to be created. These will include the UN which, for all its faults, it is the only one we will ever get. While its faults are many, it should be recognised that the UN and its agencies have been remarkably successful in putting a floor under human misery caused by war, famine and pestilence. We should not, however, expect the UN to be a 'sovereign state writ large' (see Pettersen, 2002).[24] What is true at the national level is even truer at the global level: promoting integrity and combating corruption require a range of institutions — multilateral, national, corporate and not-for-profit (see Singer, 2002).[25] We, however, must be mindful that power, people and resources that are invested in these organisations will create agency problems and potential for system abuse.[26]

Globalisation places great stress on existing patterns of global governance and on the increasingly complex interstate interactions. In this environment, international corruption systems can emerge which need to be identified, mapped, assessed for weaknesses and strategies employed to disrupt. Sometimes the corruption systems are based on loose networks. Some appear highly institutionalised. Some are sectoral (drugs, trafficking, arms, illegal logging, smuggling, resource theft). Some are interlinked with diversification and 'three-way trades' (see Neilsen, 2003). A number of different initiatives on international institutional reform have appeared in recent years, and more can be expected in the future. The success of such initiatives is important. Bringing more coherence and coordination between global environmental governance, global financial governance, and global economic development systems is a major priority (Najman, Runnalls, & Halle, 2007). The creation of institutional integrity systems makes it more likely that such reforms will be realised by the relevant global governance institutions.

Towards an Institutional Approach

A global integrity system involves many institutions and those institutions will need coalitions of leaders to create, develop and lead. The creation of a global integrity system — starting with global institutions (such as the UN and World Bank) and moving to an international system more generally should include nation states, multi-national corporations and international NGOs (see Sanzholz & Gray, 2003).[27] Such a system will not be built to a single plan but built up gradually, starting with what we have.

We need to recognise the impediments to achieving good governance values and that it is necessary to build mechanisms to deal with those impediments into the global integrity system. Sustainable globalisation requires sustainable global governance. If the powers entrusted to global institutions (multilateral agencies, multinational companies and international NGOs) are abused for personal or narrow state-based aims, global governance will break down. The Global Integrity System (GIS), similar to the NIS, needs to be designed to ensure that those powers are used for the purposes which justify those powers rather than abused.

A GIS will not be built overnight. As is the case with National Integrity Systems, it has and will continue to have a history in which the system is strengthened because politicians are forced by popular demand for action to engage in positive reforms. Wars have produced institutions such as the International Red Cross, the failed League of Nations and the much more successful UN system (which, through the IMF, World Bank and GATT/WTO also sought to deal with the crisis of the Great Depression). It produced individual criminal responsibility for crimes against humanity which, when prompted by later such crimes eventually produced the International Criminal Court. It also generated a great surge in international law making through treaties (though only marginally through the already existent but too little used International Court of Justice). The creation of these institutions occasionally generates significant norm creation and further institutional development — though not to the degree found in federations because nation states are much more successful in constraining global institutions than states/provinces have been in constraining federal institutions.

One suspects that this pattern will continue and that major crises will be necessary to achieve major reforms of global integrity systems. However, the two great headline problems of the day may well stimulate just such growth. Indeed, it could be argued that such growth and the leadership to progress are necessary if this century is not to be the last century of human civilisation.

Carbon and Climate Change — the Recent Headline Issue for Sustainable Globalisation

Globalisation is one of the key drivers of economic change. The interactions between globalisation and the environment occur at different levels, and the impacts can be both positive and negative, depending on the adaptive ability of the environment, natural resource endowments and governments' capacity to establish and put into effect acceptable environmental policies (OECD, p. 90). Unlike the increasing flows of money, goods, people and ideas across national borders that constitute the heart of globalisation, carbon flows across borders independently of human action. It is a headline issue because: (a) all the above-mentioned global flows have exacerbated climate change; and, (b) solutions involve global agreement on goals for the creation of untried institutional mechanisms. If global warming is to be halted this century, total emissions have to be capped and cut and all states will have to participate in securing that outcome.[28]

Importantly, carbon and climate changes are related to other global issues. Globalisation and environmental degradation create new security fears in an already insecure world. They impact upon the vulnerability of ecosystems and societies with the conditions of the poorest communities most affected (Najman et al., 2007).

Both war and peace make massive contributions to carbon emissions (and individual armies are more expensive than collective security forces of the kind provided for in the UN Charter but never implemented). How do we persuade those who have not caused the problem to refrain from the behaviours that made us rich? We cannot pursue means that will create poverty in other countries — let alone famine through the use of potentially food producing land for growing oil substitutes or creating carbon sinks. The question is whether the emerging economies will have 'the foresight to chart a development path that is different from that which followed those who came before', and 'whether the old "affluent" economies of the North will demonstrate a shared commitment to assist the developing world' (Najman et al., 2007, p. 21). In the light of the severity of the issues and its moral complications, we are obliged to try to find a solution that is fair and equitable (Garvey, 2008). Better global governance is a key to managing both globalisation and the global environment.[29]

Financial Globalisation — the Current Headline Issue for Sustainable Globalisation

If globalisation involves the flow of people, ideas, goods and money, the last has grown most rapidly — indeed well in excess of the flow of goods and investment that it is supposed to support. The globalisation of capital markets in the last twenty years has led to a historic degree of financial integration in the world (Venard and Hanafi, 2008). Developing countries have entrusted their enormous and growing surpluses in western banks and other financial intermediaries. Some (such as Timor Leste) have been pressed by western run multilaterals to entrust the proceeds of extractive industries to Wall Street on the basis that the income was less likely to be eroded by corruption.[30]

The amounts entrusted to such intermediaries in the US and elsewhere on the basis that these funds would be invested on a secure and conservative basis were unprecedented. It now appears that entrusted powers over vast sums of money were abused for personal gain. Many within financial intermediaries have used these funds in ways that maximised their fees while increasing the risks to their investors. The ratings practices were scandalous and incredibly insulting to well run businesses and governments whose risk was far less than 110% non-recourse mortgages on inflated values to NINJA borrowers (no income, no job, no assets). The fact that the risk models were based on the probabilities of individual defaults and ignored the possibility of an overall decline in property markets is merely more evidence of incompetence, negligence and arrogance.[31] Once such ratings could be secured, the signing up of mortgagees, the packaging of those loans, their rating and their sale to local citizens and foreigners resembles a well oiled 'corruption system'. Even though they did not see themselves as corrupt, several parties were maximising their fees while squandering profits at the expense of those who entrusted them with their funds. The unedifying subsequent sharp shift from greed to blind panic only adds to the contempt that so many have engendered.

This outcome does not mean that banks should not be rescued. The fact that they were poorly run is not the point. If they had been well run, they would not need to be rescued. Rescues are instigated to protect the wider economy, confidence and depositors who were not accepting suspiciously high rates — while seeking to ensure that the owners and managers of such banks remain as exposed as possible to the consequences of their mistakes.

Neither does this mean that all participants acted unethically or illegally. If, however, confidence in the international financial system is to be restored in the long term, and if the proceeds of developing country surpluses and western superannuation funds are to continue to be entrusted with intermediaries for investment in the globalised economy — thereby supporting sustainable globalisation rather than undermining it — then, this can only happen if there is a full investigation of what went wrong and options for the establishment of adequate financial integrity systems are debated, selected and implemented as part of the GIS. Such an investigation should include members of developing as well as developed countries and be supported by the work of international researchers, NGOs and international organisations. In this process, the Equator Principles, the UN Global Compact, and the UN Principles of Responsible Investment need to be reconsidered and implemented.

In reforming the international financial system, we should set the goal of ensuring that those who are entrusted with investing funds for others do not abuse that entrusted power to increase their wealth at the expense of those for whom they invest. At the same time, we should set the international banking system the goal of establishing a regime that is sufficiently transparent so that no rational corrupt official or tax avoider would deposit personal funds in an offshore bank. This is the single most important contribution that developed nations can make to the reduction of corruption in developing nations. While some developed nations had resisted such a goal, September 11 has stimulated the development of relevant tools for tracking the ultimate owners of those whose funds are moved across international boundaries.

A Global Financial Integrity system is a key part of any GIS and any sustainable values based Global Economic System of the kind called for by Kofi Annan a decade ago (Annan, 1999; Porritt, 2005).[32]

Recognising the Role of Individuals in Dealing With These Global Issues

While the architecture of sustainable global governance and sustainable globalisation is, and always will be, largely institutional, we should never ignore the individual dimension. We should identify our own actions that can further stated good governance values. We must recognise that we can act at three levels: as Citizens/voters; as Investors; and, as Consumers.

When we act, we have responsibility for the consequences of our actions. The fact that we are acting as consumers and investors does not excuse us from that responsibility. However, between our actions and the achievement of intended consequences lie a number of institutions:

- As citizens, we rely on parties, parliaments and bureaucracies to implement our collective choices.
- As investors, we rely on advisors, trust funds, fund managers and corporations to connect our values with our investments.
- As consumers, we rely on manufacturers, service providers, retailers and advertisers to inform our choices and deliver them.

We empower these institutions by voting, investing and consuming and must recognise that those institutions may well abuse that power and demand institutional changes to limit such abuses. Action on one front can affect action on other fronts and campaigns should press for action on all three fronts. We should especially seek to harness the ultimate owners of most corporations — superannuants. Their interests are long term and not confined to the market return on their shares. These investors have other economic interests as employees, taxpayers and parents. An action that marginally increases the return on their shares but raises unemployment or requires taxpayer funded clean-ups or bailouts are against their overall economic interests. The best entrepreneurs are those who build sustainable businesses. The problem is that the financial intermediaries who handle superannuants' money are driven by short-term incentives.

Such investors, as citizens, have values that go beyond economic interests. They are not only entitled to seek to further these through their investments but are responsible for their choices. Shareholders' values may vary but this merely means that funds should differentiate themselves on the basis of the values they seek to further. As most superannuation funds aim for diverse investments and align shareholdings with stock market indices, superannuants are becoming 'universal investors'. Any attempt by businesses to externalise their costs damages the superannuant's investments — and often the superannuants themselves. Accordingly, the externalisation of costs is not an option that superannuants can afford and neither they, nor the funds who invest their money, should be willing to adopt. There is a direct line between ethical and socially responsible investment by individuals' funds adopting and implementing the UN's Principles of Responsible Investment (PRI) and corporate social responsibility initiatives such as the Global Compact.

Conclusion

The Fitzgerald report transformed the architecture for governance in the State of Queensland, as discussed in the preceding chapters in this book. Future global governance architecture for a transnational world is complex and fraught with problems and will not follow the pattern in any particular national or subnational jurisdiction. In this chapter, I have argued that much can be learned from the approach suggested by Fitzgerald in 1989, Queensland's attempts at implementation, the exemplar it produced, and the thinking it generated. Such an approach would have ethics and values at its heart — asking, or rather demanding, of institutions that they justify themselves to the global community in terms of the benefits they provide for the global community. It would recognise the risk that those institutions might abuse their institutionalised powers in ways that could benefit the holders of power and harm others and look to the new, existing and reformed institutions that would make that abuse less likely. Above all, it would recognise that the best way to build integrity and combat corruption is not through a single overarching institution but a range of institutions that mutually support and check each other in an 'integrity system'. Queensland's institutional choice, that was inspired by Fitzgerald, developed by EARC and legislated with bi-partisan support, is an institutional necessity in a globalising world that does not have the centralised institutions that could implement a global ICAC. However, as experience has shown, the distributed 'integrity system' is superior to the Hong Kong model of a powerful single anti-corruption agency.

In global governance, the institutions to be covered by and involved in the global integrity system would include global, regional, national, subnational, corporate and civil society institutions. Such institutions have long been entrusted with power, people and resources to benefit the communities they claim to serve. The onset of globalisation, however, and the interlocking nature of its problems require these institutions to justify themselves to broader communities and recognise their role in contributing to existing global problems and joining in the solutions to those problems.

Such an approach will recognise the contributions of all governance disciplines to understanding when and why institutions fail to live up to their promises. As in other areas, I would argue that global governance reform requires ethical standard setting, legal regulation and institutional reform integrated into an 'ethics regime' or 'integrity system' (Sampford, 1994a, 1994b, 2001; Sampford & Wood, 1993).

We are a long way from securing a global integrity system. However, it is more likely and more desirable than a global, independent commission against corruption

Endnotes

1   For which the 1648 Treaty of Westphalia is a conventional landmark for a complex process that developed gradually but never operated in practice as it was imagined to operate in theory.

2   Although these disciplines were not originally separate and 18th century theorists such as Adam Smith and Jeremy Bentham would not have considered them severable.

3   In my view, the Treaty of Westphalia was a 'tyrant's charter' — a treaty of tyrants, for tyrants, by tyrants.

4   Other justifications for the acceptance of absolute power can be found in the Confucian 'mandate of heaven' and al-Ghazali's claim that: 'an evil-doing and barbarous sultan, so long as he is supported by military force, so that he could only with difficulty be deposed and that any attempt to depose him would cause unendurable strife, must of necessity be left in possession and obedience must be rendered to him, exactly as unquestioning obedience must be rendered to caliphs' (cited in Collomb, 2006, p. 63).

5   Montesquieu's image of it involving a three-way separation of powers was deeply flawed as a description, or even an interpretation, of the British constitution.

6   Voltaire and Diderot pinned their hopes in turn on Frederick the Great in Prussia, then Catherine the Great in Russia.

7   It is one of history's great ironies that Montesquieu's description was most accurate under William III and George III, because parliamentary control over the executive was largely achieved between those monarchs' reigns but disappeared with the loss of the American colonies. The Americans created a strong head of state wielding full executive power — the very thing they had rebelled against, and the British were rejecting. More importantly, one chief American objection to British rule was that they did not have the same rights as Englishmen because the Crown had more power, with fewer constraints outside the shores of England than on home soil. Despite their objection to this feature of the British Constitution, they gave the Presidency a similarly great and largely unfettered power to act outside the United States. The legal dangers of this power are exacerbated by political factors; the President, as Head of State, not facing any official Opposition Leader in the legislature, can 'wrap himself in the flag' and depict criticism of his foreign policies as disloyalty to the nation itself. The world has reaped the consequences in recent years as Presidents have initiated

wars in apparent contravention of international law and, in the case of the Bush administration, sought to detain and try prisoners captured in such wars, outside US soil, thereby claiming properly legislative and judicial powers without constitutional constraint. The final irony is that the president whose authority was used to create such systems was the third American President called 'George' who might be called 'George III of America' for both numerical and symbolic reasons!

8   The Electoral and Administrative Review Commission was established by Act of the Queensland Parliament in 1989, pursuant to a recommendation of the Fitzgerald Report (*Report of a Commission of Inquiry Pursuant to Orders in Council*, July 1989).

9   Integrity: defined as the use of entrusted power for publicly justified ends (See Dobel, 1999; Sampford, 2005).

10 This is the most commonly used definition. However, there is an ongoing debate about corruption definitions: specifically, what defines a corrupt act and in what circumstances. The definition of corruption is, therefore, complex and contested. For a fuller discussion of the arguments see, for example, Philp (1997); Philp (2002); Génaux (2004); von Alemann (2004); Philp (2005).

11 This approach is important when we examine the various domains of corruption that can exist even within a strong democracy and the potential effects. See, for example, Warren (2004).

12 See Keohane (2006) for his vision of a pluralistic, global accountability system and his analysis of the extent to which democratic principles can be applied to world politics and the implications for combating corruption.

13 This was a major conclusion of the first World Ethics Forum held in Oxford in 2006.

14 Neilsen (2003) identifies examples of exclusive corruption networks as criminal organisations such as the Mafia and the Japanese Yakuza and more subtle types of corruption networks, known as 'crony capitalism', as informal networks of large family businesses and where government officials control such activities as large loans from state bank that are not repaid, preferential government contracts, protected monopolies, investment banking and brokerage conflicts of interest, auditing, and consulting conflicts of interests etc.

15 See Duffield and Grabosky (2001) for an interesting discussion on the psychology of fraud. The authors discuss the motivation and psychological aspects of fraud. They argue that in the case of senior officials 'high flying entrepreneurs tend to be extremely ambitious to the point of appearing driven. They also appear obsessed with enhancing power and control … have a favourable impression of themselves, sometimes unrealistically so … Some develop a sense of superiority bordering on narcissism … their tendency to surround themselves with sycophants or organisational conformists who are easily dominated' (p. 4).

16 See Dahan, Doh and Guay (2006) for a discussion on the role of multinational corporations in transnational institution building.

17 Brown and Cloke (2004) warn of the tendency towards the universalising of Western norms and values in creating technical solutions to the problem of corruption in the form of particular types of economic policies and/or institutional reforms.

18 Following our argument that global governance values needed to result from dialogues between cultures seeking 'congruent' values (Sampford 1999), the Open Society Foundation funded a series of such dialogues between Muslims and Westerners led by Prof Azyumardi Azra and the author leading to the publication of Azra and Hudson (2008). Along similar lines, Castells (2008) argues that 'it is essential for state actors, and for intergovernmental institutions, such as the United Nations, to relate to civil society not only around institutional mechanisms and procedures of political representation

but in public debates in the global and public sphere. That global public sphere is built around the media communication system and Internet networks' (p. 90).

19 Theologian Hans Küng helped convene a world parliament of religions in Chicago in 1993. The Declaration of The Religions for a Global Ethic agreed by the Parliament of the World's Religions set out a global ethics statement emphasising the common values shared across different religions.

20 Mary Robinson, (UN Commissioner for Human Rights, 1997–2002) holds that the Chicago Declaration of 1993 of a global ethic and the 1993 Vienna Declaration ratifying the Universal Declaration of Human Rights provides evidence that universal values transcend particular traditions or social contexts and underpin basic standards of morally legitimate global governance.

21 The issue is a major one for which the Key Centre and the institute for Ethics, Governance and Law (IEGL) have organised a dozen workshops and a book series with Routledge on the Challenge of Globalisation (edited by Samford and Patapan).

22 Hellsten and Larbi, in this context, describe 'autonomous' as 'freedom with responsibility'.

23 Robert Keohane argues that a pluralistic accountability system 'will not come from a centralized hierarchy, but from a pluralistic, often discordant system of NGOs and networks among them' (p. 84).

24 For a discussion of peoples' values preferences and orientation towards internationalised governance see, Pettersen (2002).

25 Peter Singer argues that how well we come thought the era of globalisation (perhaps whether we come through it at all) will depend on how we respond ethically to the idea that we live in one world.

26 For example, Duffield and Gradbosky (2001) argue that 'ethics will only get us so far' and that 'there will always be a hard core of people who, with full knowledge of the difference between right and wrong, will opt for the latter' (p. 6).

27 The authors examined data from 150 countries and their study suggests that prevailing norms in international society delegitimise and stigmatise corruption. Countries that are more integrated into the international society are more exposed to economic and normative pressures against corruption. They argue that international norms have a variable effect on domestic norms, depending on the extent to which countries are integrated into international society.

28 The currently favoured approach is to set a cap and then cut total emissions with the trading of emission rights to provide incentives to those who can most efficiently cut their carbon and minimise the cost This is unsurprisingly popular in states emitting the most carbon because it effectively gives them a property right to emit — something that is acknowledged in the literature ('issuing permits free of charge (or at low cost) explicitly recognises the property rights which emitters have had in the past') (Gunasekera and Cornwell, 1998, p. 11). Giving concessions to those countries or corporations who are already engaged in the unsustainable activity effectively concedes a 'right' to engage in unsustainable activities. It also has the perverse effect of encouraging market players to look for the next unsustainable activity in which they can invest to benefit from 'grand fathered' rights. Faith in markets may be misplaced in this case. Building a workable international system to manage climate change is not a single, one-year project. Business leaders would do best to sell their elected representative on a long-term approach to managing the effects of climate change (Packard and Reinhardt, 2000).

29 The alternative approach involves the taxation of unsustainable activity rather than granting rights to it. An approach could be a 'carbon added tax' (CAT) to operate similar to a VAT. If it operates akin to a VAT, carbon taxes are passed on up the line

until paid by the consumer of the relevant goods and services. The VAT treatment of imports means that those who keep outside the system of carbon taxes would still be liable for the CAT when the goods are imported into a market within the system. It also means that the burden is on those countries which consume high carbon goods and services rather than those who produce them. Revenue could be returned to individuals through cuts in consumption tax (either across the Board or targeted in areas such as food where the poor pay more) to prevent inflationary impact while retaining a strong price signal. Indeed, it provides both negative and positive price signals as low carbon products actually decline in price (though slowly enough to avoid deflation of low carbon products). In general, we should move from taxing consumption to taxing carbon and return the proceeds to individual citizens — or to individuals globally through a global minimum income. Replacing consumption taxes with a carbon tax would significantly change the incentives for reducing green house and other emissions without affecting inflation. This is an example of how adopting a different institutional mechanism will reduce the possibility for the abuse of power.

30 The author was deeply sceptical of this approach during a World Bank mission in 2005. Not only is Timor Leste and many other countries desperate for investment, but the rate of return in developing economies should be higher than the rate of return in highly developed countries. While this means that a robust and effective integrity system needs to be completed as soon as possible, this appears to be an example of funds flowing in the wrong direction. There is a particular poignancy in this example. The author and Lt Gen John Sanderson proposed in 1999 that funds should be provided to employ unemployed Timorese (especially the 'young men with guns') to rebuild the destroyed housing stock, channelling funds through local organisations that could become the kernel for new democratic local government organisations. This proposal was rejected. It is ironic that the later investments of Timor Leste are caught up in the maelstrom generated by the attempt to provide much more expensive homes to American citizens who were not nearly as poor and not nearly as homeless as East Timorese citizens.

31 An example is the well-known case of Freddie Mac and Fannie Mae: 'As government-chartered entities, they were able to borrow money at lower rates than their competitors, as most investors took for granted that their operations were implicitly guaranteed by the government. At the same time, as publicly traded companies, they sought to maximise their revenues and returns. Critics questioned their accounting, which they said was manipulated by executives to justify their large and growing compensation' (Freddie Mac, 2009).

32 At the World Economic Forum, Davos, on 31 January 1999, the UN Secretary-General Kofi Annan challenged world business leaders to 'embrace and enact' the Global Compact, both in their individual corporate practices and by supporting appropriate public policies. The claims it makes on the global economic system are threefold: (i) respect of, and support for, human rights, (ii) the elimination of all forms of forced child labour, and (iii) a response to ecological challenge. These claims are based on the conviction that in all societies, cultures and religions people need to recognise and accept comparable ethical pillars which allow them to live together peacefully without conflict or compromise to their interest and concerns (see Annan, 1999). However, as Jonathon Porritt (2005) points out 'there are currently hundreds of signatories to the Global Compact from all around the world. But as non-governmental organisations (NGOs) have noted, there are no mechanisms for assessing the degree to which any one of them is complying with those principles *in practice,* leading to the inevitable (and not excessively cynical) conclusion that they are just in it for the UN badge' (p. 244).

References

Annan, K. (1999). *Corporate citizenship in the world economy*. Retrieved April 2, 2009, from http://www.un.org/Depts/ptd/global.htm

Azra, A., & Hudson, W. (Eds.). (2008). *Islam beyond conflict*. Aldershot: Ashgate.

Brown, E., & Cloke, J. (2004). Neoliberal reform, governance and corruption in the South: Assessing the international anti-corruption crusade. *Antipode*, 272–294.

Castells, M. (2008). The new public sphere: Global civil society, communication networks, and global governance. *The Annals of the American Academy of Political and Social Science, 616*, 78–93.

Collomb, R. (2006). *The rise and fall of the Arab empire*. Gloucestershire: Spellmount Publishing.

Dahan, N., Doh, J., & Guay, J. (2006). The role of multinational corporations in transnational institution building: A policy network perspective. *Human Relations, 59*, 1571–1599.

Dalberg-Acton, J.E.E. (1949). *Essays on freedom and power*. Boston: The Becon Press.

Dobel, J.P. (1999). *Public Integrity*. Baltimore: Johns Hopkins University Press.

Duffield, G., & Grabosky, P. (2001). The psychology of fraud. *Trends and Issues in Crime and Criminal Justice, 199*, 1–6.

Faccio, M. (2006). Politically connected firms. *American Economic Review, 96*, 369–386.

Fitzgerald, G. (1989). *Report of a Commission of Inquiry Pursuant to Orders in Council*. Brisbane, Australia: Queensland Government.

Freddie Mac. (2009, April 22). *The New York Times*. Retrieved June 17, 2009, from http://topics.nytimes.com/top/news/business/companies/freddie_mac/index.html

Garvey, J. (2008). *The ethics of climate change: Right and wrong in a warming world*. London: Continuum.

Génaux, M. (2004). Social sciences and the evolving concept of corruption. *Crime, Law and Social Change, 42*, 13–24.

Gunasekera, D., & Cornwell, A. (1998). *Essential elements of tradable permit schemes. Trading greenhouse emissions: Some Australian perspectives*. Canberra, Australia: Bureau of Transport Economics.

Hamilton, C., & Denniss, R. (2005). *Affluenza: When too much is never enough*. Sydney, Australia: Allen and Unwin.

Heidenheimer, A.J. (2004). Disjunction between corruption and democracy? A qualitative exploration. *Crime, law and Social Change, 42*, 99–109.

Hellsten, S., & Larbi, G. (2006). Public good or private good? The paradox of public and private ethics in the context of developing countries. *Public Administration and Development, 26*, 135–145.

Hobbes, T. (1991). *Leviathan*. Cambridge: Cambridge University Press.

Horton, K., & Patapan, H. (Eds.). (2006). *Globalisation and equality*. London: Routledge.

Johnson, S., Kaufmann, D., McMillan, J., & Woodruff, C. (2000). Why do firms hide? Bribes and unofficial activity after communism. *Journal of Public Economics, 76*, 495–520.

Johnson, S., & Mitton, T. (2003). Cronyism and capital controls: Evidence from Malaysia. *Journal of Financial Economics, 67*, 351–382.

Kaufmann, D., & Wei, S. (1998). *Does 'grease money' speed up the wheels of commerce?* Washington: World Bank and Harvard University.

Keohane, R. (2001). Governance in a partially globalized world: Presidential address American Political Science Association, 2000. *American Political Science Review, 95*(1), 1.

Keohane, R. (2006). Accountability in world politics. *Scandinavian Political Studies, 29*(2), 75–87.

Klochko, M., & Ordeshook, P. (2003). Corruption, cooperation and endogenous time discount rates. *Public Choice, 115*, 259.

Küng, H. (1993). *The Declaration of the Religions for a Global Ethic.* Retrieved February 16, 2009, from http://astro.temple.edu/~dislogue/Centre/kung.htm

Manzetti, L., & Wilson, C. (2007). Why do corrupt governments maintain public support? *Comparative Political Studies, 40.*

Montinola, G., & Jackman, R. (2002). Sources of corruption: A cross country study? *British Journal of Political Science, 13*(3), 147–170.

Najman, A., Runnalls, D., & Halle, M. (2007). *Environment and globalization: Five propositions.* Winnipeg, Canada: International Institute for Sustainable Development.

Neilsen, R. (2003). Corruption networks and implications for ethical corruption reform. *Journal of Business Ethics, 42*, 125–149.

OECD. (1999). *Public Sector Corruption: An international survey of prevention measures.* Paris: Author.

OECD. (2008). *Globalisation. OECD environmental outlook to 2030.* Paris: OECD.

Packard, K., & Reinhardt, F. (2000). What every executive needs to know about global warming. *Harvard Business Review, July–August*, 129–135.

Pettersen, T. (2002). Individual values and global governance: A comparative analysis of orientations towards the United Nations. *Comparative Sociology, 1*, 339–463.

Philp, M. (1997). Defining political corruption. *Political Studies, 45*, 436–462.

Philp, M. (2002). Conceptualising political corruption. In A.J. Heidenheimer & M. Johnston (Eds.), *Political corruption: Concepts and contexts.* New Jersey: Transaction Publishers.

Philp, M. (2006). Corruption definition and measurement. In C. Sampford, A. Shacklock, C. Connors & F. Galtung (Eds.), *Measuring corruption.* Aldershot: Ashgate.

Pope, J. (2000). *Confronting corruption: The elements of a National Integrity System (The TI Source Book).* Berlin: Transparency International.

Pope, J. (2008). National integrity systems: The key to building sustainable, just and honest government. In B. Head, A.J. Brown & C. Connors (Eds.), *Promoting integrity.* Aldershot: Ashgate.

Porritt, J. (2005). *Capitalism as if the world matters.* London: Earthscan.

Robinson, M. (2002). *Ethics, human rights and globalization: Second Global Ethic Lecture.* Retrieved February 16, 2009, from http://weltethos.org/dat-english/00-lecture_2-robinson.htm

Rodriguez, P., Siegel, D., Hillman, A., & Eden, L. (2006). Three lenses on the multinational enterprise: politics, corruption, and corporate social responsibility. *Journal of International Business Studies, 37*, 733–746.

Rose-Ackerman, S. (2008). Corruption and government. *International Peacekeeping, 15*, 338.

Sampford, C. (1990, July). *Law, institutions and the public–private divide (Keynote address).* Paper presented at the Australasian Law Teachers Association Conference, Brisbane, Australia.

Sampford, C. (1994a). Law, ethics and institutional design: finding philosophy, displacing ideology. *Griffith Law Review, 3*, 1.

Sampford, C. (1994b). Institutionalising public sector ethics. In N. Preston (Ed.), *Ethics for the public sector: Education and training.* Sydney, Australia: Federation Press.

Sampford, C. (1999, March). *Sovereignty and intervention.* Paper presented at the World Congress on Legal and Social Philosophy, New York.

Sampford, C. (2000, April). *Opening address: Queensland Integrity System*. Paper presented at the Joint Key Centre/Transparency International Workshop on the Queensland Integrity System, Brisbane, Australia.

Sampford, C. (2001). Australian National integrity System Assessment. In KCELJAG (Ed.), *Australian National integrity System Assessment: Queensland Handbook*. Brisbane and Melbourne, Australia: KCELJAG and TI.

Sampford, C. (2005, April). *Integrating integrity: Opening keynote address*. Paper presented at the World Ethics and Integrity Forum, Oxford.

Sampford, C., & Connors, C. (Eds.). (2006). *World ethics forum conference proceedings*. Oxford: Griffith University.

Sampford, C., Smith, R., & Brown, A. (2005). From Greek temple to bird's nest: Towards a theory of coherence and mutual accountability for National Integrity Systems. *Australian Journal of Public Administration, 64* (2), 96–108.

Sampford, C., & Wood, D. (1993). The future of business ethics: Legal regulation, ethical standards setting and institutional design. In C. Sampford & C. Coady (Eds.), *Business ethics and the law*. Sydney, Australia: Federation Press.

Sanzholz, W., & Gray, M. (2003). International integration and national corruption. *International Organizations, 57,* 761–800.

Singer, P. (2002). *One world: The ethics of globalization*. New Haven and London: Yale University Press.

Stubbs, R. (2008). The ASEAN alternative: Ideas, institutions and the challenge to 'global' governance. *The Pacific Review, 21,* 451–468.

Theobold, R. (1999). So what really is the problem about corruption. *Third World Quarterly, 20,* 503–513.

Venard, B., & Hanafi, M. (2008). Organisational isomorphism and corruption in financial institutions: Empirical research in emerging countries. *Journal of Business Ethics, 81,* 481–498.

von Alemann, U. (2004). The unknown depths of political theory: The case for a multidimensional concept of corruption. *Crime, Law and Social Change, 42,* 25–34.

Warren, M. (2004). What does corruption mean in a democracy. *American Journal of Political Science, 48,* 328–343.

LIST OF CONTRIBUTORS

Jacqueline Drew is a Lecturer in the School of Criminology and Criminal Justice at Griffith University and is an Associate Investigator in the Australian Research Council (ARC) Centre of Excellence in Policing and Security (CEPS). Dr Drew trained as a psychologist and received her PhD in Organisational Psychology from Griffith University. Her research interests include attraction and retention of police personnel; performance management within police organisations; and organisational structure and systems as they relate to innovative police strategies and operational practice.

Richard Evans is a Research Fellow at the Institute for Social Research, Swinburne University of Technology. His most recent book is *Disasters that Changed Australia*, MUP, 2009. Richard's interests include social and political history, crime and policing. He has taught subjects as diverse as media law, European history and criminology. He was a journalist for ten years before embarking on an academic career.

Jenny Fleming is Research Professor and Director of the Tasmanian Institute of Law Enforcement Studies at the University of Tasmania. A strong supporter of participatory action research with the emphasis on practitioner involvement, Professor Fleming was the chief coordinator of an ARC funded linkage project, Policing in the 21st Century with the Australian Federal Police. She was academic panel adviser to the Criminology Research Council at the Australian Institute of Criminology in Canberra from 2006-2008. She is on several Boards including the Alcohol and other Drugs Council, Crimestoppers Australia and the Australian Crime Prevention Council. Her research interests include, police management, police leadership and police practice. She has published widely both nationally and internationally in these areas. Her book (with Jen Wood), *Fighting Crime Together: the Challenge of Policing and Security Networks* was published in October 2006. She is the co-author (with Alison Wakefield) of *The Sage Dictionary of Policing*, published by Sage Publications London in 2009. Professor Fleming is currently a Chief Investigator on the ARC funded Linkage Project, Policing Just Outcomes with Victoria Police. The project looks at the police management of sexual assault.

Ross Homel AO is Foundation Professor of Criminology and Criminal Justice at Griffith University in Brisbane, Australia, and Director of the Griffith Institute for Social and Behavioural Research, a virtual network of over 100 academic staff in the social and behavioural sciences. He has held senior research management positions within Griffith University since 1993 including as Director of the highly successful Australian Research Council Key Centre for Ethics, Law, Justice and Governance between 2004 and 2007. He was responsible (with Jan Carter) for establishing a national set of research priorities to advance the wellbeing of children and young people and for setting up a new Australian Research Council research network, while undertaking a half time role with the Australian Research Alliance for Children and Youth in 2002 and 2003. Between 1994 and 1999 he was a part time Commissioner for the Queensland Criminal Justice Commission. He is Vice-President of the Council for Humanities, Arts and Social Sciences (CHASS), a Fellow of the Academy of Social Sciences and a member of the Academy Executive, and has won numerous awards for his research on the prevention of crime, violence and injuries. Professor Homel's accomplishments were recognised in January 2008 when he was appointed an Officer in the General Division of the Order of Australia (AO) 'for service to education, particularly in the field of criminology, through research into the causes of crime, early intervention and prevention methods'. In May 2008 he was recognised with an award from the Premier of Queensland as a 'Queensland Great', 'for his contribution to Queensland's reputation for research excellence, the development of social policy and justice reform and helping Queensland's disadvantaged communities'. In December 2008, he was short-listed for 2009 Australian of the Year.

Colleen Lewis is an Associate Professor in the School of Political and Social Inquiry at Monash University. Her major research interests include police accountability, complaints against police, police-government relations and models of oversight bodies such as anti-corruption commissions, integrity commissions, ombudsmen and crime commissions. She has contributed widely to a number of highly regarded research publications in the area of policing.

Tim Prenzler is a Chief Investigator in the Centre of Excellence in Policing and Security (CEPS) and a Professor in the School of Criminology and Criminal Justice, Griffith University, Brisbane. In CEPS he manages the 'Integrity Systems' Project. In teaching he has developed and taught courses in situational crime prevention, security management, criminal justice ethics, social justice and police studies. He has also contributed to a number of textbooks and co-edited *An Introduction to Crime and Criminology* (Pearson, 2009, with Hennessey Hayes). Tim's research has focused on the application of crime prevention principles to corruption and misconduct, especially misconduct amongst police and security providers. He is the co-author of *The Law of Private Security in Australia* (Thomson Lawbook, 2009, with Rick Sarre), and author of *Police Corruption: Preventing Misconduct and Maintaining Integrity* (CRC Press – Taylor and Francis, 2009) and *Ethics and Accountability in Criminal Justice* (Australian Academic Press, 2009).

Noel Preston AM has been an ethicist whose publications, commentary and research on public sector ethics focussed on Queensland politics from the Bjelke-Petersen years to the Beattie era. Previously an Associate Professor at QUT and founding Director of the Unitingcare Centre for Social Justice, he is currently adjunct Professor at Griffith University.

Janet Ransley lectures in Criminology and Criminal Justice at Griffith University. She is a member of the Key Centre for Ethics, Law, Justice and Governance, and an associate investigator in the ARC Centre of Excellence in Policing and Security. She worked previously in legal practice, and was the inaugural Director of Research for the Parliamentary Committee for Electoral and Administrative Review. Her PhD thesis dealt with the investigative role of royal commissions. She has published in the areas of police reform, inquiries and court processes, and is currently part of research teams investigating policy responses for immigration detainees, illicit drug regulation and counter-terrorism.

Charles Sampford became the Foundation Dean of law at Griffith University in 1991. He later became Director if the National Institute for Law, Ethics and Public Affairs, which was incorporated into the Key Centre for Ethics, Law, Justice and Governance (KCELJAG) at Griffith University. He is presently Director of the Institute for Ethics, Governance and Law (IEGL), a joint initiative of the United Nations University, Griffith University, Queensland University of Technology and in association with the Australian national University. He is also Convenor, ARC Governance Research Network (GovNet) and President, International Institute for Public Ethics.

Julianne Schultz AM is the editor of Griffith REVIEW. She is the author of *Reviving the Fourth Estate* (CUP, 1998), a professor in the Centre for Public Culture and Ideas at Griffith University and a member of the board of directors of the Australian Broadcasting Corporation.

David Solomon AM is an author and retired journalist. He was Chair of the Electoral and Administrative Review Commission in 1992-93 and chaired the Independent Panel that reviewed Queensland's Freedom of Information law in 2007–2008, resulting in the passage of the Right to Information Act

2009. He began serving a five-year term as Queensland Integrity Commissioner in July 2009. He has degrees from the Australian National University in Arts and Law and a Doctorate of Letters.

Kerry Wimshurst is a lecturer in the School of Criminology and Criminal Justice, Griffith University. His teaching areas include youth justice, crime and society, and the criminal justice system. His research interests are in criminal justice education, and criminal justice history.

www.ingramcontent.com/pod-product-compliance
Ingram Content Group Australia Pty Ltd
76 Discovery Rd, Dandenong South VIC 3175, AU
AUHW011249130325
408272AU00010B/38

9 781921 513350